WORLD ENGLISH

WORLD ENGLISH
From Aloha to Zed

Robert Hendrickson

John Wiley & Sons, Inc.

New York • Chichester • Weinheim • Brisbane • Singapore • Toronto

Published by John Wiley & Sons, Inc.
Published simultaneously in Canada.

Design and production by Navta Associates, Inc.

This publication is designed to provide accurate and authoritative information in regard to the subject matter covered. It is sold with the understanding that the publisher is not engaged in rendering professional services. If professional advice or other expert assistance is required, the services of a competent professional person should be sought.

Library of Congress Cataloging-in-Publication Data:

Hendrickson, Robert
World English : from aloha to zed / Robert Hendrickson
    p. cm.
  ISBN 0-471-34518-0 (acid-free paper)
    1. English language—English-speaking countries—Dictionaries.   2. English language—Foreign countries—Dictionaries.   3. English language—Dictionaries.
  I. Title.

PE2751 .H46 2001
423—dc21   00-053418

Printed in the United States of America

10 9 8 7 6 5 4 3 2 1

For my grandson Nicholas

Introduction

World English, a book for the general reader, is surprisingly the first collection I know of a large number of English words and phrases used in the many nations where English is spoken—even to a limited extent—around the world. Of these more than thirty-five hundred expressions, many are unique to the nations where they are used, some have meanings different from those of the same words in American English, and still others (such as many of those found in Japanese) have been borrowed from English and altered to better suit the mother tongue.

English is spoken, fluently or haltingly, over one-fifth of the world's surface. Anywhere from 800 million to 1.5 billion people speak the language today with some degree of proficiency, including at least 400 million native speakers, leading one writer to note that "the sun never sets on English-speaking countries" and inspiring British scholar Tom McArthur to title his study of English *The English Languages*. As the accompanying list makes clear, English is spoken as an official language (some nations have more than one official language) in forty-six countries recognized by the United Nations, and it is the native tongue in at least twelve of these. Then there are scores of countries such as Israel, Japan, and Sweden (where English is officially the "first second language") in which English is widely spoken or studied. Finally, there are the many nations where some English is spoken or understood, and the numerous English dialects—such as the southern dialect (among many more) spoken in the United States.

It would be impossible to include in one book anywhere near all the English words and phrases used in the world's hundreds of countries—that would be a daunting task for even a four-foot-high, multivolume unabridged dictionary—but in this book for the language lover I have tried to treat in an entertaining fashion a large representative sample of the different ways English is spoken around the world. Some seventy varieties of English are represented, including to a large extent the English spoken in Great Britain and the United States, which George Bernard Shaw wryly called "two nations separated by a common language." Only by focusing mainly on the differences among the various global Englishes

1

and American English (English as spoken in the United States) could I have kept this book to a reasonable length.

In treating British English, for example, *World English* covers hundreds of words such as the well-known *bobby* (a policeman, of course, to Americans), *lift* (for an elevator), and *chucker-out* (for a bouncer). I've tried to choose only the most interesting of these from among tens of thousands, giving both brief, accurate definitions of the expressions and any entertaining stories behind them. The same has been done with unique American English words and phrases, especially those from American dialects, which include the New England, New York, western, southern, and mountain ways of speech, the last mainly including expressions from the Ozark and Appalachian Mountains.

Similarly, there are plentiful examples of expressions used in all other nations where English is the native tongue. With the success of the Crocodile Dundee movies, for example, Americans have become aware of Australianisms such as *barbie* for barbecue, and *sheila* for girl. There are hundreds more in these pages. Likewise for Canadianisms. In my travels through Canada I've noticed that many Canadians don't know what you're talking about when you order a *soda* like a Coke or a Pepsi—to them *soda* is seltzer. They also commonly use *go to the washroom* for go to the bathroom, and typically end their sentences with *eh?*, as in "Nice day, eh?"—this in fact has been called "a national bad habit" there. *World English* gives scores more of such expressions, as well as Newfoundland Canadianisms.

World English also features expressions used in those countries in which English is an official language, such as South Africa and India (where twenty million to twenty-five million people speak English). Places where English is widely spoken, though not an official language, are not neglected, either.

Finally, *World English* includes an ample selection of words and phrases borrowed from English by countries where the English language is not widely or fluently spoken—where there are such efforts as this sign on a temple door in Thailand: *It Is Forbidden To Enter A Woman Even A Foreigner If Dressed As A Man.* Since World War II, due to the war itself and movies, television, modern technology, advertising, business travel, and tourism, separate English words have entered the vocabularies of most major languages and many of the smaller ones as well. These useful English words often have replaced older, unwieldy terms in the adopting language or filled a vacuum where a word was needed. In the French-language newspaper *Le Monde*, for example, one recent study found that every 166th word is English. Much the same is true in German, where several thousand English words have infiltrated the language. Italian now

Nations Recognized by the United Nations in Which English Is an Official Language*

Antigua and Barbuda

Australia

Bahamas

Barbados

Belize

Botswana

Cameroon (with French)

Canada (with French)

Dominica

Fiji

Gambia

Ghana

Grenada

Guyana

India (with Hindi)

Ireland (with Irish Gaelic)

Jamaica

Kenya (with Swahili)

Lesotho (with Sesotho)

Liberia

Malawi (with Chichewa)

Mauritius

Micronesia

Namibia

New Zealand (with Maori)

Nigeria

Pakistan (with Urdu)

Papua New Guinea (with Motu)

Philippines (with Tagalog)

Saint Kitts and Nevis

Saint Lucia

Saint Vincent and the Grenadines

Samoa (with Samoan)

Sierra Leone

Singapore (with Malay and Chinese)

Solomon Islands

South Africa (with Afrikaans)

Swaziland (with Siswati)

Tanzania (with Swahili)

Trinidad and Tobago

Uganda

United Kingdom

United States

Vanuatu (with French and Bislama)

Zambia

Zimbabwe

* Other countries, not recognized by the United Nations, also could be included. Tom McArthur, in *The English Languages* (1998), lists 113 of what he terms "territories" (nations, national possessions, colonies, etc.) where English is either an official language, a de facto official language, a second language, or a lingua franca (i.e., a language used for communication between groups of people who speak different languages). This is more than twice as many territories as the English language's nearest rival, French. McArthur goes on to give a list of 232 "territories," including the initial 113, where English is spoken to some extent, often as a global lingua franca. Even China, North Korea, Vietnam, Cuba, Iran, and Iraq are on this last list. To keep these figures in perspective, however, remember that there are some 6,700 languages spoken in the world today.

has hundreds of English words, such as *lo show* (TV), as does Spanish (*suburbio,* for suburbs). In Swahili the names of the month are taken from English.

You'll even find in these pages a handful of surprising expressions from several invented or artificial languages such as "e-mailese" computer abbreviations and (for interplanetary polyglots) "Klingon" from the universally known *Star Trek* adventures—if only because *"Beam me up, Scotty"* and similar expressions are great fun. Above all, I've tried to fashion an accurate but entertaining "reader's book" about English "as she is spoken" globally, complete with humorous anecdotes or interesting facts whenever possible.

Many people have helped me in this quest over the past few years. I would especially like to thank Professor Masayoshi Yamada of Shimane University for his invaluable help and the long, accurate lists of Japanese loanwords from English that he supplied. Professor Yamada documented the extensive use of Japanized English expressions in the Japanese language and explained that these English expressions are usually written in a special syllabic script called the Katakana alphabet. Foreign borrowings (not only English and including technical terms) total about a hundred thousand words, fully one-third of the Japanese vocabulary.

Among many other contributors, I am also indebted to Robert and Lauren Walsh for their help with Canadianisms and British English expressions. My wife, Marilyn, the heart of everything I do, was as always of invaluable help in reading hundreds of books, magazines, and newspapers in search of words and phrases. To everyone who helped I extend a heartfelt thank you, and to my readers I extend an invitation to submit other global English expressions that they feel I have neglected and should include in any future editions.

A

aandag!

Attention! The word, frequently employed in newspaper ads, derives ultimately from the Dutch *aadacht,* meaning the same.

aback BAHAMIAN

Ago. "Ten years aback we were there, but we never returned."

above snakes AMERICAN (WEST)

Above the ground. "He's a lean, rangy cowpoke, about six and a half feet above snakes."

abroad AMERICAN (SOUTH)

Heard especially among old-fashioned speakers in the American South, a trip abroad is often not a journey overseas but a trip or visit within the community, even a stroll down to the store. It can, however, mean a distance of fifty miles or more, as in the common newspaper expression "[Mr. Jones] has returned from his trip abroad."

absentee ballot AMERICAN, AUSTRALIAN

A ballot used by a voter who is unable to vote in person at the polling place. The British call it a *postal ballot* (q.v.) or a *postal vote.*

accident department BRITISH

A hospital *emergency room,* or *ER.*

according to Cocker BRITISH

Very accurate or correct, according to the rules. *According to Cocker* could just as well mean "all wrong"; however, few authorities bother to mention this. The phrase honors Edward Cocker (1631–1675), a London engraver who also taught penmanship and arithmetic. Cocker wrote a number of popular books on these subjects, and reputedly authored *Cocker's Arithmetick,* which went through 112 editions, its authority giving rise to the proverb. Then, in the late nineteenth century, documented proof was offered showing that Cocker did not write the famous book at all, that it was a forgery of his editor and publisher, so poorly done, in fact, that it set back rather than advanced the cause of elementary arithmetic.

According to Hoyle, according to Guinness, and *according to Fowler* are three similar British phrases understood wherever British English is spoken.

according to Rafferty's rules   AUSTRALIAN
According to no rules at all, no holds barred. It apparently arose in Australian boxing matches, though who the original Rafferty is—if there was one—is unknown. The expression probably has nothing to do with the British slang *Rafferty*.

ace on   BAHAMIAN
The best at, excellent or outstanding at, as in "She ace on singin'."

acorn calf   AMERICAN (WEST)
A runt or weak calf; sometimes used to describe a physically weak person. It was once believed that cows that ate too many acorns gave birth to such calves.

action replay   BRITISH
A television sports term whose U.S. counterpart is *instant replay.*

adrift   AMERICAN (NEW ENGLAND)
A seafaring term used on land in Maine and other New England states, *adrift* can mean to be tied improperly, to become untied. "That package is all adrift; you don't know your knots."

advert   BRITISH
An abbreviation of *advertisement; ad* in America.

adzoons!   SCOTTISH
An exclamation of great surprise used by older Scottish speakers. The term's origins are unknown.

aeroplane   AUSTRALIAN, BRITISH
Airplane. The British *aerodome* means an airfield or airport.

African time   SOUTH AFRICAN
A humorous term used by both whites and blacks that refers to being late, not on time.

afters   BRITISH
Dessert, the last course of lunch or dinner.

ag   SOUTH AFRICAN
A common exclamation, meaning *oh* or *ah.* "Ag, man, all I want is another chance—I know I can do it." From the Dutch *ach.*

again   JAMAICAN
Anymore, any longer, as in "She don't love him again."

aggravoke   AMERICAN (SOUTH)
Combination of *aggra*vate and pro*voke.* William Faulkner himself used this Southern slang, which means "to incite or provoke."

agley   SCOTTISH
Awry, off to one side, wrong. American mountain folk used this word in the same sense, as in "Jake's gone agley since he got in with those boys," or "That shed is all agley."

Agony Aunt   BRITISH
A tabloid lonely hearts columnist who answers questions from readers.

agricultural show   BRITISH
A state or county fair—that is, an exhibition of farm goods accompanied by competitions and entertainment.

agricultural worker   BRITISH
A farmhand or farm worker.

aided school   NEW ZEALAND
A school founded and funded by a religious organization.

air hostess   BRITISH
A female flight attendant on a commercial airliner. The term *stewardess* is used in America.

airish   AMERICAN (SOUTH)
(1) Drafty. "It's plenty airish in here." (2) One who puts on airs or acts
superior to others. "He's real airish, ain't he?"

airy-fairy   BRITISH
An intellectual. "He counted himself among the airy-fairies." As an adjective this derogatory word means completely visionary, without substance.

aisle tooth   SCOTTISH
Any of the molar teeth, so named because of their broad biting surface.

Aladdin's cave   BRITISH
A hiding place, such as a warehouse, for stolen goods that criminals are
waiting to sell or distribute.

alcool   CANADIAN
An alcoholic drink made from grain that is popular in Canada.

alight and look at your saddle   AMERICAN (WEST)
An invitation to a rider to get off his horse and visit a while, come inside
for a drink or a meal. "It's a hot day. 'Light and look at your saddle,
pardner."

all and all   JAMAICAN
Often used instead of "all," as in, "She tell all in all her friends."

all arms and legs beer   BRITISH
Slang for a very weak beer with "no body" to it, an inferior beer.

all bally-which-way   AMERICAN (WEST)
Twisted in every direction, highly confused. "Just when you think you
know that country, somehow it's twisted all bally-which-way."

all fingers and thumbs   AUSTRALIAN, BRITISH
Americans would shorten this expression, meaning lacking coordination
and skill, to *all thumbs*.

all hat and no cattle   AMERICAN (WEST)
Someone who acts rich or important but has no substance, such as a person who pretends to be a cattle baron, even dressing the part.

all his bullet holes is in the front of him AMERICAN (WEST)

He's brave, not a coward. "I ain't ashamed of him. All his bullet holes is in the front of him."

all-in insurance policy BRITISH

A policy protecting against all types of risk. An "all-risk" policy in American English.

all-in wrestling BRITISH

A wrestling match in which there are no holds barred; almost everything is permitted as long as no weapons are used.

all my eye and Betty Martin BRITISH

Baloney, bull, etc. This old saying may have originated when a British sailor, looking into a church in an Italian port, heard a beggar praying, *"An mihi, beate Martine"* (Ah, grant me, Blessed Martin) and later told his shipmates that this was nonsense that sounded to him like "All my eye and Betty Martin." Most authorities dismiss this theory, but St. Martin *is* the patron saint of beggars.

all of that! JAMAICAN

A common phrase expressing complete agreement: "All a dat, man!"

all right already AMERICAN (NEW YORK CITY)

Stop it, that's enough! Stop talking! *Enough already* is a variation. Both are common expressions influenced by Yiddish speech rhythms.

all-rounder BRITISH

A versatile cricket player who is good at all aspects of the game—batting, bowling, and fielding. What Americans would call an *all-around player.*

all the hours God sends BRITISH

All the time, every hour of the day. "He works all the hours God sends."

aloha HAWAIIAN

Probably the best known of Hawaiian words contributed to standard English. *Aloha,* meaning either "hello" or "good-bye," literally means "love" in Hawaiian and can mean "I love you" if *mi loa* is prefaced to it. It has been called the world's loveliest greeting or farewell. Hawaii is, of course, America's *Aloha State,* its anthem "Aloha 'Oe" (Farewell to Thee), written by Queen Liliuokalani.

aloha shirt   AMERICAN (HAWAIIAN)
Colorful shirts in bright prints of hula girls, palm trees, pineapples, and many other Hawaiian subjects. These shirts date back to the 1920s, when small Honolulu tailor shops began making them for the tourist trade. Native Hawaiian Ellery Chun (1909–2000) was the first to mass-produce them. Mr. Chun, a Yale graduate, coined the name *aloha shirt* in about 1933 when he began turning the shirts out at his Honolulu plant. (See also *aloha.*)

alphabet   HAWAIIAN
A letter of the alphabet, as in "My name begin with the alphabet B." This follows a Japanese practice taken from the many Japanese settlers in Hawaii, the Japanese word for *letter* being the same as that for *alphabet.*

already   HAWAIIAN
Often means "yet," as in "I called you up, but you weren't there already." This usage probably stems from a similar practice among Portuguese settlers in Hawaii.

Alsatian   BRITISH
The breed of dog commonly called a *German shepherd* or a *police dog* in the United States.

alst   AMERICAN (NEW ENGLAND)
Common in Maine for *all* or *all that.* "That's alst I heard about it."

ama   JAPANESE
A Japanese borrowing and shortening of *amateur.*

amalaita   SOUTH AFRICAN
A ruffian who fights in the streets. "A gang of amalaitas beat him senseless." From a Zulu word meaning a street desperado. Pronounced *ama-lay-ta.*

amber fluid   AUSTRALIAN
Descriptive Aussie term for beer. See also *tinner.*

amen corner   AMERICAN (SOUTH)
A group of fervent believers is called an *amen corner,* after the similarly named place near the pulpit in churches that is occupied by those who lead the responsive "amens" to the preacher's prayers.

american   JAPANESE

American coffee, meaning "weak coffee," unlike espresso or other strong brews.

Americanism   BRITISH

An American, not an Englishman, coined this expression. In 1781 Dr. John Witherspoon, president of the College of New Jersey (now Princeton), wrote a series of essays on "the general state of the language in America." He listed a number of "chief improprieties," such as Americans using "mad" for "angry," and coined the word *Americanism* to define them.

amn't I?   IRISH

Used in Ireland and Britain but rarely, if ever, in America. As odd as it may sound to some ears, the locution is preferred to "Aren't I?" by a number of good writers and is widely employed. James Joyce used it in *Dubliners,* Rumer Godden employed it in *An Episode of Sparrows,* and Rebecca West used it in one of her novels ("I'm just awful, amn't I?"). *Amn't I?* is especially popular in Ireland, the expression dating back at least two centuries there.

anancy rope   JAMAICAN

A spider web. *Anancy* derives from Anansi, the name of a cunning spider in an old African folk tale.

anchor   AMERICAN

The strongest member of a track team, the runner who runs the last leg of a relay race, has been called the *anchorman* since the late nineteenth century, the term possibly having its roots in the anchor man at the end of a tug-of-war rope. By the 1930s *anchorman* was being used for the strongest member of an American radio broadcasting team. With the rise of women in sports and television news broadcasting, the term is increasingly heard as *anchor,* not *anchorman.*

and pigs fly!   BRITISH

The American counterpart would be a sarcastic *yeah* or *sure,* both expressing disbelief. But Americans also use the similar phrase *and pigs have wings!*

angel teat   AMERICAN (OZARK MOUNTAINS)
Moonshiners call particularly good, mellow whiskey with a good bouquet *angel teat* or *angel's teat*. A synonym is *good drinkin' whiskey*.

angle with a silver hook   BRITISH
An old British expression without much currency in America. An unlucky fisherman who fails to catch anything doesn't want to go home empty-handed. Thus when he buys fish (with silver coin, in past times) to conceal his abject failure, he is said to *angle with a silver hook*.

angry teeth   SCOTTISH
Used to describe the sharp, fragmentary remains of a rainbow, which are said to forecast bad weather.

Annie Oakley   AMERICAN
Slang for a complimentary ticket. At first this was just the stage name of Phoebe Annie Oakley Mozee (1860–1926), star rifle shot with Buffalo Bill's Wild West Show. Her most famous trick was to toss a playing card into the air and shoot holes through all its pips. The riddled card reminded circus performers of their punched meal tickets, which they began to call *Annie Oakleys,* and the name was soon transferred to free railroad and press passes, both of which were customarily punched with a hole in the center. Today all complimentary passes, punched or not, are called *Annie Oakleys.*

anorak   CANADIAN
A name given to both a parka and a warm waterproof coat made by the Inuit natives from animal skins.

answer phone   BRITISH
The usual name for what Americans would call a telephone *answering machine.* The British also use the trademarked name *Ansaphone.*

anticlockwise   BRITISH
Counterclockwise in American. "To open the medicine bottle, push the top down and twist it anticlockwise."

Antsie's limit   BRITISH
A British expression with some American use. The nineteenth-century physician Edward Antsie advised his patients that more than one and a half ounces of pure alcohol a day, consumed day in and day out, will

eventually cause physical damage to the body. Stay under this limit, Antsie said, and drinking won't harm you. One and a half ounces of pure alcohol translates roughly into three one-ounce drinks of 100-proof whiskey, or four beers, or half a bottle of wine. Some experts agree with Antsie, but most refuse to generalize.

anybody   HAWAIIAN
Frequently used instead of *everybody*, as in "Anybody went to the beach today."

any joy?   BRITISH
Slang for "Have you had any luck and success?"

A-O.K.   AMERICAN
An American expression with worldwide usage. An accidental coinage, *A-O.K.* was not used by American astronaut Alan Shepard while making the first suborbital space flight, in 1961, as was widely reported. The term is actually the result of a mistake by NASA public relations officer Colonel "Shorty" Powers, who thought he heard Shepard say "A-O.K." when the astronaut, in fact, uttered a rousing "O.K." Powers liked the sound of A-O.K. so much that he reported it several times to newsmen before learning of his mistake. By then it was too late, for the term became part of the language practically overnight. See also *O.K.*

apartment   JAMAICAN
Used by Jamaicans to mean not a separate residence but a rented *room* in a house.

Apple   AMERICAN (WEST)
A derogatory name given to certain American Indians by other American Indians who believe their values are too much like those of whites; that is, they are, like an apple, red on the outside and white on the inside. See *Oreo.*

apples   AUSTRALIAN
O.K.; under control, everything's in apple-pie order. "Everything's apples, mate."

apricot sickness   SOUTH AFRICAN
The runs or the trots, often caused by eating unripe apricots or too many apricots.

argy-bargy   BRITISH
Loud arguing or squabbling. The word derives from *argue*. "Did you hear all that argy-bargy next door?"

Arizona strawberries   AMERICAN (WEST)
American cowboys and lumberjacks used this term as a humorous synonym for beans, also employing the variations *Mexican strawberries* and *prairie strawberries*. Some dried beans were pink in color, like strawberries.

armhole   BAHAMIAN
The most common term for an armpit.

around the horn!   AMERICAN (WEST)
A cry used by loggers in the Pacific Northwest when a log is swinging through the air to be loaded.

arse   BRITISH
Still used by most British for the buttocks. Americans would say *ass;* the word *arse* in this sense is rarely heard in America.

arse licker   AUSTRALIAN, BRITISH
What Americans would call an *ass kisser,* a *sycophant,* or an *apple polisher.*

arsy-varsy   BRITISH
Ass backward or vice versa, all wrong. "You've got it all arsy-varsy."

arterial road   BRITISH, NEW ZEALAND
A major highway or trunk road.

artic   BRITISH, NEW ZEALAND
Short for an *articulated lorry,* which Americans would call a *trailer truck* or *rig.*

artsy-fartsy   AMERICAN, BRITISH
Someone who tries to appear more educated or knowing about art than he is, a pretentious person. Also *arty-farty.*

arvie   SOUTH AFRICAN
Afternoon. "I spent the whole arvie at the movies." Probably a corruption
of *afternoon.*

arvo   AUSTRALIAN
Slang for *afternoon:* "It's a sunny Sunday arvo."

ary   AMERICAN (NEW ENGLAND)
An old-fashioned word meaning *either.* "Take ary one or the other."

as   IRISH
Commonly substituted for *who,* as in "There are some of us as don't
know."

as cold as charity   BRITISH
Bitterly cold. The saying alludes to the coldness encountered in the offices
of charitable or welfare organizations by people seeking help.

as different as chalk and cheese   BRITISH
Completely different, like night and day. "They're in love, but they're as
different as chalk and cheese."

ashamed   AMERICAN (OZARK MOUNTAINS)
Among hillfolk the word is used to mean modest, shy, or bashful, as in
"He was so ashamed to meet women he sat in a corner all night."

ashet   SCOTTISH
A serving dish, borrowed from the French *assiette* for same.

ashore   CANADIAN (NEWFOUNDLAND)
Used to mean "aboard" a vessel, as in "All hands come ashore, we're set
to sail."

ashy   AMERICAN (SOUTH)
Angry; ill-tempered, ill-humored. "He argued awhile and then got right
ashy about it."

as mad as a two-bob watch   AUSTRALIAN
Slang for someone extremely mad or silly. See *two-bob.*

as near as damnit

BRITISH

Very close, just about. "I'll get there by twelve, as near as damnit." The phrase was originally "As near as 'damn it' is to swearing."

assessor

BRITISH

An insurance adjustor; someone who investigates insurance claims.

assistant

BRITISH, NEW ZEALAND

A clerk, a salesperson in a store; short for *shop assistant*. In the United States an *assistant* would be a *clerk* or a *salesman*.

at all events

BRITISH

In any event. "At all events, I'll finish it by Saturday."

at close of play

BRITISH

Originally a cricket expression, this saying means *when all is said and done.*

attend to

HAWAIIAN

Often used instead of *attend,* as in "I attend to Honolulu High School."

attorney

JAMAICAN

Can mean any person who manages property for its absentee owner; not necessarily a lawyer.

aubergine

BRITISH

Eggplant. *Aubergine* is the French work for this vegetable. It is also used as an adjective meaning "black" or "dark purple."

auld

SCOTTISH

Old, as in the well-known song "Auld Lange Syne" (The Good Old Days).

Auld Sooty

SCOTTISH

The devil, one of many such names for Satan, including Auld Bobby, Auld Bogie, Auld Clootie, Auld Nick, Auld Roughy, and Auld Waghorn.

Aunt Edna   BRITISH

The creation of British playwright Terence Rattigan, *Aunt Edna* is the equivalent of the American little old lady from Dubuque—nice but provincial, very prudish, and traditional.

auntie   SOUTH AFRICAN

(1) A friendly, mostly respectful form of address to any older woman. (2) Among blacks the name for an old woman who sells liquor illegally. See also *shebeen queen*.

Aunt Sally   BRITISH

A scapegoat or a patsy, after the Aunt Sally figure used as a target in an old British carnival game.

au pair   AMERICAN, BRITISH

A young woman, often foreign, who receives room and board and a small salary in return for housework. The term is becoming more common in the United States, especially to describe one who watches children.

Aussie salute   AUSTRALIAN

A humorous term for waving a hand in the air to swat or scare off flies.

away from   JAMAICAN

Except for. As in "He always live here away from a year in America."

away to the woods   BRITISH

Gone crazy. "He's away to the woods, I'm afraid."

awful   CANADIAN (NEWFOUNDLAND)

Instead of having a negative connotation, the word means remarkable or exceptional, as in "He gave her an awful present, beautiful and very expensive."

ayuh   AMERICAN (NEW ENGLAND)

Yes, though the word has shades of meaning ranging from the affirmative to the sarcastic. Chiefly heard in Maine, *ayuh* (EYE-uh) is used throughout New England in variations such as *eyah, ayeh, eeyuh, ehyuh, aaay-yuh,* and even *ayup*. A touchstone of New England speech, it possibly derives from the nautical *aye* (yes). Another theory has *ayuh* coming from the old Scots American *aye-yes,* meaning the same.

baaad AMERICAN

Bad, when slowly pronounced *baaad,* has long been American black slang for something or someone good, and recently this meaning has come into general usage to a limited extent. The variation is so old that it is found in the American Creole language Gullah three centuries ago, when *baaad* was used by slaves as an expression of admiration for another slave who successfully flouted the white men's rules.

baas SOUTH AFRICAN

Boss, master. This usage as a form of address from a black to a white man is dead in Namibia, where it has been banned by law, and it is fast dying in South Africa. It derives from the Dutch for *master.*

babbalaas SOUTH AFRICAN

A classic hangover after a hard night's drinking. The word derives ultimately from a Zulu word meaning the same. "He's got a bad case of the babbalaas."

baboon rock SOUTH AFRICAN

Rocky soil that is not suited for farming. "We couldn't make a living on that baboon rock."

baby in the bushes AMERICAN (APPALACHIAN MOUNTAINS)

A euphemism for a child born to an unwed mother.

baby-watcher BRITISH

What would be called a *baby-sitter* in America.

bachelor party AMERICAN

See *stag party.*

bachelor's tart AUSTRALIAN

A piece of bread with jam spread on it. See *damper.*

back AMERICAN (OZARK MOUNTAINS)

An old-fashioned term meaning to address an envelope, from the days when letters were folded and addressed on the back. "As soon as I back this letter, I'll mail it."

back bacon   CANADIAN
An oval-shaped bacon with very little fat that is sometimes called *Canadian bacon.*

back end of the year   BRITISH
Fall or autumn, usually heard in Lancashire.

the back-blocks   AUSTRALIAN
Arid back country, far from any settlement.

backchat   BRITISH
Rude remarks to someone older or in authority. Americans would call this *backtalk.*

backhanders   BRITISH
Graft or kickbacks paid to officials or law enforcement authorities.

the back of beyond   BRITISH
Any remote place far removed from the world.

back-up wife   BAHAMIAN
A humorous term for a mistress of a married man.

backward thoughts   BRITISH
Second thoughts. "He had backward thoughts about his proposal."

bad cess to you   IRISH
Bad luck to you. Many people on hearing the Irish expression *bad cess to you* assume that the *cess* in the term is a corruption of the word *success.* This, however, isn't the case. The expression originated in Ireland, where *cess* meant an assessment or land tax. The phrase thus means, "May your taxes be raised."

baddies   SCOTTISH
Wicked youngsters. "They are awful baddies up to no good."

bad form   BRITISH
Bad manners or inappropriate behavior. The term has some use in the United States.

bad growl fella   AUSTRALIAN PIDGIN
Any crabby, cranky person, man or woman. For other forms of pidgin see
mary.

badlands   AMERICAN, CANADIAN
Dry, rocky areas where little grows.

the Bad Man   AMERICAN (OZARK MOUNTAINS)
A name highlanders have for the devil. *The Good Man* is a name for God.

bad-minded   JAMAICAN
Can mean an ungenerous person or an evil-minded person, depending on
the context.

badmouth   AMERICAN
To speak ill of someone. Probably originating among African American
speakers and possibly deriving from a Vai or a Mandingo African expression, to badmouth was at first used mostly by southern blacks but is now
used nationwide.

bad patch   BRITISH
A bad or a rough time. "He had a bad patch of it for a few weeks."

bad scran   IRISH
Bad luck, as in "Bad scran to you!" Perhaps *scran* here comes from *scran-
nel,* food or victuals.

bad show!   BRITISH
Too bad, tough luck; or a rebuke telling someone he or she should have
done better.

bagging   BRITISH
A British term meaning a snack, something eaten between meals.

bag lady   AMERICAN
Short for shopping bag lady, a homeless woman who carries all her possessions in shopping bags. The expression *bag man* also is used. Both are
familiar today in the United Kingdom as well. A *bag lady* also can be a

woman who collects or delivers illegal payments such as bribes, and a woman who deals in drugs.

bagman   AMERICAN, AUSTRALIAN, BRITISH

The word has different meanings in different countries. Australian slang for a tramp, *bagman* means a commercial traveler or traveling salesman in Britain (a drummer who carries bags of samples). In America a *bagman* can mean a racketeer or anyone assigned to collect a bribe, extortion, or kidnapping ransom. It also can mean a man who deals in drugs. (A *bag man* is a homeless man.)

bag of fruit   AUSTRALIAN

Rhyming slang for a man's suit, as in "He wore his best bag of fruit."

bags of   BRITISH

Lots of, piles of, an abundance. "He always has bags of money to spend."

bairn   SCOTTISH

A child, a son or daughter, or a childish person of any age. *Bairn* derives from the Old Scottish word *bearn,* meaning the same.

bait   BRITISH

A term meaning a midday snack; the term is used mainly by farmers.

baked potato   AMERICAN

See *jacket potato.*

bakgat   SOUTH AFRICAN

Slang, its origin unknown, for great, splendid, beautiful, excellent. "He's a bakgat guy."

bakore   SOUTH AFRICAN

Large, protruding ears. "The one over there with the bakore did it." The word derives from the Afrikaans *bak,* bowl, plus *or,* ear, and is pronounced *back-or-e.*

bald-faced shirt   AMERICAN (WEST)

A cowboy's name for a man's stiff dress shirt that may derive from the use of *baldface* for a cow with a long white marking down the center of its face.

ballocks   BRITISH
Slang for the balls or testicles. The word has some currency in the United
States.

balmy   BRITISH, AUSTRALIAN
Eccentric in behavior, slightly crazy. The word has some American usage.
It is possibly a variation of *barmy*, meaning the same.

bandicoot   AUSTRALIAN
A thief who steals vegetables out of the ground. Like the Australian
marsupial they are named for, human bandicoots usually steal root
vegetables, leaving their tops protruding from the ground to forestall
suspicion.

bandiet   SOUTH AFRICAN
A convict or a prisoner, the word deriving from the Dutch *bandiet*, a robber, and pronounced *ban-dit*.

banfaxed   IRISH
(1) Destroyed, totally ruined. "Her car was banfaxed in the crash." (2)
Totally drunk or stoned on drugs. (3) Defeated completely.

bang   SOUTH AFRICAN
Frightened, afraid. "He's too bang to go outside." An Afrikaans word that
derives from the Dutch *bang*, meaning the same.

bang-bellied   JAMAICAN
Having a big belly, one that "bangs" up and down as one moves about.

bangers   AUSTRALIAN, BRITISH
Sausages—because they often split open with a slight bang while cooking.

bang on   BRITISH
Exactly right, dead on. The term was originally the military *bang on target.*

banker   AUSTRALIAN, CANADIAN
In Australia, a river that floods, rising over its banks and causing great
damage; in Canada, a fisherman who works the Grand Banks, or a fishing boat that operates off the Grand Banks.

bank holiday   BRITISH, NEW ZEALAND
A legal holiday, when banks are closed.

banshee   IRISH
The banshee is an evil old hag of Irish folklore who sits on the roofs of houses and wails of coming death. Also to howl like a banshee.

barbie   AUSTRALIAN
A barbecue: "Let's slip some shrimp on the barbie tonight."

barmy   AUSTRALIAN, BRITISH
Daft, eccentric, crazy. First recorded in England, but used in Australia for more than a century. Also spelled *balmy.*

barnacle   CANADIAN (NEWFOUNDLAND)
Can be used to mean a despicable, bad, or vicious person. A *barnacle's breed* is a bad youngster.

barney   AUSTRALIAN, BRITISH
An argument, a quarrel, a fight. "They had a real barney over it."

barnyard beauty   SCOTTISH
An old expression, rare today, that means an attractive, buxom country girl.

barrack   AUSTRALIAN, BRITISH
To root for a football team or any sports team by shouting loud, often coarse encouragement to the players. *Barrack* possibly derives from the Australian *barrack* meaning to banter.

barrier cream   BRITISH
Suntan lotion or *sunscreen lotion* would be the names of this cream in the United States.

barrister   BRITISH
In America, *lawyer* or *attorney* describes anyone who does any kind of legal work, whereas in England a *barrister* is an attorney who does trial work and a *solicitor* (q.v.) one who does general legal work.

basting big AMERICAN (NEW ENGLAND)

An expression used mostly in Maine for something very large of its kind, as in "That's a bastin' big lobster." *Baster,* from which this expression derives, also means something very large, and was probably first a euphemism for bastard, as in expressions such as "He's a big baster, ain't he?" *Baster* rhymes with *faster.*

batch-mate INDIAN

A classmate or another student in one's school.

bathe BRITISH

A synonym for *swim,* as in "He went for a bathe in the river." Americans rarely if ever use *bathe* in this way.

bathers AUSTRALIAN

Another word for a bathing suit, as in "He slipped into his bathers." See also *cozzie, togs.*

bathing box SOUTH AFRICAN

A bathhouse or locker for changing one's clothes that is commonly built on South African beaches, often erected on stilts near the water.

battalion JAPANESE

In Japan this word means a zombie, of all things. *Battalion* came to mean zombies in Japan after a Japanese distributor in 1985 rather arbitrarily changed the name of the film *The Return of the Living Dead* to *Battalion.* Japanese moviegoers thought that *battalion* referred to the zombies in the picture and began calling all zombies *battalions.*

battler AUSTRALIAN

A person who fights hard against all obstacles, no matter how great, to make a living or to accomplish something. In America the word *battler* is usually confined to boxing and other sports.

bay AMERICAN (SOUTH)

In South Carolina a *bay* refers to a low, swampy area with many bay trees, also called bay laurels *(Laurus nobilis);* in Florida a *bay* is a watergrass meadow or flooded forest of cypresses and other trees. The word is not used in these senses anywhere else.

baygles   IRISH
Bad-mannered children. "Get those baygles out of here!" Heard mainly in Northern Ireland.

bazoo   CANADIAN
Heard in Montreal as a slang term for any old heap of a car.

beat me a picture   KENYAN
Take my picture or photograph. "Beat me a picture I will send to my family."

to be in at the death   BRITISH
To be present when something ends. "He wanted to be in at the death of the game."

to be crook with a sheila   AUSTRALIAN
To be on bad terms with a young woman (a sheila).

to be mad on someone   BRITISH
To be mad about or crazy in love with someone, as in "She's mad on him."

to be made redundant   BRITISH
A euphemism for to be laid off or fired from work.

to be on Queer Street   BRITISH
In days past the Latin term *quaere,* meaning "enquire," was noted on a person's application for a loan if there were strong suspicions about his credit history. From this practice came the British expression *to be on Queer Street,* to be in bad trouble.

bes   MALAYSIAN
Great, fantastic, fabulous; a clipping of the English word *best.*

to be short a shingle   AUSTRALIAN, BRITISH
To be simpleminded, stupid, one brick shy of a load.

to be sold   BRITISH
To be tricked, deceived, or hoaxed.

beach box   BRITISH
In the United States this would be called a *bathhouse, locker,* or *cabana,* a small structure on or just off the beach that is used for changing one's clothes.

beal   AMERICAN (APPALACHIAN MOUNTAINS)
To fester, be infected. "With the birth of her baby, his wife came down with a bealed breast."

"Beam me up, Scotty"   AMERICAN, INTERGALACTIC
This has become a very popular American humorous expression, often used on bumper stickers as well as in conversation for "get me out of here, free me from this mess," etc. It originally requested instant transportation back to the starship *Enterprise,* a frequent order Captain Kirk gave (but never exactly in those words) to chief engineer Montgomery "Scotty" Scott on the immensely popular television series *Star Trek,* which premiered in 1966. Trekkies and interplanetary polyglots will be interested to know that "Beam me up!" in Klingon is *Hljol.* The word *Klingon* itself has become a synonym for any barbaric, warlike person, the Klingons in the series being savage, warlike beings from the planet Klingon.

bear   AMERICAN
Slang among truckers for police, especially highway patrol officers. Suggested by the forest ranger hat worn by Smokey the Bear in conservation ads and commercials, which is similar to the hat worn by highway patrol officers. A *bear in the air* is a helicopter patrol.

beastly   BRITISH
Unpleasant, disagreeable, terrible, as in "Beastly night out there."

beast with a belly full of bedsprings   AMERICAN (WEST)
A colorful cowboy rodeo term for a bucking horse. "It was my turn out of the chutes—on a beast with a belly full of bedsprings."

beatin'est   AMERICAN (SOUTH)
Most unusual, remarkable, surprising. "He's the beatin'est child I ever saw."

beat up   BRITISH
To pick someone up to go somewhere. "I'll beat you up about six o'clock."

beautiful   SCOTTISH
Besides its usual uses beautiful can mean delicious, as in "That's a beautiful pudding, lass."

beaver   BRITISH, AMERICAN
A term meaning a "snack." In American slang *beaver* means a woman's pubic hair or an erotic magazine or film, among other things.

beaver away at   BRITISH
To work at consistently. Perhaps influenced by the Americanism *busy as a beaver.*

bedclothes   HAWAIIAN
Often used to mean both men's and women's pajamas as well as sheets and blankets.

bedonderd   SOUTH AFRICAN
Crazy, extremely stubborn. Ultimately derives from a Dutch word meaning the same.

bedsitter   BRITISH
What Americans would term a studio, or one-room, apartment. Often abbreviated to *bedsit.*

been gone   BAHAMIAN
Insane, crazy. "He been gone years now, never come back."

been to   SOUTH AFRICAN
A name South Africans have for any South African who constantly brags about having been to Britain. "He's just another boastful been to."

beer and skittles   BRITISH
A life of ease with no worries; fun and games. *Skittles,* a British tavern game of ninepins in which a wooden ball or disk is used to knock down the pins, takes its name from the Scandinavian *skutill,* "shuttle." This game, similar to shuffleboard, has been played since the early seventeenth century in taverns, where *beer and skittles* became an expression for a relaxed, laid-back lifestyle in which people want no more from life, and no less, than their beer and a game of skittles.

beer boep
SOUTH AFRICAN
A beer belly, pot belly. *Boep* is Afrikaans for a paunch or pot belly.

beetle-brained
BRITISH
An extremely stupid, obstinate person. The term, first recorded in 1604, derives from the Old English *betl*, "a hammer," a *betl* or *beetle-brained* person having a head as hard as a hammer head.

beetroot
BRITISH
The British word for the vegetable Americans always call a *beet*. A *beet* in England is another root vegetable, often called the *sugar beet*.

before you can say knife
BRITISH
Before you can say Jack Robinson—that is, very quickly, instantly.

begorra
IRISH
A mild oath that is an alteration of *by God* and is always associated with the Irish.

belly-god
JAMAICAN
A greedy person, a glutton who looks the part, big belly and all.

beltway
AMERICAN
A highway encircling an urban area. Also called a *belt*, a *belt highway*, or a *belt parkway*.

benastied
AMERICAN (OZARK MOUNTAINS)
Fouled, covered with vomit, feces, dirt, etc., as in "It got so he benastied himself drinking every night," or "Don't benasty the child's mind with such stories."

Benedict Arnold
AMERICAN
The term has been used in America to mean a traitor for more than two hundred years. Familiar is the story of how American general Benedict Arnold plotted to deliver the West Point garrison to British major John André, how the plot failed with André's capture, and how Arnold fled to the British Army. Less familiar are the facts that Arnold was a brilliant soldier and that his treason was provoked by shabby treatment at the hands of superiors.

bent   BRITISH
Slang for crooked or dishonest, as in "He's a bent copper [a dishonest policeman]."

berk   BRITISH
Slang for a fool, a dope, someone nobody respects. The word was not suggested by *jerk,* another synonym, but is of unknown origin. The word, also spelled *burk,* is commonly heard in Australia.

bespoke tailoring   BRITISH
Americans would call this custom tailoring, clothes custom-made for someone.

best boy   AMERICAN
This term, often puzzling to moviegoers when seen in film credits, simply means the chief assistant of the electrician, or gaffer, on a movie or television set.

best maid   SCOTTISH
What would be called the *maid of honor* at a wedding in the United States, a female counterpart of *best man.* The British call the *maid of honor* the *chief bridesmaid.*

the best of British luck!   BRITISH
An ironic saying meaning "lots of luck," I wish you good luck in what is obviously a lost cause.

best parlor   AMERICAN (NEW ENGLAND)
The living room in a house in which guests are entertained and the best furniture is kept.

between a rock and a hard place   AMERICAN
A century ago if someone was badly in need of money, he or she was said to be between a rock and a hard place. The expression was probably born in Arizona during a financial panic in the early 1900s, but over the years its meaning changed and it came to mean being in any tight spot, having to make a hard decision.

between grass and hay   AMERICAN
Between boyhood and manhood; an old-fashioned expression heard nationally that originated in New England.

between the lights

SCOTTISH

An old term meaning twilight that is still occasionally heard.

beyond beyond, beyond the beyond

IRISH

Beyond all reason, totally unreasonable. "That plan of his is beyond beyond."

b.f.

BRITISH

A euphemism for a *bloody fool,* a damned fool. "Bloody" remains a somewhat offensive term in Britain. *Blinking* is another euphemism for *bloody,* as is *blooming.*

bickies

AUSTRALIAN

Short for biscuits (always cookies, not crackers). The term is also heard in England.

big

AMERICAN (SOUTH)

(1) As an adverb, *big* can mean "very, exceedingly," as in "He got big rich." (2) Pregnant. "If you hadn't said you were big, he wouldn't have married you." (3) As a verb, to make or become pregnant; to have sex with. "Sarah won't tell who bigged her."

big-and-so-so

JAMAICAN

Anyone or anything that is large but not very good. A *big-and-so-so* mango, for example, is a large mango variety that isn't very tasty.

big bug

BRITISH

An important person, often a self-important person. Americans would say a *big wheel,* a *big gun,* or a *big shot.*

big eye

BAHAMIAN

A person who has the *big eye* is someone very greedy or gluttonous.

big fella rain

AUSTRALIAN PIDGIN

The wet or rainy season in Australia, as in "Big fella rain come soon." A lake or any large body of water is called *big fella watta.*

big kahuna

AMERICAN (HAWAII)

Originally *kahuna* meant "a priest or wise man"; then, in the 1950s, it also came to mean an expert surfer, and by the 1980s it took on the meaning of "an important person or thing," this last usually in the form of *big kahuna:* "He's the big kahuna around here."

big mother   SOUTH AFRICAN
An older sister of any mother. A *small mother* is a younger sister of any mother.

big-noter   AUSTRALIAN
A braggart who boasts about his or her status, usually exaggerating it. *To big-note* means to boast.

big wheel   AMERICAN, BRITISH
In the United States a "big wheel" is slang for an important or self-important person, while in Britain it just means the Ferris wheel in an amusement park.

big word book   AMERICAN (OZARK MOUNTAINS)
A colorful term for a dictionary still heard among older speakers.

bijou   BRITISH
This word has the general meaning of a small, exquisite trinket, but in British it also means a small but attractive and fashionable building. "That's a bijou residence."

bill   BRITISH
Americans call for the *check* in a restaurant, but Britons always call for the *bill*.

Bill   BRITISH
Slang for a policeman. *The Bill* refers to the police in general.

billabong   AUSTRALIAN
(1) A dead-end channel of water, the offshoot of a river. (2) A stream filled with water in the rainy season. (3) A stagnant pool of water. The word derives from a Wiradhuri Aboriginal word of southeastern Australia.

billiard saloon   BRITISH
See *pool hall.*

billibue SCOTTISH

A great noise or excitement, or uproar, a hullabaloo.

billingsgate BRITISH

Coarse and abusive language, similar to the talk of the fishwives in the Billingsgate fish market along the Thames River in London. The area was named for the man who built the gate below London Bridge leading to the old walled city. But exactly who built Billing's Gate is really unknown. This British word has some American currency.

billycan AUSTRALIAN

Any can in which water or food can be carried and boiled over a fire; also *billy.* The term derives from the Aboriginal Australian *billa,* "water."

bin BRITISH

A mental hospital, a looney bin. "He's been in the bin three years now."

bioscope SOUTH AFRICAN

The cinema, the movies. "He's gone to the bioscope every night." The term derives from the movie projector called a *bioscope.*

bird BRITISH

A pretty or smashing girl; the word is said to derive from *burd,* an obsolete dialect word meaning "maiden."

Biro BRITISH, IRISH

A trademarked name (pronounced *buy-ro*), sometimes used generically, for a ballpoint pen. The Biro, invented by a Hungarian immigrant named Biro, was the first ballpoint.

biscuit AUSTRALIAN, BRITISH

What Americans would call a *cookie.*

bissom SCOTTISH

An old-fashioned word meaning "a lewd, worthless woman." The British *besom* means an old hag or crone.

bitch SCOTTISH

Can be used as a contemptuous term for a man in Scottish, as it sometimes is in U.S. slang.

bite one's teeth   SOUTH AFRICAN
To be firm and unyielding. "We've got to bite our teeth until help comes."

bite the dust   AMERICAN
To die. Whenever we hear of another desperado *biting the dust* in Western films, we are hearing an almost literal translation of a line found in Homer's *Iliad,* written thousands of years ago. American poet William Cullen Bryant translated the words in 1870: ". . . his fellow warriors, many a one, Fall round him to earth and bite the dust." Earlier, Alexander Pope had eloquently translated the phrase as "bite the bloody sand" and poet William Cowper had it, literally, as "bite the ground."

bit of goods   BRITISH
A pretty or attractive girl; similar terms are a *bit of fluff,* a *hot number,* and a *bit of stuff.*

bitty   AUSTRALIAN
Something made up of different things that don't fit together. "The novel was quite bitty, each chapter written by a different author."

blackbeetle   BRITISH
A name generally used for the cockroach, which may be black but is not a beetle.

black Christmas   AMERICAN (CUMBERLAND MOUNTAINS)
A Christmas or Christmas season without any snow. "We had a black Christmas last year. You need a white Christmas for a good crop year." (Snow adds nitrogen to the soil and is widely called "poor man's manure" because it fertilizes the soil, producing better crops.)

black-coat worker   BRITISH
An office worker. The British version of the American *white-collar worker.*

blackjock   SOUTH AFRICAN
City policemen; so named because of their black uniforms.

blackleg   BRITISH
A labor scab, a strikebreaker.

blackspot AMERICAN, BRITISH
Used in America for a disease of roses and other plants, in Britain *blackspot* means a dangerous spot in the road, where road signs with a black dot on them indicate dangerous areas.

blaps SOUTH AFRICAN
A blunder, gaff, or blooper. "He commits a blaps every time he opens his mouth." An Afrikaans word.

blastie SCOTTISH
A derogatory term for a dwarf or someone else very short.

blate SCOTTISH
Very shy. The word may derive from *blater* for a sheep.

blaw SCOTTISH
A commonly heard word meaning "to blow."

bleaky JAMAICAN
Dull, foggy, or overcast weather. "It sure looks like a bleaky day."

blerry SOUTH AFRICAN
A corruption of the British *bloody* or *bleeding,* meaning lousy, damned, etc. "Get that blerry car out of here!"

blether SCOTTISH
To talk nonsense or foolishness. "He blethered on, the blithering fool."

blighter BRITISH
A person of low, obnoxious character, although the word has lost some of its force and is used almost affectionately in terms such as *a lucky blighter.*

blik SOUTH AFRICAN
A type of South African music named for the sound *(blik)* emanating from cheap guitars or banjos.

blimey! BRITISH
A euphemistic oath that is probably a contraction of *God blind me!*

blind as a one-eyed mule in a root cellar   AMERICAN (WEST)
Completely blind, unable to see or understand. "That umpire is blind as a one-eyed mule in a root cellar."

blind road   BRITISH
What Americans would call a *dead-end street;* a blind road has no "eye" or passage through it.

blinker   SCOTTISH
A star in the sky, or a pretty girl glittering with beauty.

block of flats   BRITISH
An apartment building.

block of ice   NEW ZEALAND
An ice cube. In England, where the term originated, the American *ice cube* is mainly used today.

bloke   BRITISH
A guy, fellow, man, chap, male friend. The word's origin is unknown, and while the word is chiefly British, dating back to the mid-nineteenth century, it has limited usage in America.

bloodnound   AMERICAN (SOUTH)
A bullfrog; the word is heard chiefly in South Carolina. Also known as a *bloodynoun.*

bloody   AUSTRALIAN, BRITISH
Eric Partridge's *Words!* has a two-thousand-word essay on *bloody,* which became an objectionable adjective in Britain in the early 1800s, though it had been respectable enough for a century before. Meaning "very," it may have become objectionable because it suggested menstruation, but Partridge believed that "the idea of blood suffices" to explain the squeamishness. *Bloody* is often inserted for emphasis within words, as in *abso-bloody-lutely.* Though it originated in England, the term has become typical of Australian speech, among the most overworked adjectives in the national vocabulary. While the British commonly use it to mean "lousy" or "damned," Australians employ *bloody* to give emphasis to any expression, as in "You're bloody right, mate, let's have a bloody beer."

bloody cow!   AUSTRALIAN

A common expletive similar to the American *holy cow!*

bloomer   BRITISH

A blunder in speech, a *blooper. Bloomers* in current American speech is a
humorous term for girls' or women's underpants (their name deriving
from the name of a costume worn by American feminist Amelia Jenks
Bloomer). *Bloomers* in Britain, however, are blunders in speech, or *bloopers,* as they would be called in America.

bloomin'   BRITISH

Often used as an intensifier, as in "It's not bloomin' likely."

blower   AUSTRALIAN, BRITISH

Slang for a telephone. Perhaps from the slang *blower* for a very talkative
person.

blow that for a lark!   BRITISH

I've had enough of this. "Inside work? Blow that for a lark, I like working
outside." Also *Sod that for a lark!*

bludge   AUSTRALIAN, NEW ZEALAND

(1) To avoid work. (2) To sponge on someone. "He constantly bludged on
me." A *bludger* is a slacker who depends on others to do his work for him.

blue   AMERICAN (NEW ENGLAND)

Synonymous for a blueberry. "He picked a bucket of fine, ripe blues."

bluebottle   BRITISH

Another name for a policeman, after the blue police uniforms. See *bobby.*

blue-brick universities   BRITISH

Patterned on "blue blood," this is a nickname for universities with the
highest prestige and pedigrees, such as Cambridge and Oxford.

bluey   AUSTRALIAN

A dog used for herding cattle (see *blue heeler*) or, for some unknown reason, a red-haired person.

blue-eyed boy   BRITISH
A favorite or pet; a *fair-haired boy* in America.

blue John   AMERICAN (OZARK MOUNTAINS)
(1) Skim milk, because it often has a bluish tint. (2) Sour or slightly sour milk.

bluenose   AMERICAN (NEW ENGLAND)
A person of rigid puritanical habits. The term was first applied to lumbermen and fishermen of northern New England and referred to the color of their noses, the blue induced by long exposure to cold weather. Later the word was applied to the aristocratic inhabitants of Boston's Back Bay area, possibly in allusion to their apparently "frigid" manner. *Bluenose* also is used as an opprobrious nickname for Nova Scotians, but there the word probably derives from the name of a popular Nova Scotian potato.

boat   AMERICAN
A large, often gas-guzzling yet very comfortable American car.

bob   BRITISH
The British slang word *bob,* long a shilling, now means five pence. It has been suggested that the word, familiar to all British-speaking peoples, may come from the name of Sir Robert (Bob) Walpole (1676–1745). The first earl of Walpole was intimately connected with money in his posts as army paymaster, first commissioner of the treasury, chancellor of the Exchequer, and finally as England's prime minister. But the word *bob* isn't recorded until about 1810, some sixty-five years after Walpole's death, so the derivation remains uncertain.

bobbasheely   AMERICAN (SOUTH)
To walk in no great rush but to move on, to saunter. A *bobbasheely* also can mean "a very close friend"; in fact, the word is said to derive from a Choctaw Indian word meaning "my brother."

bobby   BRITISH
The British *bobby* is among the most familiar of eponymous words, despite the fact that "copper" or "cop" is more often used today by Britons to describe a policeman. The well-known word honors Sir Robert Peel, British home secretary (1828–1930) when the Metropolitan Police Act

remodeled London's police force. Peel, whose wealthy father bought him his seat in Parliament, first won fame as chief secretary for Ireland, where he was nicknamed "Orange Peel" for his support of the Protestant "Orangemen." At this time he established the Irish constabulary under the Peace Preservation Act (1814), and his policemen were soon called "Peel's Bloody Gang" and then *peelers*. *Peelers* remained the name for both Irish and London police for many years, *bobby* and *robert* not being recorded in print until about 1851. *Peeler* is still commonly used in Ireland. Other names the British have for a police officer include *constable, pointsman* (for a traffic cop), *P.C.* (for police constable), and *bogey* (underworld slang).

Bob's your uncle!   BRITISH
That's it, that'll be all right, you've got it right, there you go! The term only dates back to the 1880s, but no one has been able to convincingly identify the real "Bob" in the phrase, if indeed there was one.

bod   AMERICAN, AUSTRALIAN, BRITISH
To Americans *bod* is slang for body ("That's some bod"), but both Australians and Britons use it to mean a person, as in "Some bod came uninvited."

bodega   AMERICAN
Originally a small Hispanic grocery store, often selling a large variety of items and including a wine shop, but now used to mean any small grocery store. *Bodega* derives from the Spanish for "storehouse."

boffin   AUSTRALIAN, BRITISH
A specialist, especially a scientist, who knows a lot about his field but next to nothing about anything else.

bog   AUSTRALIAN, BRITISH
Slang for a toilet, as in "I'm going to nip down to the bog." *Bog paper* is toilet paper.

bogey   AUSTRALIAN
A swimming hole; also called a *bogey hole*.

bogger   IRISH
Someone from the country; a hick or a hayseed.

bogle   SCOTTISH
A boogeyman, phantom, scarecrow. "Be good or the bogles will get you."

bog off   BRITISH
To go away, leave. "They bogged off home earlier than usual."

bog standard   BRITISH
Something completely ordinary, without anything special added, as in "It's a bog standard car, a car without extras."

bogtrotter   IRISH
A derogatory term meaning any Irishman; after the many bogs in Ireland.

bogus   HAWAIIAN
Means not "false" but "boastful" in the Hawaiian da kine dialect. "He give us this bogus talk."

bok   SOUTH AFRICAN
A lover; from the Afrikaans *bok,* meaning flame, boyfriend. Also can mean any avid, eager person.

Bollywood   INDIAN
A word coined in India to describe the motion picture industry in Bombay.

bomb   AMERICAN, BRITISH
Bomb, in reference to theatrical productions, has completely opposite meanings in England and America. When a play *bombs* in America it is a complete flop—a *bomb.* When a play *bombs* in England it is a great success—a *bomb.* The British use seems to be built on the great explosive force of a real bomb, while the American usage is based upon the utter destruction a bomb creates.

bombo   AUSTRALIAN
Whiskey, or cheap wine, especially if heavily fortified.

bone to pick   AMERICAN
A difficult subject to discuss. "I've got a bone to pick with you." The British would say a *crow to peck.*

boney SOUTH AFRICAN
A motorbike; the term possibly derives from *boneshaker.*

bonk BRITISH
Slang for "to have sexual intercourse." "There they were bonking away."

bonnet BRITISH, SCOTTISH
Not a woman's hat. In Scotland, a man's or a boy's brimless round cap; in Britain, the hood of a car (the hinged cover of the engine compartment).

bonny SCOTTISH
Lovely, first-rate. "'Tis a bonny dress she's wearin'."

bonny clabber IRISH
A drink of sour buttermilk. From the Gaelic *bainne,* milk, and *claba,* thick or thickened.

bonspiel SCOTTISH
A curling competition between two teams. Curling is a Scottish game in which players on opposite teams slide heavy stones toward a circle at either end of the ice.

bonzer AUSTRALIAN
A regular guy who can be counted on to perform well at whatever he does. "He's a real bonzer to have on your team." Also called a *bottler.* Also can be anything excellent, exceptional, very pleasant.

boob AMERICAN, BRITISH
In America *boob* is slang for either a stupid person or a woman's breast. In Britain the word means to be put in jail, as in "He was boobed last night."

booking office AUSTRALIAN
The ticket window in a railway station.

boot BRITISH, AMERICAN (SOUTH)
The trunk (storage compartment) of a car. Chiefly a British term, the word was sometimes used in Georgia and other southern states early in the twentieth century but apparently has little or no use there today.

boozer   AUSTRALIAN
A *boozer* is not a drunkard in Australia, where the word means a bar or a saloon. "Meet me at the boozer."

bore   AUSTRALIAN
(1) A water hole for cattle. (2) An artesian well.

borrow   HAWAIIAN
Means *use,* as in "May I borrow your telephone?" This corresponds to a similar practice in Chinese among the early Chinese settlers in Hawaii.

bothie   IRISH
A hut, small cottage, or house. The term derives from a Gaelic word meaning hut.

bottle   BRITISH
Slang for courage, guts, strength. Perhaps from bottles of gin, whiskey, etc., that can bolster a drinker.

bottle shop   AUSTRALIAN
What would be called a *liquor store* or a *package store* in the United States.

bounder   BRITISH
A well-known old term for a boor, a bad-mannered, poorly raised person, often an unprincipled man who takes advantage of women.

bouzing   SCOTTISH
Boozing, drinking. "We sat bouzing at the nappy [ale]."

bovver boy   BRITISH
A rowdy who enjoys fighting and picking fights. *Bovver* also means violent behavior, and *bovver boots* are heavy, thick boots often used for kicking opponents in fights. *Bovver* is a Cockney pronunciation of *bother.*

bowl over   AMERICAN, BRITISH
Apparently this term, meaning to surprise greatly, is a British expression coined in the late nineteenth century. It is said to have derived from a cricket term describing the bowler throwing the ball to the batsman.

box
BRITISH
A television; similar to the U.S. slang *tube*. "Anything on the box tonight?"

boxty
IRISH
A potato. "They hadn't a boxty to their name in The Famine."

boys of the bulldog breed
BRITISH
Pugnacious men, often sailors, often were called *boys of the bulldog breed*. The words come from the popular nineteenth-century song "Sons of the Sea, All British Born." Bulldogs are a brave, tenacious breed formerly used in bull-baiting.

bra
JAMAICAN, SOUTH AFRICAN
Can be used to mean "brother" or as the equivalent of "Mr." applied to any man. As black slang for *brother* the term is also heard in South Africa. The U.S. equivalent is *bro*.

braces
BRITISH
Suspenders. The word *suspenders* is used in Britain to mean what Americans call garters—that is, elastic devices to hold up socks—or a garter belt.

brae
SCOTTISH
A hillside or a slope. Also heard in northern England.

brag
AMERICAN (SOUTH)
Excellent; fit to be boasted about. A prize dog, for example, is a *brag dog;* superlative cotton is *brag cotton.*

brak
SOUTH AFRICAN
A mongrel dog; from the French *braque,* hound. Also *brakkie.*

brassed off
NEW ZEALAND, AUSTRALIAN
Angry. "He was brassed off at him."

braw
SCOTTISH
(1) Fine, good-looking, pleasant, excellent in any respect. (2) Finely or splendidly dressed. (3) Gaudily dressed.

breakdown gang   BRITISH
What would be a *wrecking crew* in America. *Breakdown gangs* often work
with a *breakdown crane,* a wrecker boom.

breakdown truck   BRITISH
The British term for what Americans would call a *tow truck.*

break in   AMERICAN
(1) To wear or use in order to make comfortable, as in "I'm breaking in
this new pair of shoes." (2) To train someone for a job. "He broke in his
replacement." (3) To interrupt. "He broke in with his usual stupid
remarks." (4) To enter by force. "He broke into the store."

break one's manners   AMERICAN (SOUTH)
To become intentionally rude. "Don't break your manners, Jody."

breathalized   BRITISH
To be stopped by the police and have one's breath tested for alcohol use.
The term is not heard in the United States, although *Breathalyzer,* a trade-
mark, is.

breed a scab on one's nose   AMERICAN (WEST)
A warning to someone that he or she is raising or stirring up trouble, is
looking for a punch on the nose. "Keep talking like that you'll breed a
scab on your nose."

breeks   SCOTTISH
Trousers; a form of *breeches.* Also heard in northern England.

breker   SOUTH AFRICAN
A tough, leather-jacketed motorcyclist. "The brekers were all over the road
last night." Pronounced *breaker.*

brekkers   BRITISH
Slang among the upper class and their imitators for breakfast.

bride   JAMAICAN
Can be applied to the bridegroom as well as the bride at a wedding. The
bridegroom in Jamaican is the best man.

Bristols   BRITISH
British rhyming slang made the slang *titties* (for breasts) into *Bristol Cities* (because they come in pairs) and later dropped the second word, as is frequently the case in rhyming slang, and made *Bristol* plural—so that *Bristols* became slang for female breasts. See also *charlies*.

broke   HAWAIIAN
Often used to mean *tore,* as in "My shirt broke on the nail."

brokkie   SOUTH AFRICAN
A small piece or morsel; from the Afrikaans *brokke,* meaning the same. Pronounced *brock-ie.*

brolly   BRITISH, AUSTRALIAN
Slang for an umbrella. First recorded in 1873. *Gamp* (q.v.) also is commonly used.

brother belong me   AUSTRALIAN PIDGIN
A friend or an acquaintance. "Him brother belong me." For other forms of pidgin see *mary.*

broth of a lad   IRISH
A big, sturdy young man. "He was a broth of a lad."

brucktummuck   JAMAICAN
A very steep hill. One that strains the stomach of anyone trying to climb it.

brum   BRITISH
Counterfeit or cheap merchandise is called *brum* after the city of Birmingham, England, which was often pronounced *Brummagem* locally in the seventeenth century. The city had a reputation as a manufacturing center of cheap trinkets and a place where counterfeit coins were made.

bub   AMERICAN
An old-fashioned term of address to a man, often in an angry tone. "Listen, bub, you better get out of here."

bubba   AMERICAN (SOUTH)
Bubba, chiefly in the South, is a term of address meaning "brother" and is used by friends as well as relatives.

bubbler   AUSTRALIAN
A descriptive term for a water fountain.

bubkes   AMERICAN
Usually pronounced *BUB-kiss,* this Yiddish word, from the Russian for "beans," means nothing or very little, a small amount, something trivial. "You know what I got for the job? Bubkes!"

buck   AMERICAN, CANADIAN, SOUTH AFRICAN
In the United States and Canada, a dollar; in South Africa, a *rand.* Also Hollywood slang for a hundred thousand dollars: "He brought the movie in at under ten bucks."

bucket   AUSTRALIAN
To blame a person for something or everything; to dump a bucket of blame on him or her. "Don't bucket me about your troubles."

buckhorse   BRITISH
Old slang for a punch or other blow. If you gave him a few shillings, the fighter John Smith, who went by the ring name of *Buckhorse,* would let you punch him on the side of the head as hard as you could. The well-known boxer saw his name enter the language beginning in about 1850— that is, if he saw anything but stars after a while.

Buckley's chance   AUSTRALIAN
Little or no chance. Possibly from the name of cornered nineteenth-century outlaw John Buckley, "whose chance of escape was made hopeless," according to a contemporary report.

bucko   IRISH
A young man or lad. "See here, now, me fine bucko."

bucks party   AUSTRALIAN
A party for a man who is getting married; a *bachelor party.* See also *stag party.*

buddy   CANADIAN (NEWFOUNDLAND)
Can mean an unknown man as well as a friend or a fellow, as in "Who's that buddy coming down the road?"

buddy sap   AMERICAN (NEW ENGLAND)
Maple sap dark in color and strong in flavor. Maple syrup is buddy when made from sap running at the time the maple buds begin to open.

bug   AMERICAN
A word used among fishermen for a lobster. "He took more than fifty bugs today."

bugger   BRITISH
Bugger in British never means a child, as it does in American expressions such as "He's just a little bugger." A *bugger* in England is a sodomite, and *to bugger* is to sodomize—in fact, use of the word in print was actionable in England for many years. *Bugger* in this sense, which is sometimes heard in America, derives, down a tortuous path, from the medieval Latin *Bulgarus,* meaning "both a Bulgarian and a sodomite." The word first referred to a Bulgarian and then to the Bulgarian Albigenses or Bulgarian Heretics, an eleventh-century religious sect whose monks and nuns were believed to practice sodomy.

bugger all   AUSTRALIAN, BRITISH
Slang for "damn all," "damn everything." The words also can mean "nothing," as in "I know bugger all about it."

buggered   AUSTRALIAN
Among Australian speakers *buggered* has no sexual connotations, meaning simply to be tired, exhausted. See also *bugger.*

bugger off!   BRITISH
British slang for "Get the hell out of here!"

bughouse   AMERICAN, SOUTH AFRICAN
Originally the name for a rundown movie theater (much as Americans would call such a theater "the Itch"), but now a name for movie houses in general. "We took our kids to the bughouse yesterday." *Bughouse* means "crazy" in American slang, as in "He's gone bughouse."

build a fire under   AMERICAN

Hillfolk may be responsible for this common national expression, meaning to stir someone into action. Mountain people, it is said, sometimes built fires under their mules to get the beasts moving when they were standing four legs spread and refusing to budge despite every other tactic.

bulkie   SCOTTISH

A policeman.

bumble   BRITISH

The beadle Bumble in Dickens's *Oliver Twist* is a self-important, domineering parish official. His name has come to be used for all such officious bureaucrats.

bumbye   HAWAIIAN

By and by, in a while. "Bumbye we go beach." Also *bymbye*.

bumf   BRITISH

What Americans would call *gobbledygook*. *Bumf* is a shortening of *bum fodder*, "toilet paper," and also refers to the reams of directives issued by government agencies. The *bum* in *bum fodder* refers, of course, to the buttocks.

bumfuzzle   AMERICAN (APPALACHIAN MOUNTAINS)

To confuse. "You bumfuzzled everybody with that story."

bumpy   SCOTTISH

Another word used for the buttocks or bum.

bundu   SOUTH AFRICAN

Wild, remote country, like the Australian *outback* (q.v.); from the African Shona language *bundo*, grasslands.

bung   AUSTRALIAN

To throw, as in "Bung a tinner [can of beer] over here."

bung-ho!   BRITISH

Used both as a synonym for *cheerio!* (q.v.), good-bye, and as a toast like the more popular *cheers* (q.v.).

buppie   SOUTH AFRICAN
An acronym (patterned on the U.S. *yuppie*) for a black urban professional person.

burgled   BRITISH
Americans would say *burglarized*. "This house was burgled."

burke   BRITISH
To smother or strangle someone to death, though in relatively recent times it has also come to mean to hush up, to suppress something, especially a rumor or relevant fact in an argument. Both meanings commemorate a murderer. William Burke (1792–1829) was an Irish laborer who with his confederate William Hare murdered some thirty people and sold their bodies to anatomists, smothering their victims so no marks would be left on them. Burke was hanged, but Hare turned state's evidence and went free.

burn   SCOTTISH
A small stream; a brook. From the Old English *burna; to burn*, set afire, comes from another Old English word.

burnt to a frazzle   BRITISH
Completely burned, ruined. "The roast she made was burnt to a frazzle."

buryin'   AMERICAN (NEW ENGLAND)
An expression heard in Maine for *funeral*. "We had his buryin' yesterday."

bushed   AUSTRALIAN, AMERICAN
In Australia, to be lost in *bush* country or to be confused, bewildered. In America, to be tired, worn out.

bushie   AUSTRALIAN
Someone living in the bush, far from civilization. Also called a *bushman*.

bushranger   AUSTRALIAN
An old-time outlaw like the famous Ned Kelly, "scourge of the bush," who became an Australian folk hero.

bushwalking   AUSTRALIAN
What the Aussies call hiking in wilderness areas. "Ten of them went out
bushwalking."

business wahine   HAWAIIAN
A prostitute; *wahine* means woman in the native Hawaiian language.

buster   AUSTRALIAN
A high, cold, southerly wind. *Buster* also means anything of great size.

busy as a cat with fur on fire   AMERICAN
Very busy indeed. The expression is said to have been coined by American cartoonist T. A. Dorgan ("TAD") early in the twentieth century.

butcher's   BRITISH
A look at something. "Give us a butcher's at your present." The term is
from the Cockney rhyming slang *butcher's hook,* which means a look.

buttered eggs   BRITISH
Still used for what Americans call scrambled eggs, though the latter term
is more popular in Britain today.

butt in   AMERICAN
To meddle in someone else's business or interrupt a conversation. A
buttinsky is someone who butts in.

Buttondownhemd   GERMAN
A button-down shirt. One of the well over a thousand words adopted
or adapted by the Germans, this one combining German and English.
Others include *der clown, der Toaster, der Computer, der Swimming pool,
das Apartment, der Hobby, die Cocktail-Party, der Drink, der Boss, das
Baby, die Chips* (french fries), *der Teenager,* and *das Rock and Roll.* Adjectives such as *happy, simple,* and *super!* are used in German without initial capital letters.

butty   SCOTTISH
Another word for a sandwich. Also heard in Northern Ireland.

bwana   SWAHILI
Boss. This is *not* an English word, despite its frequent use as an often
servile form of address to Great White Hunters in so many old movies set

in Africa. It comes directly from Swahili, the first or second language of millions of Africans.

bway   JAMAICAN
Boys. "Them bway don't go to school."

bya   JAMAICAN
To sing a baby to sleep with a lullaby, to "rockabye" the baby.

by a short head   BRITISH
A track term meaning to win by a small distance, less than a horse's head. The American equivalent would be *by a nose.*

by-election   BRITISH
What Americans would call a *special election,* held between regular elections, as to fill an office that has come open unexpectedly.

by guess and by God   AMERICAN (OZARK MOUNTAINS)
To do something randomly, without much careful planning, is to do it by *guess and by God.* The planner hopes that God will see it through. "He did it by guess and by God and it worked for him."

by half   BRITISH
The expression, which has some currency in America, means "much too much," as in "She's too proud by half."

B.Y.O.   AUSTRALIAN
A restaurant without a liquor license where you can bring your own wine or liquor.

cabinet   AMERICAN
The term for a milkshake in Boston.

caboose   CANADIAN
A cabin on wheels moved from place to place and used by lumberjacks.

ca'canny   SCOTTISH

This Scots expression for "go easily, don't exert yourself" is used by trade unions in Scotland when they want to bring pressure on their employers without going on strike. It amounts, in effect, to what Americans would call a *slowdown*.

cack-handed   BRITISH

Though it literally means "left-handed," this word is used to mean clumsy, awkward.

cad   *British*

A vulgar, bad-mannered man without any gentlemanly qualities. The word derives from the French *cadet*, which once meant a younger member of a noble family. Although the word is known in America, it is not widely used there.

caird   SCOTTISH

A tramp, Gypsy, any wanderer. Also heard in northern England, the word derives from the Gaelic *ceard* for a smith, perhaps because smiths traveled extensively in their work.

calabash cousins   HAWAIIAN

A blend from Spanish and English meaning two close friends, so close they drink from the same calabash or bowl.

call box   BRITISH

In America a *call box* would be called a *telephone booth*. Britons also call it a *kiosk*.

calluses on one's feet   AMERICAN (APPALACHIAN MOUNTAINS)

Said of any child born fewer than nine months after his or her parents were married, because the child would have to walk fast to make a nine-month trip in less time. "He was born with calluses on his feet."

callyhootin'   AMERICAN (SOUTH)

Moving at a breakneck pace, very rapidly and noisily; moving recklessly; moving lickety-split. "Here comes a callyhootin'!" It possibly derives, according to one source, from "the confusion and noise that accompanies the musical instrument called a calliope."

camp bed BRITISH
A cot. Also called a *safari bed,* this light, folding cot is made of canvas stretched over a metal frame.

candy floss BRITISH
The *cotton candy* often sold at fairs, circuses, amusement parks, etc.

candy store AMERICAN
What the British call a *sweetshop* (q.v.) or a *confectioner's* (q.v.).

canny SCOTTISH
(1) Steady, gentle. (2) Snug, quiet. *Canny* in its usual sense of careful, shrewd, and thrifty is also heard in Scotland.

can't pour piss out of a boot AMERICAN (WEST)
Slang for can't do the simplest things. "When it comes to ranchin', he can't pour piss out of a boot."

cantrip SCOTTISH
A trick or a mischievous prank, often one played by children.

can't say boo to a goose BRITISH
The phrase describes someone very shy or timid.

can't see to can't see AMERICAN (SOUTH)
Before dawn to after dusk. "I was out hunting from can't see to can't see."

canty SCOTTISH, AUSTRALIAN
In Scotland *canty* means "cheerful," while in Australia its meaning is "disagreeable, irritable."

caravan BRITISH
A car trailer with living quarters.

cariole CANADIAN
(1) A light sled pulled by a horse. (2) A one-person sled pulled by dogs.

carline SCOTTISH
A term for a witch, a hag, an old woman.

car park   BRITISH
Called a *parking lot* or a *parking field* in the United States.

carriage   BRITISH
A railroad coach. A *coach* is the usual word for an intercity bus in Britain.

carry coals to Newcastle   BRITISH
England's Newcastle-upon-Tyne was the first coal port in the world, the initial charter granted to the town for the digging of coal given by Henry III in 1239. The fact that no one in his right mind would import coal into this coal-mining county gave rise in the nineteenth century to the expression *to carry coals to Newcastle,* "to do something superfluous, to take something where it is already plentiful." The phrase has limited use in the United States.

carry on   BRITISH
Get on with whatever you were doing. "Well, carry on now!" A *carry-on* can also mean a love affair in Britain, deriving from "carrying on with."

carve-up   BRITISH
Slang for a war, or a battle in a war.

cascate   BAHAMIAN
To throw up, vomit; the word possibly derives from *cascade,* one meaning of which is "to vomit."

catamaran   CANADIAN
Can mean a heavy sled used to haul logs as well as the two-hulled sailboat connected by a frame.

catapult   BRITISH
A slingshot; the British term is never used in this sense in the United States.

catch colt   AMERICAN (WEST)
A western euphemism for an illegitimate child, called an *old-field colt* and a *woods colt* in other U.S. regions. Originally the term meant a colt that wasn't the result of its owner intentionally breeding its parents.

catch someone bending   BRITISH
To surprise someone, catch him from behind or at any disadvantage.

catch you up   BRITISH
Catch up with you, as in "You go on ahead, I'll catch you up."

cat on a hot tin roof   AMERICAN
Best known today as the title of Tennessee Williams's famous play, the expression has been in wide use since the turn of the twentieth century. Apparently it came to the South and then the rest of the country via a similar British phrase, *like a cat on hot bricks,* which has been traced back to about 1880 and which also means "someone ill at ease, uncomfortable, not at home in a place or situation."

cattle singer   AMERICAN (WEST)
A cowboy able to calm restless cattle, even in some cases those on the verge of a stampede, by singing to them.

caught bang to rights   BRITISH
Caught red-handed. "He was caught bang to rights by the constable."

cave!   BRITISH
Used by schoolboy lookouts to warn others in a group that a policeman or teacher or any adult is coming and that they'd better clear out or stop what they're doing. *Cave* is Latin for "beware." In America the warning would be *chickee!* (q.v.), as in "Chickee, the cops!" or *cheezit!* (q.v.). The Scottish equivalent is *shote!*

ceilidh   IRISH
A gathering where people pair off and dance traditional dances, a caller shouting out the moves and steps. *Ceilidha* (pronounced KAY-lee) have become very popular recently. The term is also used in Canada and Scotland.

chaff   SOUTH AFRICAN
To get fresh with a woman verbally, especially when she is alone. "He chaffed her unmercifully."

chaklata   JAMAICAN
An early morning light breakfast, the first meal of the day. The word derives from *chocolate.*

chalkie   AUSTRALIAN
Slang for a schoolteacher, because teachers often write with chalk on blackboards. See also *schoolie.*

champers   BRITISH
A slang synonym for champagne. "Have a glass of champers with me."
Also heard in America.

chance child   BRITISH
A euphemism for an illegitimate child.

changing room   BRITISH
A locker room at a gymnasium or pool.

chap   AMERICAN, BRITISH
A guy, fellow, man. A *chapman* was formerly a common term for a wan-
dering peddler or merchant. *Chap* is simply an abbreviation of *chapman*—
a *good chapman*, or *chap*, became in time a *good fellow*. The word is
sometimes heard in the United States. In the American Ozarks, however,
chap is never used for an adult; there it means a male child usually and
even a little girl occasionally.

Charley More   BRITISH
An old term meaning "honest," "Charley More—the fair (or square)
thing"—was the legend on the huge tavern sign of a Maltese publican in
about 1840. His name became synonymous with fair or straight dealing,
and *Charley More* became a British naval term for one who is honest and
upright, though the term is not much used anymore.

charlie   BRITISH
Slang for a fool or a jerk, a patsy who will fall for any obvious scheme.

charlies   BRITISH
The British slang *charlies* for a woman's breasts, one etymologist suggests,
derives from "the opulent charms displayed by the mistresses of Charles
II." According to this theory *charlies* was originally *Charlie's* because they
were "playthings belonging to the king." In any case, a number of things
have been named *charley* or *charlies* by the British. Long before policemen were dubbed *bobbies,* London night watchmen were called *Charleys,*
or *Charlies.* The obsolete designation is believed to derive from the name
of Charles I, who extended and improved the London night watch to curb
street offenses in 1640. Charles I, beheaded by Cromwell in 1649, definitely wore a short, triangular beard called a *Charlie* that is now known
as a *Vandyke. Charley* was also the term for a fox used by the British for

almost a century, beginning in the late 1700s. The eponym here is brilliant British politician and foreign secretary Charles James Fox (1749–1806), who constantly outfoxed the opposition. See also *bobby; Bristols.*

chawan cut   HAWAIIAN

A haircut that looks as if it had been done with a bowl. The word *chawan,* introduced by Japanese settlers, means "bowl."

cheapjack goods   BRITISH

Shoddy, cheap merchandise often sold in bargain stores. The word has some currency in the United States.

check it out   AMERICAN

To look at, pay attention to. This expression is probably military slang dating back to World War II.

cheechako   CANADIAN

A newcomer or tenderfoot, the word taken from Chinook jargon in Yukon gold rush days and still used, as in "Welcome to the Yukon, cheechako." Also heard in Alaska.

cheerio!   BRITISH

Good-bye or good health. Used as a toast and when parting. See also *bung-ho!*

cheers   BRITISH, IRISH, SOUTH AFRICAN

In South Africa, good-bye, as in "Cheers, I'll see you later." In Britain either a toast or as a synonym for "thanks," as when acknowledging a small favor. The word is also used with the latter meaning in Ireland. See also *slainte.*

cheezit   AMERICAN

Cheezit or *cheese it,* meaning to stop what you are doing immediately, has been a slang expression for almost two centuries, while "Cheese it, the cops!" (Stop what you are doing and get out of here quickly!) goes back at least a hundred years. See also *cave!*

chemist   BRITISH

A drugstore or a pharmacy. Also called a *chemist's shop.*

cheque book farmer   SOUTH AFRICAN
A gentleman farmer, one who doesn't have to depend on what he grows
for his living.

cheque card   BRITISH
What would be called a *credit card* or a *bank card* by Americans.

chesterfield   AMERICAN, BRITISH, CANADIAN
Three different meanings here: The British call a large, overstuffed sofa a
chesterfield, while the Canadians apply the name to *any* sofa and Americans sometimes use it for a man's velvet-collared overcoat with concealed buttons. The couch and the man's overcoat called a chesterfield
were introduced in the nineteenth century. Both may have been named
in honor of Philip Dormer Stanhope, the fourth earl of Chesterfield
(1694–1773), but it is more likely that they commemorate a later earl of
Chesterfield, who may even have invented them. Just which earl no one
knows.

chew up the scenery   AMERICAN
To overact or ham it up. Originally only a theatrical expression, these
words can be traced to their inventor, author Dorothy Parker, who first
used them in a 1930 theater review: "More glutton than artist . . . he com-
mences to chew up the scenery."

chiak, chiike   AUSTRALIAN
Cheek, impudence. The word is a corruption of *cheek. To chiak* is to tease,
ridicule.

chickee   AMERICAN
(1) Someone who serves as a lookout in a crime such as a break-in or a
burglary. "You guys go in, I'll play chickee." (2) A cry made by a criminal
or schoolboy lookout meaning stop what you're doing and get out of there,
as in "Chickee, the cops!"

chicken flesh   BRITISH
What Americans would call *goose pimples* or *gooseflesh.*

chickens today, feathers tomorrow   AMERICAN
An old saying roughly equivalent to "here today, gone tomorrow," or life
is short.

Chic Sale   AMERICAN
An outhouse. Among the most ignominious fates suffered by an American actor befell vaudeville comedian Chic Sale, an early twentieth-century performer whose act was very popular throughout the country. Sale
was noted for his comedy routine about building an outhouse, and even
wrote a book about his specialty. He is hardly remembered today, except
in this term, in use since the 1920s.

chief cook and bottle washer   AMERICAN
A humorous name for someone doing a lot of menial work.

chief editor   BRITISH
What Americans would call the editor in chief of any publication.

child-minder   BRITISH
In America and Australia a *child-minder* would be called a *baby-sitter.*

chilly bin   NEW ZEALAND
A cooler used for picnics, etc., to keep beer and food cold.

chin chin   BRITISH
Used by the British to mean hello or good-bye. Relatively few Americans
have been greeted by anyone using this expression, but it is an oriental
greeting often encountered in literature since the early nineteenth century.
There is no connection here with the lower jaw, the word for which derives
from the Old English *cin. Chin chin* is just a corruption of the Chinese salu-
tation *ts'ing ts'ing.*

china plate   AUSTRALIAN
Aussie rhyming slang for mate, as in "Me old china plate." Also heard as
china alone.

Chinese burn   BRITISH
A twisting of the skin of the wrist so that it burns; usually practiced by
schoolboys. Called an *Indian burn* in the United States.

chinwag   BRITISH
Small talk, chatter, or gossip. "They do more chinwag than work."

chip in BRITISH
To interrupt, or to *butt in,* as Americans would say. "Every time I opened my mouth, he would chip in."

chips BRITISH
French fries, as in *fish and chips.* A *chippy* is a shop where fish and chips are made and sold, this far from its American meaning of a prostitute.

chisler IRISH
Slang for a kid, a child, a young lad. "He riz (raised) three chislers." Also *chiseler.*

chit AMERICAN, BRITISH
A British and American term for a voucher of money owed for food or drink, though the British also use it to mean any I.O.U. The word derives from the Hindustani *citthi,* "a short note." In British colonial India, Hindu civil servants seem to have been in the habit of writing an inordinate amount of *citthis* about every conceivable matter. The British found this practice time-consuming and inefficient, criticizing it so often that the word *citthi* eventually became the easier-to-pronounce *chitty* and then *chit* in their vocabulary. They used *chit* for the notes they signed for drinks and food at their clubs. The *chit* that means a young, often insignificant person or a child goes back much farther in time ("a chit of a girl"). Found in the works of John Wycliffe, it refers to the young of an animal and probably derives from *kitten* or *kit.*

choke rag AMERICAN (WEST)
Cowboys invented this humorous disdainful word for a necktie.

chokey BRITISH
Slang for any prison. "He was sent to the chokey for ten years." *Chokey* derives from the Hindustani *chauki,* for a prison building.

cholmondely AMERICAN
Spelled *cholmondely* and pronounced *chumley,* this an old South Carolinian way to say *chimney.*

chommie SOUTH AFRICAN
Buddy, pal, friend; from *chum,* meaning the same.

choo-choo   AMERICAN
Imitative of the sound of a train locomotive, this baby-talk expression has
for a century meant either the sound of a locomotive, or a locomotive itself,
or a train itself (which is sometimes called a *choo-choo train*). The train
can be a real train or a toy train.

chook   AUSTRALIAN
A chicken. In Australia domesticated chooks live in *chook houses*, not
chicken coops. *Chook* can also be used as a term of affection.

chop   BRITISH
Can refer to dismissal from a job, or death, the ultimate dismissal. "Too
bad he had to get the chop."

chop box   GHANAIAN
Used in Ghana and other parts of West Africa to mean a food storage box.
"He put the vegetables in the chop box."

Chrissie   AUSTRALIAN
A common slang term for Christmas. See also *pressies.*

Christmas gift!   AMERICAN (SOUTH)
A greeting used on Christmas morning, with the first person saying it traditionally receiving a gift. The custom, which has been traced back to as
early as 1844, is no longer observed, but *Christmas gift!*, which used to
be a far more popular Christmas greeting than *Merry Christmas!*, is still
heard among older people.

Christmas tree   CANADIAN (NEWFOUNDLAND)
Often used to mean a Christmas party, as in "He came home late from the
Christmas tree."

chuck a mental   AUSTRALIAN
Slang for to throw a fit, lose one's temper. "He really chucked a mental
when his team lost."

chucker-out   BRITISH
British for the American *bouncer,* a person who acts as a guard in a disco,
nightclub, brothel, or bar, someone who throws out unruly people. The

British term seems to have originated in about 1880, while the older American word dates back to Civil War days.

chump chip   AUSTRALIAN
A thick piece of lamb or other meat. "Put the chump chips on the barbie."

chunder   AUSTRALIAN
To vomit. As a noun *chunder* means vomit, while *chunderous* means revolting, nauseating.

chuntering   BRITISH, NORTHERN ENGLAND
To grumble or to grouse. "There he goes chuntering to himself again."

chutzpah   AMERICAN
Chutzpah (HUTS-pah) derives from a Hebrew word meaning "insolence, audacity." Signifying impudence, gall, brazen nerve, incredible cheek, and unmitigated audacity in Yiddish and in American slang, it more often today indicates an admirable quality in a person. Leo Rosten gives the classic definition of *chutzpah* in *The Joys of Yiddish:* "That quality enshrined in a man who, having killed his mother and father, throws himself on the mercy of the court because he is an orphan." The word is becoming familiar in Britain as well.

cigarette punch   BRITISH
A powerful, bone-breaking uppercut to the jaw of someone who has relaxed and begun to open his mouth after being offered a cigarette. Invented by the Cockney career criminal Ronnie Kray (1934–1995), who, along with his twin brother, Reggie (d. 2000), ran London's underworld from about 1955 to 1970, heading a crime family called the Firm. The Firm also is a nickname for the American CIA.

Civil War   AMERICAN, BRITISH
To the British, the Civil War refers to the war between Charles I and Parliament (1642–1646). To Americans the Civil War was, of course, the War of Secession (1861–1865) between the North and the South.

clatter   IRISH
To hit someone. "He clattered him good." The word also means to make loud noises by hitting hard objects against one another.

claw out   AMERICAN (NEW ENGLAND)
An old term, probably nautical in origin, meaning to make excuses or extricate oneself from a difficult situation. "He sure clawed out of that one."

Clayton's   AUSTRALIAN
Something that isn't authentic. *Clayton's* was originally the name of a soda touted as an alcohol substitute.

cleg   SCOTTISH
A name for the common horsefly, or for the gadflies that annoy livestock.

clerk   BRITISH
Not a salesperson in Britain but an office employee. Pronounced *clark*. A *clerk of the weather* is an imaginary character of folklore said to control the weather.

clever   AMERICAN (OZARK MOUNTAINS)
(1) The word usually means generous, kind, and friendly among hillfolk, not intelligent or sly, which it means in most other areas. "He has a good heart, a very clever man." (2) Beneficial, advantageous. "Their rich uncle promised to do something clever for them." (3) Hospitable. "She treated them as clever as anybody."

clever dick   BRITISH
A wise guy, joker, know-it-all. Originally school slang of the late nineteenth century.

clink   CANADIAN (NEWFOUNDLAND)
A hard blow with the fist. "He gave him a clink in the face."

clinking good   BRITISH
Excellent, terrific, as in "It was a clinking good game, what?"

clocker   AMERICAN
A low-level drug dealer who sells dope on a street corner. *Clocker* probably derives from the older slang *clock*, to watch for a prospective victim of a crime or to watch for a customer.

closet   BRITISH
(1) Any small room. (2) A small conference room. "We'll meet in the closet."

close up sun   JAMAICAN
The time just before darkness; dusk.

clutch   AMERICAN
A crucial moment, and someone who doesn't freeze up at such a time is a clutch performer. The term originated in baseball about eighty years ago in the form of a *clutch hitter*.

C.M.G.   BRITISH
Initials for *Call Me God*, a term used derisively for any self-important person. "There goes C.M.G."

coach   BRITISH
A long-distance bus; an intercity bus.

cobber   AUSTRALIAN
A friend, comrade, companion.

coble   SCOTTISH
A kind of flat-bottomed rowboat commonly used by fishermen.

cock a snook   BRITISH
To thumb one's nose defiantly at someone or something. The origin of *snook* here is unknown.

cockaty   JAMAICAN
Someone boastful, vain, selfish. Said to derive from the African Tur language *kakate*, meaning unruly, unmanageable, selfish.

cocker   BRITISH
Slang for a male friend. "They've been cockers since way back." Also called a *cock*.

cockney, Cockney   BRITISH
The British term *cockney* literally means a "cock's egg," deriving from the Middle English *cokeney*. The word first meant a foolish child or a foolish

person who did not know a good egg from a cock's egg (a small egg with no yolk). Country people next applied the term to city people in general, then to Londoners, and finally to London East Enders, people said to be born within sound of the bells of St. Mary-le-Bow (Bow Bells) who share a characteristic accent called *Cockney.* Actually, people who speak Cockney are found in London far out of earshot of Bow Bells.

cocky   AUSTRALIAN
(1) A nickname for a native Aussie bird, the cockatoo. (2) An Australian farmer.

codfish aristocracy   AMERICAN
The term *codfish aristocracy,* for a pretentious, newly rich person, apparently originated in the Boston area. It's hard to think of any group haughtier than the Lowells and the Cabots (who spoke only to God in the land of the bean and the cod), but the Boston *nouveau riche* who made their money from the codfishing industry in the late eighteenth century apparently gave a grandiose imitation of those haughty Yankees in Back Bay Boston.

codswallop   BRITISH
A British word meaning baloney, bull, hot air, etc. Unfortunately, despite many attempts, no one has determined the term's origin.

coffin clock   SCOTTISH
A grandfather's clock, after its shape, which somewhat resembles a coffin.

Cold-Ass Mary   AMERICAN
Slang for a cold woman, unresponsive sexually, perhaps frigid. "She's the original Cold-Ass Mary."

cold-blooded   AMERICAN (WEST)
Said of an animal, especially a horse, that isn't a Thoroughbred, that is the result of inferior breeding. Such a horse is called a *cold blood,* and a Thoroughbred is called a *hot blood* or *pure.*

cold enough to freeze the balls off a brass monkey   AUSTRALIAN
In Australia, the saying is as above; in Canada it is often the euphemistic *freeze the ears off a brass monkey.* One source indicates this is a late-nine-

teenth-century Australian saying for very, very cold indeed, but others claim it for America and Ireland. The origin of the term is unknown.

coldie   AUSTRALIAN
Slang for a beer, which is always served cold in Australia. See also *amber fluid.*

colleen   IRISH
An Irish girl. The word derives from the Irish Gaelic *cailin,* which in turn comes from Old Irish. Gaelic, incidentally, is still spoken by some six hundred thousand people in Ireland.

college   BRITISH
In Britain, the word does not always mean an institution of higher learning, as it does in the United States (with the exception of terms such as the Electoral College). In Britain a college can also be a prep school, and an association of scholars within a university.

collegiate   CANADIAN
The name Canadians use for secondary school.

Colonel   AMERICAN (SOUTH)
An honorary title in the South, as are *Major* and *General,* since the eighteenth century. Novelist William Faulkner explained it this way in *The Town,* 1957: "Jefferson, Mississippi, the whole South for that matter, was still full at that time of men called General or Colonel or Major because their fathers or grandfathers had been generals or colonels or majors or maybe just privates, in Confederate armies, or who had contributed to the campaign funds of successful state governors." The unofficial title of respect is also used in an ironic or joking sense.

colonial goose   NEW ZEALAND
A humorous term for stuffed lamb or mutton.

to come a cropper   BRITISH
To fall head over heels, to fail, or to be struck by some misfortune. This British expression originally meant only to fall head over heels from a horse—when a horse falls neck and crop (back), it falls completely, all together in one heap. The phrase has some currency outside Britain today.

to come a stummer AUSTRALIAN
To fail financially in any business venture.

come-day, go-day BRITISH
Used to describe a happy-go-lucky person who lives for the moment and lets nothing bother him or her.

to come down BRITISH
To graduate from a university; *to be sent down* means to be expelled from a university.

to come down like a ton of bricks on someone AMERICAN
To be very severe with someone, to come down hard on him or her. This Americanism dates back to the nineteenth century and resembles the British *come down like a thousand bricks on him*. It has been pointed out that the British expression is more technically accurate, in that bricks aren't sold or measured by the ton.

come right SOUTH AFRICAN
Be all right, turn out well. "It will all come right sooner or later."

to come the raw prawn AUSTRALIAN
To pull a fast one. "You can't come the raw prawn with me." The expression's origin is unknown.

come-see AMERICAN (SOUTH)
A lovely word in the Gullah dialect for a delicate child, one who has come to see this world and decide whether or not it wishes to stay, which is to say its life may be very brief.

come-to-help-us JAMAICAN
A prolific variety of yam that seeds itself and keeps a long time in the earth, helping people in hard times. Also called *come-here-fe-help*.

to come to holts AUSTRALIAN
To argue. "They came to holts over who saw her first."

to come up trumps BRITISH
To do better than one thought. "I came up trumps on the examination."

commercial traveler   BRITISH
What in the United States would be called a *traveling salesman.*

commoner   BRITISH
A man or a woman below the rank of peer. British statesman William Pitt
the elder was called *the Great Commoner* before he became the earl of
Chatham.

compere   BRITISH
A word sometimes used for a master of ceremonies at a variety show or
at a television or movie awards ceremony.

conchie   AUSTRALIAN, BRITISH
A person who is too conscientious and works too hard, often trying to
impress someone. In British *conchie* (pronounced in both countries
KON-chee) is slang for a conscientious objector, especially during World
War I.

confectioner's   BRITISH
A *candy store* (q.v.). Also called a *sweetshop* (q.v.).

conjurer   BRITISH
The usual word for what Americans would call a magician, though *conjurer* has some currency in America.

conk   AMERICAN
A straightened hairstyle sometimes worn by African Americans. It probably takes its name from the slang *conk* for head and/or from the commercial preparation Congolene used to straighten hair. The term is used
widely throughout the United States. Also called a *process.*

conker   BRITISH
This name for the horse chestnut is used mainly in England, but the British
game called *conkers* is sometimes played by children in the United States.
In the game, a horse chestnut is hollowed out with a penknife and is knot-
ted to one end of a length of string. The children then swing their strings,
trying to break each other's conkers. The game may have first been called
"conqueror," which was corrupted to *conker,* which in turn gave its name
to the horse chestnut used in the game. It could, however, derive from the
French *conque,* a "shell," because the game was originally played with

shells instead of horse chestnuts. *Conker* is also used by the British as the name for the rubber match or playoff match in the game of darts.

consarn   AMERICAN (NEW ENGLAND)
A euphemism for *damn*. Jabez Stone's mother frequently admonishes him for using *consarn* in Stephen Vincent Benét's story "The Devil and Daniel Webster."

constable   BRITISH
Constable, for "a police officer," comes from the late Latin *comes stabuli*—any count, or officer, of the stable, or "master of the horse," under the Theodosian Code in about A.D. 438. In England, the word first meant the chief officer of the court or of the nation's military forces. The title is usually reserved for police officers up to the rank of sergeant. See *bobby*.

conversation fluid   AMERICAN (WEST)
Used in the West for whiskey, especially potent moonshine that loosens the inhibitions and the vocal cords.

convertible   AMERICAN
A car with a folding top that can be lowered and raised depending on the weather. The British call this a *drop-head*.

coo   SCOTTISH
Typical Scottish pronunciation and spelling of *cow*.

coo!   BRITISH
A Cockney exclamation of great surprise. See also *Cockney*.

coo-ee   AUSTRALIAN
An old Australian cry for hailing someone. The *ee* sound is stretched out.

cooker   BRITISH, IRISH
The common British word for a kitchen stove. The term is never heard in the United States, where *stove* and *range* are used.

cooldrink   SOUTH AFRICAN
A cold drink of any kind. "He took three bottles off the cooldrink shelf."

cool head main thing   HAWAIIAN
Slang for "don't panic," "keep a cool head," "don't get excited."

to cool out   JAMAICAN
To unwind, be relaxed. Also heard in American slang, where it means to cool off, calm down, and, more recently, to subdue or to kill.

to cop   AUSTRALIAN
To take a look at, as in "Cop those legs, mate."

to cop it sweet   AUSTRALIAN
To be very fortunate, lucky. "He copped it sweet when he married her."

copper   BRITISH
British slang (with some American use) for a police officer. The term doesn't derive from the large copper buttons worn by members of the first London police force, nor any other police officer. Neither was it originally an acronym meaning constabulary of police or anything similar. *Cop* can be traced back to the verb *cop,* which was first recorded in the sense of "to catch or capture" in early eighteenth-century England. It took about a century and a half, but the verb was eventually adopted as a name for a policeman, who, of course, caught or captured crooks. See also *bobby.*

corbie   SCOTTISH
A raven or a crow. From the Middle English *corbie,* raven.

corn   BRITISH, AMERICAN
When in Keats's "Ode to a Nightingale" a homesick Ruth stands "in tears amid the alien corn" (the phrase is Keats's own and not from the King James Bible), she is standing in a field of wheat or rye, any grain but New World corn, or maize. The English have always used the word *corn* to describe all grains used for food and never specifically for the grain that built the Mayan and Incan Empires. *Corn* derives from the Old Teutonic *kurnom,* which is akin to *granum,* the Latin word for grain. *Kurnom* eventually became the Old Saxon *korn* and then *corn* in Old English. The semantic confusion arose when settlers in America named corn on the cob "Indian corn" soon after Squanto brought ears to the starving Puritan colony in Massachusetts; the settlers then dropped the qualifying adjective over the years. Although the British are today increasingly using the term *sweet corn* for American corn, they commonly call New World corn

maize, a word that derives from the Spanish *maiz,* which has its origins in *mahiz,* a Caribbean Indian tribe's name for the plant.

cornet   BRITISH
The cone into which a scoop of ice cream is placed.

cornish pasty   BRITISH
A kind of turnover filled with meat and vegetables that originated in Cornwall, England. *Pasty* here is pronounced *pahsty.*

corns   HAWAIIAN
A common shortening of *corn on the cob.* "We put corns on the barbecue."

coronach   SCOTTISH
A funeral hymn or lament; a slow, mournful musical composition. Pronounced *kor-o-nach.*

cosh   BRITISH
A billyclub or blackjack ("It happened so fast the guards couldn't get their coshes out") or to be hit on the head with a blackjack or other weapon ("The guards coshed him").

cossie   SOUTH AFRICAN
A swimsuit or bathing suit; the word is an abbreviation of *costume.*

costermonger   BRITISH
A pushcart vendor of fruits and vegetables. A *costermonger* was originally an apple-seller, selling large apples called *costards.*

cost the earth   BRITISH
Very dear or expensive. "It cost the earth to build that house of his."

cottage country   CANADIAN
An area in the wilderness by a stream or a lake; vacationland.

cotton   BRITISH
A synonym for sewing thread. A *cotton reel* is a spool of thread.

cotton candy   AMERICAN

See *spun sugar.*

cotton pickin'   AMERICAN (SOUTH)

Despicable, wretched, damned; now sometimes used in a humorous sense. The expression has its roots in the inferior status of poor farmers and field hands in the southern United States. "Keep your cotton pickin' hands off me" is commonly heard.

                                         AMERICAN (APPALACHIAN
couldn't hit the ground with his ole hat   MOUNTAINS)

Is dead drunk. "He drank so much he couldn't hit the ground with his ole hat."

coulee   AMERICAN (WEST)

A deep ravine or gulch with sloping sides, formed by running water, that is often dry in summer; also can be a small valley or a small stream. The word derives from the French *couler* (to flow). The famous Grand Coulee Dam is at the end of the deep, dry canyon called Grand Coulee that is cut by the Columbia River in Washington State.

counter   AMERICAN (NEW ENGLAND)

A Maine lobster that is big enough to be kept under the state's legal limits law; called a *keeper* in other places.

courage   AMERICAN (SOUTH)

Sexual desire or potency. "He told the doctor that he had sexual problems, couldn't get his courage up."

courgette   BRITISH

A squash, especially the squash Americans call a *zucchini.*

cousin   HAWAIIAN

A common term of address for anyone. *Cuz* is used similarly in the mainland United States.

cowabunga!   AUSTRALIAN

Cowabunga! has recently come to be used as a general cry of delight, due to the popularization of it by the cartoon character Bart Simpson of television fame. Originating in Australian surfing sometime in the 1960s, *cowabunga!* is still shouted by surfers at the beginning of a good ride or wave.

coward   SOUTH AFRICAN
South African black slang for bad or cruel. "He did something coward to her."

cowboy   BRITISH
The American word is used in Britain to mean an incompetent workman, such as a roofer, who causes more trouble than he fixes.

cow cocky   NEW ZEALAND
Someone who runs a small dairy by himself without any but family help.

cowcumber   AMERICAN (SOUTH)
A name for the cucumber in North Carolina, Louisiana, and other southern states, especially among older speakers.

cowlick   AMERICAN (WEST)
(1) Places along branches or streams where drinking cattle eat or lick out great holes; the term is unrelated to *cowlick* meaning an unruly tuft of hair. (2) A salt lick (block) purchased for cattle to lick.

cozzie   AUSTRALIAN
Common slang for any swimsuit, swimming trunks. See also *bathers, cossie, togs.*

cracker   AMERICAN (SOUTH)
A poor white person, especially one from Georgia (the Cracker State), so called, perhaps, from their use of cracked corn. Originally the expression was *corncracker,* one who cracks corn to make grits or cornmeal. When, after the Civil War, many people in the South became too poor to buy cornmeal and had to make their own, *cracker* came to mean a backwoodsman and then a poor white, generally a person living in the southern states of Georgia or Florida. Others say that *cracker* was originally applied to Florida cowboys and derived from their cracking their whips as they herded cattle. In any case, the term is generally an offensive one and is now regarded as a racial epithet. Many people, however, are proud to call themselves *Georgia crackers, Florida crackers,* etc., just as long as they're doing the calling.

crackers   BRITISH
Mentally unbalanced, crazy, nuts, cracked, as in "He's gone crackers."

crack hardy   NEW ZEALAND
To put on a brave face, act as if everything is all right when it isn't.

cracking good   BRITISH
Outstanding, excellent. "That was a cracking good story she told."

cranky   JAMAICAN
Very thin or sickly, in poor health. "He's our cranky man." In the central
Pennsylvania mountains of the United States, *cranky* means cheerful or
high-spirited.

crapper   BRITISH, AMERICAN
A name for the modern flush toilet, which was invented by English
plumber Thomas Crapper in the 1870s.

crash   AMERICAN
Slang for "sleep," as in "We found a place to crash."

crawler lane   BRITISH
What Americans would call the slow lane for cars traveling on highways.

crazy as a shithouse rat   AMERICAN (WEST)
Very crazy. "'These guys are crazy as shithouse rats."

creamery can   IRISH
A churn for making butter.

to create   AUSTRALIAN, BRITISH
To be angry. "She really created when she heard about it." The nearest
American gets to this is in uses such as "She really created a scene when
she heard about it."

creepie   IRISH
A very low stool used for many purposes.

crekey! BRITISH
Said when something surprises you. Equivalent to the American *gee!* or *gee whiz!*

crib AMERICAN
Crib for a residence is not contemporary; it has been recorded as criminal slang as far back as the early nineteenth century and is probably older than that.

cricket BRITISH
(1) The national sport of Britain. (2) Fair, right, gentlemanly; according to the rules of cricket.

Crippen BRITISH
Any man wild and unkempt in appearance, but more commonly a doctor-murderer, of whom there have been too many. Dr. Hawley Harvey Crippen, murderer, killed his wife, Cora, and was hanged for his crime on November 23, 1910. Dr. Crippen, born in the United States, received his medical education in London and settled there with his wife, who had previously appeared unsuccessfully in opera and on the music hall stage. Crippen fell in love with his secretary and on New Year's Eve 1909 poisoned his wife, dissected the body, and, after destroying what he could by fire, interred the remains in his cellar. He and Ethel le Neve, who disguised herself as a boy, eventually fled England, but in the English Channel the boat captain recognized them from their pictures and wired Scotland Yard to come aboard.

crisp BRITISH
A potato chip; short for *potato crisp.*

critical list AMERICAN
A hospital patient who has unstable and abnormal vital signs that indicate that he is hovering near death is said to be in *critical condition* and on the hospital's *critical list* of patients. See *danger list.*

crocodile MALAYSIAN
Someone who chases women; a womanizer.

crocus sack AMERICAN (SOUTH)
A gunnysack, a sack made of coarse material like burlap; so named because crocus, or saffron, was first shipped in sacks made of this material. Also called a *croker sack, tow sack,* and *grass sack* in the South.

crook   AUSTRALIAN
(1) To be sick. "He's been crook all week." (2) To be angry or cross with someone. "He got so crook with him I thought he was going to hit him."

crook drama   BRITISH
A crime show or series on television. The term is rarely, if ever, heard in the United States.

crosswalk   AMERICAN
See *zebra*.

to cruel   AUSTRALIAN
To ruin, as in "We cruelled our chance to win."

crumbs!   BRITISH
A common exclamation of disappointment or surprise.

crumpet   BRITISH
A small, unsweetened cake made from batter.

crunchy   SOUTH AFRICAN
An offensive slang term, its origin unknown, for an Afrikaner, a white, Afrikaans-speaking South African. *Hairyback* is another such word.

cry all the way to the bank   AMERICAN
An expression usually said by or of someone who may not be a critical success but nevertheless makes lots of money. The origin of the saying is unknown, but it is often attributed to the popular American pianist Liberace.

cuddle   BRITISH
A hug, as in "Give us a cuddle."

cuddling   AUSTRALIAN
Necking or making out. "Her mother caught her cuddling on the couch."

cuddy   SCOTTISH
A nickname for a donkey. Also used to describe a stupid person.

cuffs AMERICAN
See *turn-ups.*

cufuffle BRITISH
Commotion, disorder, fuss. Also spelled *kerfuffle.*

culpable homicide SCOTTISH
Manslaughter. This term is used only in Scotland.

cumshaw BRITISH
A tip or gratuity. The term came into the language early in the nineteenth century from the Chinese Amoy. The Chinese words it derives from were a traditional beggar's phrase that has a literal meaning of "grateful thanks."

cunny JAMAICAN
Cunning, clever, shrewd, tricky. "Cunny better than strength."

cuppa char BRITISH, AUSTRALIAN
Slang for a cup of tea; often shortened to *a cuppa. Char* is a corruption of *cha,* which means tea, deriving from the Mandarin *ch'a* for the same. *Tea* itself comes to us from the Chinese Amoy *t'e. Cuppa* is also heard in Australia.

curiosity delay AMERICAN (BOSTON)
A delay in traffic caused by drivers slowing down to view an accident. Called *rubbernecking* in New York and elsewhere.

curlicism BRITISH
Literary indecency. John Arbuthnot remarked that publisher Edmund Curll's inaccurate biographies were "one of the new terrors of death," but Curll (1683–1747) was more notorious for the obscene books he published. Today "the unspeakable Curll" would have been a rich man, but in his time he was fined, put in a pillory, and imprisoned for his efforts. Among the greats who lampooned him were Jonathan Swift and Alexander Pope, who described him as "a fly in amber." No one has identified the anonymous wit who coined the word *curlicism* from his name.

curling   CANADIAN, SCOTTISH
An ice sport played with flat, round stones that are slid toward a mark.

curl up/down   AMERICAN, BRITISH
While Americans *curl up* with a book, etc., the British *curl down* with one.

currach   IRISH, SCOTTISH
A small round or wide boat made of wickerwork or laths and covered with a waterproof layer such as oiled cloth or animal skins. Pronounced *Kur-ah*. Also called a *coracle*.

curse of Scotland   SCOTTISH
The nine of diamonds playing card. The name may have been suggested by the coat of arms of the earl of Stair, who was hated in Scotland for helping bring about the union with England in 1707. But there are several other possible derivations.

cushlamachree   IRISH
Cushlamachree is one of the few Gaelic locutions that Irish immigrants retained after being in America awhile. The expression is a corruption of the Gaelic *cuisle me chroidhe*, "vein of my heart." Pronounced *cushla-ma-chree*.

cut along   BRITISH
Leave, depart, cut out. "Cut along and get to school on time."

cut a rusty   AMERICAN (MOUNTAINS)
To show off, behave foolishly. "I cussed and laughed . . . I tooted my horn. I cut a rusty."

cut a stick   AUSTRALIAN
In days past Australians often cut a staff before taking a trip. Thus *cut a stick* came to mean "to leave, to go."

cut it wild aloose and see where it lights   AMERICAN (WEST)
Free something from control and see what happens. "I'd as soon cut the whole thing wild aloose and see where it lights. The hell with the regulations."

cut lunch   AUSTRALIAN
Sandwiches brought to work for lunch. *Cut lunch commandos* are soldiers serving at headquarters, not in action.

cut tail   BAHAMIAN
To leave hastily, as in "We cut tail out of there before they come."

cutter   CANADIAN
A small wooden sleigh used mainly by children.

cut-throat   BRITISH
A humorous name for a sharp, straight-edge razor.

cutty   SCOTTISH
A word applied to anything short, such as a short person, a short-tempered person, or a short stool (a *cutty stool*).

c.v.   BRITISH, AMERICAN
Short for *curriculum vitae,* what Americans would call a résumé. "He asked to see my *c.v.*" *C.v.* is used in the United States, chiefly among academics.

cymling head   BRITISH
A stupid person, after the small, round variety of melon or squash called the cymling *(Cucurbita pepo melopepo)*. In the United States the melon is often called a *simling,* which better shows its origins, for its name derives from its shape, which resembles the fruitcake called a simnel cake. Other names for the cymling are the *scallop squash* and the *pattycake squash.*

Da   IRISH
A widely used term meaning a father, grandfather, or any respected elderly man.

daddied   AMERICAN (OZARK MOUNTAINS)
Fathered a child illegitimately. "He daddied that child; you can tell jist to look at it."

daft   BRITISH, SCOTTISH
Foolish or crazy. In Scotland the word means merry or playful.

dag   SOUTH AFRICAN, AUSTRALIAN
(1) In South Africa, an abbreviation of the Afrikaans greeting *goie day,*
meaning "good day." (2) In Australia, a character, a nerd.

dairy   NEW ZEALAND
A convenience store where many items, not just milk and dairy products,
can be bought.

daltonism   BRITISH
Color blindness. So determined was British scientist John Dalton
(1766–1844) to solve the mystery of color blindness that he willed his
eyes for study after his death. His pioneering research into the problem
was based on observations of himself, his brother, and other similarly
afflicted persons.

Dame Partington   BRITISH
Anyone futilely trying to hold back progress or natural forces. The legen-
day Dame Partington had tried to mop up the Atlantic Ocean, which was
flooding her cottage in Devon. English politician and author Sydney Smith
alluded to her in an 1831 speech condemning the opposition of the House
of Lords to reform measures.

damn all   BRITISH
Nothing at all, not a damned thing, as in "I know damn all about it."

damper   AUSTRALIAN
A name for bread made of flour and water baked in the ashes of a fire
damped so that the glowing embers can bake it without burning it. First
made by Australian Aboriginal peoples.

dandelion   CANADIAN (NEWFOUNDLAND)
A hard, bold stare. "She gave him a dandelion." Also *a dandelion look.*
The origin of the term is unknown.

dander   SCOTTISH
To stroll aimlessly without any definite purpose. "He dandered along the
road."

dandy dude
JAMAICAN

A man dressed to the nines, done up in style. See also *dasher.*

danger list
BRITISH

The list of hospital patients who are critically ill. The American synonym would be *critical list.* "He's better now; they've taken him off the danger list."

dankie
SOUTH AFRICAN

Thanks, thank you, thanks a lot; from the Dutch *dankje* meaning the same.

darbies
BRITISH

Darbies is an old British expression for handcuffs, but the word oddly enough derives from the name of a usurer. It seems that a shrewd sixteenth-century lawyer and moneylender named Derby drew up an iron-clad bond that left no loopholes for debtors to escape through. This contract, used extensively by usurers, came to be called *Father Derbie's bands.* Because they were also impossible to "unlock," it wasn't long before all manacles were known as *derbies,* too, the word often pronounced *darbies.*

Darby and Joan
BRITISH

Any mutually affectionate and contented old married couple.

> Old Darby, with Joan by his side,
> You're often regarded with wonder:
> He's dropsical, she is sore-eyed,
> Yet they're never happy asunder.

This verse by Henry Woodfall was printed in the *Gentleman's Magazine* in 1735 under the title of "The Joys of Love Never Forgot: a song." The ballad praises, in a number of stanzas, John Darby and his wife Joan, who lived in London. Woodfall had served an apprenticeship under John Darby, who, with his wife, were widely known for their good works and faithfulness. The term has little currency in the United States.

darg
SCOTTISH

(1) A full day's work. (2) Any job. Also heard in northern England.

dasher
JAMAICAN

A dashing man, a dandy, a great lover. See also *dandy dude.*

dating agency   BRITISH
What Americans and Australians would usually call a *dating service.*

dauncy   AMERICAN (SMOKY MOUNTAINS)
(1) A word, common in the Smokies, meaning "mincy about eating"—
that is, fastidious, overly nice. (2) Weak, frail, unwell, dizzy. "He's so
dauncy he can't hardly walk." (3) Stupid or confused. *Dauncy* is held by
some to be a contraction of *damn sick.*

davenport   AMERICAN, BRITISH
A desk in Britain, a sofa in the United States.

davy   BRITISH
In England *davy* has been used for *affidavit* since at least 1764, which
gives us the common British expression *I'll take my davy of it:* I'll vouch
that it's true.

dawdle   SCOTTISH
A old name for any lazy, indolent person, male or female. "He's an old
dawdle."

a day after the fair   BRITISH
Not in time, too late. "He came a day after the fair, when we didn't need
him anymore."

day clean   BAHAMIAN
Dawn, daybreak. "He get up before day clean for the job."

day-lazy   AMERICAN (NEW ENGLAND)
An old euphemism for *damned lazy.* "That day-lazy rascal is up to no
good."

dead bolt lock   AMERICAN
A lock bolt moved into position by the turning of a knob or key rather
than by spring action. The British call it a *mortise lock.*

dead cat on the line   AMERICAN (SOUTH)
Something is suspicious, something wrong. When William Safire asked
readers of his nationally syndicated word column for help in explaining

this expression, an old man in Louisiana scrawled a letter explaining that the expression has its roots in fishing for catfish, when trotlines with many hooks on them are set in the water. The lines are checked every day, so if a fisherman checks a neighbor's line and finds a dead catfish (cat) on the line, he knows there is something wrong, suspicious, or fishy going on (his neighbor may be ill, in trouble, etc.).

dead end street
AMERICAN

A street with no exit. The term has also come to mean no hope of progress, advancement, etc.

deadly nevergreen
BRITISH

A humorous term for the gallows in England since the late eighteenth century, because the gallows have no leaves but "bear fruit all the year round."

dead man's flower
CANADIAN (NEWFOUNDLAND)

A name for spirea *(Spiraea latifolia),* from the folk belief that if a child picked this common white flower his or her father would die.

dead presidents
AMERICAN

Slang for paper money of any denomination, the term was first recorded in New York's Harlem in 1944.

dead-set
AUSTRALIAN

Genuine, bona fide, as in "She's a dead-set movie star."

dead story
JAMAICAN

An occurrence one hasn't seen oneself, thus leaving it open to doubt. Its opposite is a *live story.*

dead to rights
BRITISH

See *red-handed.*

dead water
JAMAICAN

Water used to wash a corpse before burial. It must not be stepped in once disposed of, according to a Jamaican superstition, or very bad luck will befall you.

dead-yard   JAMAICAN
A cemetery; also called *burying yard*. "You don't want to walk in the
dead-yard when the moon is full."

dear boy   BRITISH
Often used in Britain as a form of address; never so used in the United
States. "No, dear boy, you don't have to come in tomorrow."

death duty (duties)   BRITISH
A death tax paid to the government on a dead person's estate. Americans
call it an *inheritance tax* or an *estate tax.*

death makes no promise   BAHAMIAN
Death strikes at any time with no warning; you never know when it will
come.

December is thirteen months long   CANADIAN
A humorous saying referring to Canada's long, severe winters, especially
in northern Canada.

decent   AMERICAN (SOUTH)
Hill people still do not frequently use the word *decent*. H. L. Mencken
explained this taboo, regarding the South, in *The American Language*
(1919): "Fifty years ago the word *decent* was indecent . . . no Southern
woman was supposed to have any notion of the difference between *decent*
and *indecent.*"

deck of cards   AMERICAN
See *pack of cards.*

deep cold   AMERICAN (NEW ENGLAND)
Heard for *bitter freezing cold* in Maine. "Sheets hung out in deep cold
become stiff as boards."

deep-laid plans   BRITISH
Plans that are carefully and secretly made over a period of time, not made
impulsively.

de facto AUSTRALIAN
Someone who lives with a person as a husband or wife though they aren't legally married. "John and his de facto will be here for dinner."

dekko IRISH
A look. "Let us have a dekko at it." The Australians and the British say *take a dekko,* take a look at.

del WELSH
A Welsh word that is a term of endearment. "Come sit by me, del."

Delhi belly AMERICAN
See *Montezuma's revenge.*

dem JAMAICAN
Commonly used in Jamaican speech for *their.* "We drive in dem car."

deoch-an-doris IRISH, SCOTTISH
A farewell drink; a stirrup cup, that is, a drink for a mounted rider ready to depart. From the Gaelic for "drink at the door." It is also called *doch-an-dorach.*

depart JAPANESE
A Japanese department store.

departmental store BRITISH
A version of the American *department store,* from which the British term derives. The term *department store* isn't recorded until 1887, when a New York establishment advertised itself as H. H. Heyn's Department Store, though the idea of separate departments in American stores can be found in print at least forty years earlier.

derail AMERICAN (MAINE)
Heard in Maine for a cheap, toxic alcoholic drink, something like antifreeze strained through cloth or cotton.

derby BRITISH, AMERICAN
The American name for a version of the dome-shaped felt hat that the British call a *bowler.* The man it honors is memorialized by the Derby at

Epsom Downs and the American Kentucky Derby at Churchill Downs..
The twelfth earl of Derby, Edward Stanley (d. 1834), had a great interest
in horse racing. The Derby named after him became so popular that many
Americans attended it. After the Civil War, American spectators at the
"Blue Ribbon of the Turf" noticed that sportsmen often wore odd-shaped
bowler hats. A number were brought back home, where it is said that a
Connecticut manufacturer made a stiff felt, narrow-brimmed version that
an unknown New York store clerk sold as "hats like they wear at the
Derby." In any event, *derby* became the American term for *bowler,* the
most popular headwear for men until the 1920s.

derebar   MALAYSIAN
A Malaysian borrowing and alteration of the word *driver.*

derms   SOUTH AFRICAN
(1) Slang for guts, courage; from the Dutch *darm,* intestines. (2) A word
for sheep intestines used for sausagemaking.

desert canary   AMERICAN (WEST)
A humorous name for a burro or small donkey because of its loud, unmu-
sical bray.

destroy   AMERICAN (MOUNTAINS)
To make an unmarried girl or woman pregnant. "He did destroy her, but
they soon were married."

destructor   BRITISH
A common term for an *incinerator* in an apartment building.

devil rain   JAMAICAN
Rain that occurs while the sun is shining. According to one superstition,
it is a result of the devil and his wife fighting over a hambone.

dewar flask   BRITISH
The *dewar flask,* the original thermos bottle, is named for its inventor, Sir
James Dewar (1842–1923), a Scottish chemist and physicist who devised
the vacuum-jacketed vessel in 1892 for the storage of liquid gases at low
temperatures. Originally a trademark, the word is now often spelled without a capital.

to dice   SOUTH AFRICAN
To race cars on public roads, speeding and changing lanes with no regard for safety. "Dicing drivers caused a terrible accident last night."

dicky   AUSTRALIAN
Weak and failing. "He's had a dicky heart for years now."

diddekoy   BRITISH
A disparaging name for a Gypsy.

diddledees   AMERICAN (NEW ENGLAND)
An unusual word Nantucketers and other New Englanders use for fallen pine needles. It may derive from the Falkland Island shrub called the *diddledee,* which was a source of kindling for whalers, the name transferred to Nantucket pine needles, which also were used as kindling. Such pine needles have been called *pins, shats, spills, straws, tugs,* and *twinkles* in other sections of the United States.

dig over   BRITISH
To turn over the soil in a garden; to weed or cultivate a garden.

digs   BRITISH
Rooms or lodgings. Sometimes, though rarely, used in the United States, where *pad* is the slang equivalent.

dik   SOUTH AFRICAN
A stupid person, as in "What a dik he is." The word derives from the Afrikaans *dik,* meaning dense.

dill   AUSTRALIAN, BRITISH
A fool. "His mate is quite a dill." Possibly derives from the British word *dilly,* half-witted, or from a combination of *dippy* and *silly.* Also *dilly.*

dilly bag   AUSTRALIAN
(1) A bag or basket woven of reeds and used by Aboriginal women. (2) Any small bag or basket.

dime novel   AMERICAN
See *penny dreadful.*

dingbat   AUSTRALIAN, AMERICAN
Dingbat has served over the years as an American slang term for "a gadget, money, buns or biscuits, and a hobo or bum." But the contemptuous use of the word for a "nut," an ineffectual, bumbling fool, probably comes directly from the Australian *dingbat,* meaning "eccentric or mad."

dink   AMERICAN (WEST)
A term for an animal or a person found wanting, from a small or deformed calf to a horse that doesn't perform well to a person who leaves much to be desired. "I'm sorry I voted for that dink."

dinkum   AUSTRALIAN
Genuine or reliable. *Hard dinkum* means hard work, and *dinkums* in World War I was the nickname of Australian troops. See also *fair dinkum.*

dinky   SOUTH AFRICAN
Any bottle of wine. Originally the brand name *Dinki.*

dinna ken   SCOTTISH
Don't know. "Ah dinna ken the answer."

dirty-great   AUSTRALIAN, BRITISH
Very big. "He's a dirty-great brute of a man." Also *dirty-big.*

dirty weekend   BRITISH
A weekend devoted to love and sex, usually between two married people after they ship the children off for a day or so.

dis   AMERICAN
To show disrespect for, to disparage. Originally black slang, dating back to the 1980s; now widely heard. "He shouldn't have dissed him."

dish towel   AMERICAN
A small towel used to dry plates and silverware. The British call it a *tea towel* (q.v.) or a *drying-up cloth* (q.v.).

dishy   BRITISH
Said of a man who is personable and attractive in looks or appearance.

dismal Jimmy   BRITISH
Someone who is rarely or ever happy about anything. The American slang
equivalent would be a *gloomy Gus.*

district attorney   AMERICAN (WEST)
Any dish containing cheap or unmentionable ingredients, such as sweet-
breads, guts, and kidneys. So named because of cowboys' feelings about
legal authorities. Also called *son-of-a-bitch stew.*

divan   BRITISH
A sofa or couch; the term has limited use in the United States. *Divan* has
an involved but logical history. Originating as a Persian word meaning "a
brochure," it came to mean, in order: "a collection of poems"; "a regis-
ter"; "a military pay book"; "a room in which an account book was kept";
"an account office or custom house"; "a court"; "a great hall"; and, finally,
by the late seventeenth century, "the chief piece of furniture in a great
hall"!

DIY   AUSTRALIAN, BRITISH
An abbreviation for the "do-it-yourself" projects so popular among home-
owners.

DJ   BRITISH, AMERICAN
In Britain, a common abbreviation meaning *dinner jacket.* In America, DJ
stands for a disc jockey, as does *deejay.*

to do a Brodie   AMERICAN
As a result of his famous leap off the Brooklyn Bridge, Steve Brodie's
name became a byword—in the form of to *do (or pull) a Brodie*—for "taking a great chance, even taking a suicidal leap." Brodie made his jump
from the Manhattan side of the Brooklyn Bridge on July 23, 1886, to win
a two-hundred-dollar barroom bet.

to do a moonlight flit   BRITISH
To leave secretly from a hotel, restaurant, etc., without paying for something.

to do a ton   BRITISH
Slang for to drive a car at more than a hundred miles an hour. "He did a
ton coming down here."

to dob   AUSTRALIAN
To secretly inform on someone. A *dobber* is an informer.

Does a bear shit in the woods?   AMERICAN (WEST)
Absolutely, certainly. "Can I do it? Does a bear shit in the woods?"

dog   AMERICAN
(1) A hot dog. (2) A homely woman or man. (3) Anything, such as a race-horse, that doesn't perform well.

dog collar   BRITISH
Humorous slang for a cleric's collar.

dog-end   BRITISH
The butt of a cigarette; also called *fag-end.*

dog my cats   AMERICAN (SOUTH)
An exclamation of surprise. "Well, dog my cats if he ain't come home!"

a dog's breakfast   BRITISH
Any mess or conglomeration. So named from the leftovers often scraped off dinner plates and fed to dogs.

dogga   SOUTH AFRICAN
Marijuana *(Cannabis sativa).* Dogga possibly derives from an African language.

dogged   AMERICAN (SOUTH)
Damned. "Dogged if they don't look just alike, Percy."

dogger   CANADIAN (NEWFOUNDLAND)
A young boy who follows and spies upon couples in lovers' lanes, etc.

dogie   AMERICAN (WEST)
A calf, a yearling, a motherless calf, a poor worthless calf, a steer, or even a lamb or a horse. The American cowboy has been shouting "git along, little dogie" for more than a century, but etymologists differ about the origin of the word. Some think it derives from "dough-guts," referring to the bloated bellies of such calves; others think that *dogie* is a clipped form of

the Spanish *adobe* (mud); possibly it referred to cows so small that they were playfully called "doggies," and the pronunciation changed. Since some American cowboys were black, there is also the possibility that the Bambara *dogo* (small, short) is the source, or the Afro-Creole *dogi,* meaning the same.

the dole   BRITISH
Government payments to the poor. Americans would usually call this *welfare,* though *the dole* has limited usage in the United States.

domkop   SOUTH AFRICAN
A fool or a stupid person; related to the German word *Dummkopf.*

donk   AUSTRALIAN
Slang for a fool or a jerk. "He's the donk of donks."

donkey's years   BRITISH
A very long time. The usual explanation for this expression, which is first recorded in 1916, is that *donkey's years* is a play on *donkey's ears,* which are very long.

don't Bogart that joint   AMERICAN
In his films Humphrey Bogart often left cigarettes dangling from his mouth without smoking them. This led to the counterculture expression *Don't Bogart that joint*—that is, "don't take so long with, don't hog that stick of marijuana; smoke and pass it on to the next person."

don't come the acid   BRITISH
Don't be a wise guy; don't give me any of your wise "acid" (vitriolic) answers.

don't even think about it   AMERICAN
A stern warning to someone who might be about to do something. "She gave them a look that said, *don't even think about it.*"

don't fence me in   AMERICAN
Give me freedom, elbow room. The expression was coined in a poem written by Bob Fletcher, a Westerner. Cole Porter bought the rights to the poem, revised the lyrics, and wrote music for the song "Don't Fence Me

In," which originally appeared in the film *Hollywood Canteen* (1944). Iron-ically, Porter was crippled in a riding accident.

don't get your knickers in a twist   BRITISH, IRISH
Don't get confused, annoyed, worried. *Knickers* in Britain and Ireland are women's underwear.

don't give a monkey's   BRITISH
A British euphemism for *don't give a monkey's fuck,* or *don't give a mon-key's shit*—that is, don't care at all about something or someone. The term was originally military slang.

don't give a rap   IRISH
Not to care in the slightest. Counterfeiters took advantage of the scarcity of copper coins in the early eighteenth century and began flooding Ire-land with bogus halfpence. These worthless coins became known as raps and inspired the expressions *not worth a rap* and *I don't give a rap.*

don't give a rat's ass   AMERICAN
A common if not proper expression meaning one couldn't care less, doesn't give a damn.

don't give holy things to hounds   BRITISH
Don't cast pearls before swine, as the biblical saying goes.

don't know enough to pound sand in a rat hole   AMERICAN
Extremely stupid. "He don't know enough to pound sand in a rat hole."

don't like the cut of his jib   AMERICAN
The cut of the jib, or triangular headsail of a ship, indicates the ship's char-acter to a sailor. *Jib* also means face in sailor's talk. Thus *don't like the cut of his jib,* a nautical phrase that probably came ashore in America a century ago, translates as "I'm suspicious of him; I don't like his manner, or the expression on his face."

doofus   AMERICAN
Originally American slang dating back to the late 1950s or early 1960s meaning a fool, a jerk, a dope, or any combination of the three. Some writers claim the word is an alteration of *goofus* for the same, while oth-ers say it is of Yiddish or German origin. It also can mean the penis.

doolally   BRITISH
Nuts, bonkers. British troops in India during the nineteenth century waited in the town of Deolali for troopships to take them home after their enlistment expired. Deolali, which they pronounced *Doolally*, became the scene of so much aberrant behavior among soldiers with too much time on their hands that the town's name became synonymous with their crazy behavior.

dooley   AMERICAN (SOUTH)
Another word for a sweet potato in the South; possibly named after someone who developed a superior variety.

doomster   SCOTTISH
An old name for a judge who frequently pronounces the death penalty.

doon   SCOTTISH
Typical Scottish pronunciation and spelling of down. "He went doon the hill."

doona   BRITISH
Do not, as in "I doona want to come." Heard mostly in Lancaster dialect. Also spelled *dunna.*

door-knocker salesman   BRITISH
What Americans would call a door-to-door salesman.

to do over   AUSTRALIAN, BRITISH
To violently attack someone. "They'll do him over if he talks." The American equivalent is *work* (him or her) *over.*

dope   AMERICAN (SOUTH)
"Gimme a dope" still means "Give me a Coca-Cola" in the South, especially among teenagers, and dates back to the nineteenth century, when the fabled soft drink was touted as a tonic and contained a minute amount of cocaine. Coca-Cola's inventor, druggist John S. Pemberton, brewed the drink in his backyard and knew it was done when he smelled the cooked cocaine.

dosh   AUSTRALIAN, BRITISH
Slang for money. "He's got no dosh at all on him."

to do someone brown   BRITISH
Slang for to deceive someone, trick him or her, or pull the wool over his or her eyes.

doss   BRITISH
(1) A bed. (2) To sleep outside, in a vacant house, in doorways, etc., as homeless people do. (3) Something that is easy, not very difficult. "That test was a doss." (4) A *doss house* is a flophouse.

to doss about   BRITISH, IRISH
To fool around, doing very little work; to *goof off* in American slang. Also to *doss around,* or, in Ireland, to *doss off.*

doss down   BRITISH
To lie down and sleep anywhere. "Don't bother about me, I'll doss on the floor."

dosser   BRITISH, IRISH
(1) A shiftless, lazy person. (2) A homeless person without means.

to do the dirty on   AUSTRALIAN, BRITISH
To pull something on someone, take advantage of someone behind his or her back.

do trading   AMERICAN (NEW ENGLAND)
A phrase used primarily in New England for *shopping.*

dotty   BRITISH
Used to describe someone slightly crazy or eccentric. "He's a bit dotty."

double-barreled   BRITISH
Any hyphenated family name, such as Melville-White or Shakespeare-Dickens.

double cousins   AMERICAN (OZARK MOUNTAINS)
A term common in the Ozarks for all the children of two sisters who are married to two brothers. "John here is my double cousin."

douce   SCOTTISH
Sweet, said especially of a person. A borrowing of the French *doux* or *douce.* "That wee lass is very douce."

doughnut   AMERICAN, BRITISH
Unlike the American *doughnut,* the British namesake has no hole in the
middle—it is what is known in America as a *jelly doughnut,* a bun with
jelly in the center. American doughnuts go back to the time of the Pilgrims,
who learned to make these "nuts" of fried sweet dough in Holland before
coming to the New World. It is to the Pennsylvania Dutch that Americans
owe the hole in the middle of the doughnut, or *sinker,* as the doughnut is
sometimes called. Also, in American English, a small tire kept in a car's
trunk and used to replace a flat tire for short distances.

down among the dead men   BRITISH
Someone who is dead drunk, hardly able to move.

downgone   AMERICAN (MOUNTAINS)
In poor health, presenting a poor appearance. "He's some downgone Santa
Claus."

downs   BRITISH
Rolling, grassy hills used for grazing animals. Also *down.*

down the pan   BRITISH
The pan is the toilet bowl in British, so down the pan means something
being flushed away, something dispensed with.

the dozens   AMERICAN (AFRICAN AMERICAN)
The art of hurling invective at one's enemies is an ancient one, and American slaves probably brought the verbal exchange now called *the dozens*
or *dirty dozens* with them from Africa, basing it on the Tuareg and Galla
game in which two opponents cursed one another until one man lost his
temper, began fighting with his hands instead of his mouth, and was considered the loser. Alive and thriving today among blacks, the game takes
its name not from dozen, "twelve," but probably from the Americanism
bulldoze, which meant "to bullwhip someone," especially a slave, the
insults in the game likened to whiplashes.

drack   AUSTRALIAN
An unattractive, slovenly person. "How could she marry that drack?"

draper's shop   BRITISH
A dry goods store. The former designation may come from stores run by
New England merchants, many of whom were shipowners and importers

in Colonial times. Two chief imports were rum and bolts of calico, which were traditionally carried on opposite sides of the store—a wet-goods side containing the rum, and a dry-goods side for the calico. "Wet goods" disappeared from the language, but stores that sell fabric are still called *dry goods stores* in the United States.

drawing pin   BRITISH
The British *drawing pin,* or *pushpin,* is what Americans would call a thumbtack.

dressed up like a dog's dinner   BRITISH
Overdressed in flashy clothes; the origin of the term is unknown.

to dress the bed   BRITISH
To make the bed; pull up the covers, etc. "The maid dressed the bed."

drink off dead Nelson   CANADIAN (NEWFOUNDLAND)
To drink alcohol copiously and indiscriminately. Lord Horatio Nelson, England's greatest naval hero, was killed at the Battle of Trafalgar in 1805, and his body was brought back to England for burial. The fabled hero became the subject of many legends, including one claiming that his body was brought home preserved in rum. This led to the British slang expression *Nelson's blood* for rum and the Newfoundland expression recorded here.

drinking hole   AMERICAN (WEST)
Any place where liquor is sold, from a saloon or honkytonk to a nightclub. Also *watering hole.*

drinking-up time   BRITISH
The time allowed customers to finish their last drinks before a pub closes.

drink one over the eight   BRITISH
To get slightly drunk, though why nine drinks would get one only "slightly" drunk is questionable.

driving hui   HAWAIIAN
A carpool that takes children to school; the Chinese *hui* here means "club."

drongo
AUSTRALIAN
A fool; a lazy, stupid, useless person. One Australian source gives as the origin of the word a racehorse called Drongo, whose performances on the track were disappointing. The horse had been named after an Australian bird called the *drongo* (this name perhaps from an Aboriginal language).

dronkie
SOUTH AFRICAN
A drunk or alcoholic; from the Afrikaans *dronk,* meaning drink.

droob
AUSTRALIAN
A person who is considered a contemptible fool, or jerk. Also *drube.*

to drop a brick
BRITISH
To do something embarrassing or to make an embarrassing remark. Also called *drop a clanger.*

to drop a dime
AMERICAN
To make a phone call to the police informing on someone. A *dime-dropper* is a *rat,* a *snitch,* a *stool pigeon.* The term dates back to the 1960s, when a phone call cost a dime.

drop-head
BRITISH
See *convertible.*

to drop off the hooks
BRITISH
Slang for to die, to kick the bucket. Possibly nautical in origin.

to drop one's aitches
BRITISH
To fail to pronounce the letter *h* when it should be pronounced at the start of words, which is not considered proper by some Britons. Also *drop one's haitches.*

to drop one's bundle
NEW ZEALAND
To lose one's nerve, to panic in any difficult situation.

dross
SCOTTISH
Scrap coal used to supplement more expensive coal.

dry goods store
AMERICAN
See *draper's shop.*

dryhead   JAMAICAN
An insulting term for a man bald or partially bald.

drying-up cloth   BRITISH
What Americans would call a *dish towel* or a *dish cloth.*

dual carriageway   BRITISH
A divided highway, each side going in opposite directions.

ducky   BRITISH
Dear; darling; sweetheart. Also *ducks, duck.*

dud cheque   BRITISH
A bad check. "He gave him a dud cheque."

duff   AUSTRALIAN, AMERICAN
(1) In Australia, to steal cattle by changing the brand, a *duffer* being an
Australian cattle thief. (2) To steal anything by altering its appearance. (3)
In America, *duff* can mean the buttocks; the decaying leaves on a forest
floor; to work hard; and a New England pudding made from flour, water,
and raisins or other fruit.

duff up   BRITISH
To rough someone up by hitting him or her repeatedly. "They duffed him
up because he went to the police."

duh!   AMERICAN
An exclamation used to make fun of someone after that person has spoken, indicating that he or she is dumb or has said or done something stupid or obvious. The expression dates back to the early 1940s, and may
have been introduced or popularized by ventriloquist Edgar Bergen's
dummy Mortimer Snerd, a rustic moron who constantly had the word put
in his mouth.

dumbwaiter   BRITISH, AMERICAN
A revolving tabletop server that Americans call a *lazy Susan* (q.v.). It is
said that the first use of the term dates back to about seventy-five years
ago, when the device was named after some servant it replaced, Susan
being a common name for servants at the time. But it could just as well

be the creation of some unheralded advertising copywriter. Therefore, *lazy* may not mean a lazy servant at all, referring instead to a hostess too lazy to pass the snacks around, or to the ease with which guests can rotate the device on the spindle and bring the sections containing different foods directly in front of them. In America, a dumbwaiter is a small, usually hand-operated elevator used to carry food and drink.

dummy BRITISH
See *pacifier.*

dumper AUSTRALIAN
Surfer language for a big wave that dumps you rather than lets you ride it into shore.

dump truck AMERICAN
See *tipper truck.*

dunny AUSTRALIAN
An outdoor bathroom, or any toilet. From the old slang *donegan* for a toilet, which may come from an obsolete word meaning excrement.

durgen AMERICAN (OZARK MOUNTAINS)
An uncouth, unpolished, clumsy person. "Most of the people around here have some manners, but he's a real durgen." The origin of the term is unknown. Pronounced *dur-gen,* rhyming with *surgeon.*

dust bunnies AMERICAN
See *slut's wool.*

dust devil AMERICAN
A small whirlwind that swirls dust and debris high in the air.

dustman BRITISH
A garbageman. A garbage can is called a *dustbin* and a garbage truck a *dustcart* or *dustbin lorry.*

duvet BRITISH
Pronounced doo-VAY. A quilt or a comforter. Also called a *continental quilt* by the British. Australians call it a *doona.*

D.V.

When someone writes or says "I'll be home next week, D.V.," he or she is saying "I'll be home next week, God willing," *D.V.* being an abbreviation of the Latin *deo volente.* First recorded in 1873, the term appeared in church publications before that and is still heard occasionally.

dying for hungry

Starving, very hungry. "Nothin' to eat all day, dyin' for hungry."

E

ear basher

A very talkative person, someone who talks your ear off, as Americans would say. Also called an *ear lasher.*

earth

A marijuana cigarette; the word's origin in this sense is unknown.

to earth a wire

To ground a wire. "The electrician earthed a wire."

easy come, easy go

See *light come, light go.*

easy meat

Slang for something easy to do, a cinch, as in "That test was easy meat."

to eat crow

To be forced to do something very disagreeable, as the crow is considered to be very distasteful and tough eating; to eat one's own words.

eat humble pie

To suffer humiliation, to apologize, or to abase oneself. The expression is rarely used in America, where the usual equivalent is to *eat crow.* To *eat humble pie* was probably born as a pun. The *humble* in this pie has nothing to do etymologically with the word *humble,* "lowly," which is from the Latin *humilis,* "low or slight." Umbles or numbles (from the Latin *lumbulus,* "little loin") were the innards—the heart, liver, and entrails—of deer and were often made into a pie. When the lord of a manor and his guests dined on venison, the menials ate umble pie made from the innards of the deer. Anyone who ate umble pie was therefore in a position of inferiority—he or she was humbled—and some anonymous punster in the time of William the Conqueror, realizing this, changed *umble pie* to *humble pie,* the pun all the more effective because in several British dialects, especially the Cockney, the *h* is silent and *humble* is pronounced *umble* anyway. So the play upon words yielded the common expression *to eat humble pie.*

eat the Yank way   BRITISH
To hold the fork in the right hand, as Americans usually do.

een   SCOTTISH
Typically the plural of *eye.* "He no can lookit into her een."

editor in chief   AMERICAN
See *chief editor.*

eh?   CANADIAN
A Canadian expression meaning approximately "Isn't it?" that is frequently used at the end of a sentence, as in, "Nice day, eh?"

eighty-six   AMERICAN
To murder someone or to put an end to something. "Eighty-six his ass, I don't want to see him again." The expression derives from the restaurant waiter slang *eighty-six,* which, among other things, means to "deny an unwelcome customer service" or to cancel an order ("eighty-six the eggs"), or which directs the cashier's attention to a customer trying to leave a lunchroom without paying his check. The code word has been used in restaurants and bars since the 1920s, but the extended uses of *eighty-six* have only been around for half as long. Its origin is unknown.

elding   SCOTTISH
Firewood or peat used to make a fire in a stove or a fireplace.

elevenses   BRITISH
A snack, such as coffee and cake, commonly eaten at about eleven o'clock in the morning. Similar to the American *coffee break.* "What did you have for elevenses?"

embarrassed JAMAICAN

Pregnant or castrated. It is a great insult for a woman to be called an *embarrassed sow* or a man to be called an *embarrassed hog,* which means he is castrated.

eme SCOTTISH

An uncle or a very close friend, a best friend.

endive BRITISH

What Americans would usually call *chicory.* Britons call endive *chicory.*

Enjoy! AMERICAN

A common expression meaning have a good time, enjoy yourself, be happy. Often heard as *Enjoy, enjoy!,* the term was influenced by Yiddish syntax.

enough already AMERICAN

Said when someone has gone too far or something has been carried on too long, etc. Either Yiddish in origin or influenced by Yiddish speech patterns.

enough to make a cat laugh BRITISH

Something so ludicrous that no one would take it seriously.

entrée NEW ZEALAND

In New Zealand an entrée is the first course of a meal, an appetizer, not the main course, as it is in the United States and Britain.

esky AUSTRALIAN

A cooler often carried in a car. First a brand name but now used generically. Few Aussies are without one.

esquire AMERICAN, BRITISH

A courtesy title used after someone's name. *Esquire* is mainly used in American English today as a title of respect after an attorney's name, a usage applied to both male and female lawyers in recent times. In British English, however, the title is commonly used after the name of any man. *Esquire* began life as the title given to a knight's personal attendant, one training to be a knight himself. Such attendants carried the knight's shield, hence their name, from the Old English *esquier,* shield bearer.

estate car   BRITISH
A large passenger car with a tailgate and rear seats that fold down. What Americans commonly call a *station wagon.*

even hands   SCOTTISH
An equal bargain. "It was an even hands trade we made."

everything's all tiggerty-boo   BRITISH
The American *O.K.* (q.v.) is generally replacing *right-o* in England, but *right-o* is still heard, as is its synonym *tiggerty-boo,* especially in the above expression. The *tiggerty* here (sometimes pronounced *tickerty*) is from the Hindustani *teega* and is said to have been introduced to Britain by Lord Mountbatten.

everything that opens and shuts   BRITISH
Everything but the kitchen sink; "loaded" (relating to automobiles); every convenience.

every way's likely   CANADIAN (NEWFOUNDLAND)
Anything, even the unexpected, can happen; don't ever rule out anything at all.

Eve-teasing   INDIAN
The teasing and sometimes harassing of young women. "The police warned him about Eve-teasing."

excuse the expression   AMERICAN
Pardon my language. A common saying influenced by Yiddish.

expats   BRITISH
Expatriates. "There are a lot of expats living over there in America."

extra time   AUSTRALIAN, BRITISH
The overtime period in football and other games. "The game went into extra time."

eye   SOUTH AFRICAN
Can be used to mean the source of a river or a spring. "The eye of the river's about four miles from here."

eyes AMERICAN (SOUTH)
Burners on a stove. "All four eyes of the stove were going."

eye water BAHAMIAN, TRINIDADIAN
Tears, as in "Eye water run down her face when he leave." The term is a translation of a West African–language word.

ey-oop me dook BRITISH
A greeting heard only in Nottingham that means approximately "Hello, dear."

F

face AMERICAN
According to Douglas Le Vien, a former New York City Police detective, as stated in the *New York Times* (March 15, 1992), a *face* is slang for "a guy who looks like a mobster's supposed to look. . . . They [the mob] send him to scare the hell out of someone, like 'Go send a face.'"

face of a robber's horse CANADIAN (NEWFOUNDLAND)
To have the *face of a robber's horse* means to be brazen, shameless. "What gall he has. He has the face of a robber's horse to come here after what he did."

face washer AUSTRALIAN
What Americans would call a washcloth or a facecloth and Britons would call a flannel.

facey JAMAICAN
Rude, impudent, cheeky. "What a facey gal she is."

fact-and-a-half JAMAICAN
A humorous term for a lie, a great exaggeration. "That's a fact-and-a-half, mon."

fag BRITISH, IRISH
(1) A slang term for a cigarette that is well known in the United States, through song and story, but is rarely used. (2) A younger schoolboy who is forced to work for an older one. (3) To wear someone out. (4) An offensive term for a male homosexual (also a derogatory term in the United States).

fag end   BRITISH
An old term, whose origin is unknown, that can mean the end of a fag,
or cigarette, or the last part of anything, as in "The fag end of a leg of
mutton."

fagged   AUSTRALIAN, BRITISH
Tired, beat, bored. "I'm too fagged to do any more."

fair   IRISH
Quite, as in "That's a fair old job," that's quite a job.

fair dinkum   AUSTRALIAN
True, real, genuine. "That's fair dinkum, mate." Probably derives from an
old word meaning the same.

fair go   AUSTRALIAN
An equal chance or opportunity. "We had a fair go at it and lost."

fairy cake   BRITISH
A common term for an individual frosted cake, what in America is a cup-
cake. *Fairy floss* is cotton candy.

F-all   BRITISH
A euphemism for *fucking-all*, which means "nothing." "He comes to work
but does f-all."

fancy   BRITISH
(1) Wish, desire. "Does he fancy another drink?" (2) To be attracted to.
("Do you fancy tall men?") Sometimes heard in the United States.

fancy dress party   AUSTRALIAN, BRITISH
A masquerade party. *Fancy dress* is the costume one wears to such a party.

fancy-shmancy   AMERICAN
Something so fancy that it is pretentious, a blending of Yiddish and English, the Yiddish in this case being the *shm* that is often prefixed to a word
in a mocking way. Other examples are *Santa-Shmanta* and *Oedipus-
Schmedipus*.

to fang   AUSTRALIAN
To drive at a dangerous speed. "They fanged down the hill and crashed into a tree."

farm to the walls of the barn   AMERICAN (WEST)
Plant a crop extensively, using all available land. "He farmed right up to the walls of the barn."

fart about/around   BRITISH, AMERICAN
Slang for to waste time, fool around, especially at work.

fast   JAMAICAN
Meddlesome, impudent. "He fast with my business."

Father Christmas   BRITISH
The preferred name for the American Santa Claus. Americans never use *Father Christmas,* though the British also use *Santa Claus.*

Father God and Sonny Jesus!   AMERICAN (NEW ENGLAND)
An exclamation heard in Maine and other parts of New England.

father-in-law   SCOTTISH
A synonym for a stepfather, not for the father of one's husband or wife.

faunch   AMERICAN (WEST)
Rant and rave. "Who cares? Let him faunch on and on."

faut   SCOTTISH
Typical Scottish pronunciation and spelling of *fault.* "It's no me faut."

feckin'   IRISH
A euphemistic pronunciation of *fuckin'.* "What is he feckin' doin'?"

fed up to the back teeth   AUSTRALIAN, BRITISH
Extremely annoyed with something or somebody. "I'm fed up to the back teeth with this job."

feeling off   AUSTRALIAN
Said of a person who is ill, as in "I was feeling off yesterday."

feesty JAMAICAN
Very impudent. "Roger so feesty all the time." Possibly a variation of *feisty.*

feh! AMERICAN
A common Yiddish exclamation of disgust similar to *pew! ugh!* or *yuck!* "Feh! This I don't like."

fell SCOTTISH
Very. "He's a fell wee one, he is." In England's North a *fell* means a mountain or a hill.

fella AUSTRALIAN PIDGIN
Can mean a person or any thing, as in "Big stone fella," a mountain or a hill, or "Big fella watta," a lake. For other forms of pidgin see *mary.*

fellow-mad BRITISH
Said of a teenager or a young woman who is boy crazy.

fender bender AMERICAN
An accident on a road or in a parking lot that causes no injuries to drivers and passengers and little damage to the cars. The British call a fender a *wing.*

fenky-fenky JAMAICAN
Puny, slight, a poor worker. The word's origin is unknown, and it also can mean cowardly.

fernenst IRISH
In front of, opposite. Sometimes heard in Scotland. Pronounced *fern-enst;* rhymes with *against.*

a few snags short of a barbie AUSTRALIAN
A little crazy, "three bricks shy of a load," as the American version of the saying goes. See also *snag, barbie.*

to fiddle BRITISH
Slang for to cheat; a *fiddle* is a small-time cheat, a *two-bit cheat* in American slang.

Fiddler's Green   BRITISH
A British expression meaning the traditional heaven for mariners. Since the nineteenth century, British sailors have called heaven *Fiddler's Green*, "a place of unlimited rum and tobacco."

fieta   SOUTH AFRICAN
A loud lout or a ruffian. "He's a political fieta." The word, pronounced *fit-ah*, derives from Fieta, the name of a slum in Johannesburg.

fifty-seven varieties of a fool   AMERICAN
A complete fool; the expression probably derives from the popular Heinz 57 varieties of canned food.

to fight like Kilkenny cats   IRISH
To fight bitterly until the end. During the Irish rebellion of 1798, Hessian mercenaries stationed in Kilkenny amused themselves by tying two cats by their tails and throwing them over a clothesline to fight to the death. Just before an officer interrupted their banned "sport" unexpectedly one day, a quick-thinking trooper reportedly cut off the two tails and let the cats escape, telling the colonel that the soldiers had nothing to do with the fight—the two cats had just devoured each other except for their tails. The above tale may have inspired the expression *to fight like Kilkenny cats*, but most authorities go along with Jonathan Swift, who, more conservatively, prefers the explanation that cats in the phrase refers to men. It seems that in the seventeenth century, residents of Englishtown and Irishtown in Kilkenny—which was bisected by a stream—were constantly fighting over boundary lines and were compared to battling cats.

films   BRITISH
See *movies*.

the filth   BRITISH
Underworld slang for the cops, as in "Cheese it, the filth!"

finger-smith   JAMAICAN
A thief, pickpocket, or safecracker.

fir apple   BRITISH
A pine cone that is roundish in shape.

to fire AMERICAN

To discharge a worker from a job.

a first BRITISH

First-class honors at a university. Below them are *seconds* and *thirds*.

first belly pain JAMAICAN

A humorous term for a woman's firstborn child.

first floor BRITISH, AMERICAN

In Britain the first floor in a building is the American second floor, whereas Americans use *first floor* interchangeably with *ground floor*.

first footer SCOTTISH

The first person to enter the house after midnight on New Year's Eve. Also called a *first foot*.

First Nations CANADIAN

A Canadian synonym for the U.S. term *Native American*. However, Canadians also use *Native Canadian*.

firth SCOTTISH

A long, narrow inlet of the sea, an estuary. Also *frith*.

fish 'n chips BRITISH

Pieces of fish fried in batter and served with French fries (chips). The dish is no longer served wrapped in newspaper, as it was traditionally. Also called *chippie*.

fivepins CANADIAN

A popular national bowling game.

fiver BRITISH

A five-pound note. "You owe me a fiver, my friend."

flannel BRITISH

(1) Unnecessary, often deceptive words or talk. "Leave out the flannel and get to the point." (2) The British word for what Americans would call a washcloth or a facecloth.

flashlight AMERICAN
See *torch.*

to flash one's Dover AUSTRALIAN
To open a clasp knife. *Dover* is the brand name of a popular knife much used in the brush.

flat BRITISH
A suite of rooms. What Americans call an *apartment.* While many Americans are familiar with the British *flat,* it is seldom used in America except in the old expression *cold-water flat* (one that had no running hot water). See also *squat.*

flat tire AMERICAN
See *puncture.*

flea market AMERICAN
These bargain markets have nothing to do with fleas. *Flea market* has been an American expression as far back as Dutch colonial days, when there was the Vallie (Valley) Market at the foot of Maiden Lane in downtown Manhattan. The Vallie Market came to be abbreviated to *Vlie Market,* and this was soon being pronounced *Flea Market.*

fleck BRITISH
Small pieces of lint or dirt that cling to fabrics. The word is sometimes heard in the United States but originated in England.

fley SCOTTISH
To frighten, fill with terror. From an Old English word meaning the same.

flit SCOTTISH, AMERICAN
To move to another house; not to move about rapidly and nimbly, the word's meaning in the United States.

floor-through AMERICAN (NEW YORK CITY)
A word encountered only in New York City for an apartment in a small apartment building such as a brownstone that takes up an entire floor. "They rented a nice floor-through."

flyscreen AUSTRALIAN
A fine-netted screen fit into an open window to keep out flies and other insects.

flyting SCOTTISH
A contest of cursing between two people that has been known since ancient times, often in the form of poetry. Pronounced *flighting.*

foo foo JAMAICAN
A fool, someone simpleminded, stupid, easy to fool. The expression is also heard as *fool-fool.*

foosty SCOTTISH
Moldy or musty. "That piece of bread has turned foosty."

foot bottom JAMAICAN
The sole of the foot.

footer BRITISH
Slang for rugby or soccer. "They were playing footer in the street."

footpath AUSTRALIAN
The part of a street reserved for pedestrians. What Americans would call a *sidewalk* and what the British would call a *footway* (q.v.) or *pavement.*

footway BRITISH
See *footpath.*

for Africa SOUTH AFRICAN
A large amount. "A brewery truck crashed and it was beer for Africa."

for beans AMERICAN
With the minimal degree of skill. "He can't play for beans."

forby SCOTTISH
Close by, near. "It's forby here, right around the corner."

force BRITISH
Heard mainly in northern England for a waterfall.

fork   AUSTRALIAN
A jockey, suggested by the way his or her legs fork over the horse he or she is riding.

fortnight   BRITISH
Two weeks. Rarely heard in America anymore, this term is still commonly used by Britons.

for toffee   BRITISH
For beans, for nothing, as in "He can't play for toffee."

forty miles of bad road   AMERICAN (WEST)
A very ugly or unattractive person or place. "One looked like forty miles of bad road, and the other looked like he went on ten miles longer."

forty-shilling word   JAMAICAN
An old term for a "dirty word," dating back to a time when one could be fined forty shillings for using an indecent expression.

for why?   HAWAIIAN
Why? As in "For why you tell lies all the time?"

fossick   AUSTRALIAN
At first this word meant only to search for gold by reworking waste piles called *washings*. Then it came to mean to rummage or to search around for anything, as in "I was fossicking among some papers and found an old letter from her." Chiefly Australian, this word of unknown origin has some currency in England and the United States.

four-by-two   BRITISH
A piece of wood that would be a *two-by-four* in America; in England the larger measurement is given first.

four-legged word   AMERICAN (WEST)
A humorous term for any long, polysyllabic word, often scholarly, frequently pretentious.

frame   AMERICAN (APPALACHIAN MOUNTAINS)
Skeleton. "The frames of them dead rebels laid up there in the hills."

frappé   AMERICAN (NEW ENGLAND)
What is called a milkshake—a drink made of milk, flavored syrup, and
ice cream—in some places is often called a frappé in New England, where
a *milkshake* is made of milk and syrup. The word is pronounced *frap*.

free bowels   BAHAMIAN
Diarrhea. "She has medicine to stop free bowels."

Freephone number   BRITISH
A toll-free telephone number; a British trademark. The American equivalent is an *800 number*.

French fries   AMERICAN
See *chips*.

French letter   BRITISH
A condom. The French call it an *English letter*. Both of these derogatory
terms are meant to suggest an envelope.

French toast   AMERICAN, BRITISH
In England *French toast* is simply sliced bread fried in bacon fat or butter.
In America French toast is sliced bread soaked in a mixture of eggs and
milk before frying.

fresher   AUSTRALIAN, BRITISH
Slang for a freshman at a college; equivalent to the American *frosh*.

frigidaire   PORTUGUESE
The word is a borrowing of the familiar trade name, but is used to mean,
of all things, a frying pan.

from a child   BRITISH
Since childhood, as in "He's lived there from a child."

from A to izzard   BRITISH
Chiefly British in usage and rare today, *from A to izzard* means *from A to
Z*, from alpha to omega, from beginning to end. *Izzard* here may be a 1597
variation of *zed* (z), according to the *O.E.D.*

from away   AMERICAN (NEW ENGLAND)
Used to describe anyone residing in Maine who doesn't hail from the state.
Heard in one tourist center: "He's from away, she's from away—some-
times it seems the whole state's from away."

from time   BAHAMIAN
For a long time. "She ain't been here from time."

front name   BRITISH
A humorous term for one's first, or given, name.

frost   BRITISH
Something that is a complete failure, a bomb or a bust. "That play was a
frost."

fruiterer   BRITISH
A fruit seller or a fruit store. The name is used by a few fancy fruit stores
in the United States.

fruit machine   AUSTRALIAN
A slot machine; after the pictures of fruit that appear when you put in a
coin and pull the handle. A favorite American synonym is *one-armed
bandit*.

fruit parlor   JAPANESE
This borrowing from English means *ice cream parlor* in Japan, perhaps
because ice cream parlors use fruit as toppings for ice cream sundaes, etc.

fryin' size   AMERICAN (WEST)
Said of a young person or a runt. "He's just about fryin' size, and he's
struttin' around givin' orders."

fub   AMERICAN (NEW ENGLAND)
Used in Maine and New Hampshire to mean "putter or fuss about doing
unworthwhile things." "He fubbed around with his car all day and it still
won't start."

fubar   AMERICAN
A euphemistic army acronym made up of the initials of "*f*ucked *u*p *b*eyond
*a*ll *r*ecognition"—that is, completely screwed up, botched up, confused.

full as a goog   AUSTRALIAN
A goog or a googie is an egg, and to be *full as a goog* is to be drunk, full of alcohol.

full of fiemes   SOUTH AFRICAN
To be fussy or capricious; pronounced *fim-is*. "One wouldn't do this and the other wouldn't do that—they were all full of fiemes." From an Afrikaans expression meaning to be full of whims.

full of the joys of spring   AUSTRALIAN, BRITISH
Very happy. "She's full of the joys of spring today."

full stop   BRITISH
The dot at the end of a declarative sentence. What Americans would generally call a *period*. Has limited use in the United States.

to fum fum   JAMAICAN
To flog or to beat. "He fum fum him." The origin of the term is unknown.

function fish   BRITISH
Food served at large gatherings—dinners, banquets, etc.—called *rubber chicken* in the United States.

fundi   SOUTH AFRICAN
Any expert; apparently from a Swahili word meaning an artisan.

fun-fair   BRITISH
Carnival or fair.

fuse   SOUTH AFRICAN
Slang for a cigarette. "Give me a fuse, will you?"

fus fus   JAMAICAN
The very first; an iteration of *first*. "It was the fus fus time he ever saw her."

futz around   AMERICAN
To fool around, play; often used as a euphemism for *fuck around*. *Futz,* possibly deriving from the Yiddish *arumfartzen,* was first recorded in

1929. "We futzed around all day" means we accomplished nothing, wasted the day. "Don't futz around with it" means don't touch it, don't mess around with it, leave it alone.

gala   BRITISH
A sports competition. "He attended the swimming gala."

galah   AUSTRALIAN
A fool. "He made a galah of himself." The word comes from the name of the cockatoo called the galah, a bird whose raucous call seems foolishly talkative. The galah bird itself takes its name from an Australian Aboriginal language.

gallinipper   JAMAICAN
A large mosquito, or some other large stinging insect.

game as Ned Kelly   AUSTRALIAN
It cost nearly half a million dollars to capture Australia's Kelly gang, even though the band was only four in number. Ned Kelly (1854–1880), son of a transported Belfast convict and a convicted horse thief himself, took to the hills with his brother Daniel when the latter was charged with horse stealing. Joined by two other desperadoes, the brothers held up towns and robbed banks for two years until the police finally caught up with them. Ned Kelly became something of a folk hero, and the great deprivations he suffered led to the phrase *game as Ned Kelly*. When the gang was traced at last to a wooden shanty hideout, police riddled it with bullets, burned the shack down, and found Ned Kelly alive and dressed in a suit of armor. He was tried, convicted, and hanged for his crimes.

gammon   BRITISH
(1) A thick slice of ham, salted and cured, from the buttock or thigh of a hog. (2) A slang term for nonsense.

gammy leg   BRITISH
Injured. "He played the whole time with a gammy leg."

gamp   BRITISH
An umbrella, especially an untidy one. The word comes to us from Charles Dickens's *The Life and Adventures of Martin Chuzzlewit* (1843–1844), in

which the garrulous and disreputable nurse Sarah Gamp always carries a bulky cotton umbrella. Sometimes her name is used for a midwife as well. *Brolly* (q.v.), first recorded in 1873, is more commonly used British slang and Australian for an umbrella today.

ganja   JAMAICAN
Marijuana. It is from a Hindi word, ganja having been introduced to Jamaica by East Indians in the nineteenth century.

ganted   AMERICAN (WEST)
Thin, gaunt, drawn. "'You look real ganted today."

gaol   BRITISH
Americans spell the word *jail,* though both words are pronounced the same. Other British variants in spelling include *cheque* (check), *manoeuvre* (maneuver), *tyre* (tire), and *kerb* (curb).

garage sale   AMERICAN
A sale of things people no longer want, held inside their garage or out in the yard, usually on weekends.

garbo   AUSTRALIAN
No connection here with the legendary Swedish movie star. *Garbo* is short for a *garbage* man or sanitation worker.

gasoline, gas   AMERICAN
A fuel used chiefly for automobiles. The British call it *petrol.*

gasper   BRITISH
Slang for a cigarette or a *fag* (q.v.), for obvious reasons.

gatcher   CANADIAN (NEWFOUNDLAND)
A vain, boastful person. To *gatch* means to behave boastfully, to show off.

Gawblimey!   BRITISH
A Cockney exclamation meaning God bless me!

gazumping   AUSTRALIAN, BRITISH
A term used in real-estate transactions that refers to the practice of a seller refusing to honor an agreement with a buyer and selling his property to

someone else for more money. The term has recently had some currency in the United States.

g'day   AUSTRALIAN
Good day, hello. "G'day, mate."

geld   SOUTH AFRICAN
Money; from the Afrikaans *geld* meaning the same.

gen   BRITISH
Slang for inside information, the real dope. The word is a shortening of *general information.*

gender bender   AMERICAN
Slang for a sex-change operation. Based on *fender bender* (q.v.).

general delivery   AMERICAN
Mail delivery to a specific post office, where it is held for pickup by the person to whom it is addressed.

gentoo   SOUTH AFRICAN
A prostitute. The word may come from a disparaging Hindi term for a Hindu who speaks Telugu rather than Hindi, but it probably derives from the name of the *Gentoo,* a U.S. ship transporting young female servants to Africa in 1846 that was wrecked on the South African coast. The women were saved but lost all their belongings and were forced to work as prostitutes in *gentoo houses* to support themselves.

the gents   AUSTRALIAN, BRITISH
A public toilet for men.

get down   HAWAIIAN
Get out, as in "We all get down from the car and walk."

to get icebergs down your back   BRITISH
To be nervous, to get the jitters.

get lost   AMERICAN
(1) Slang for to get out of here, get out of sight, stop bothering me; as in "A dollar? Get lost. I haven't got a dollar myself." (2) Often said during an

argument when one person expresses an idea unacceptable to the other. "Get lost, ya creep!"

get next to   BAHAMIAN
To become sexually intimate with somebody. "He tryin' to get next to her." Can also mean to catch up with someone and to take revenge on a person.

get off the dime   AMERICAN
To get started, take some action, as in "You'd better get off the dime while you still have time." Originally a term used by floor managers in 1930s dance halls, telling dancers to move from an almost stationary position. Ten cents was the cost of a dance.

to get one's monkey up   BRITISH
Monkeys have quick tempers, which suggested the phrase *to get one's monkey up,* "to become angry," an expression that is British in origin and is first recorded in a popular 1853 song.

to get one's spurs tangled   AMERICAN (WEST)
To be confused, disoriented. "He took so many blows to the head he got his spurs tangled."

get outta here!   AMERICAN
A common reply, expressive of disbelief, to an absurd claim or the like. "I'm making ten thousand a week," someone might say, and the slang reply would be "Get outta here!" or "Get the hell outta here!" or "Get up outta here!" or just "Get out!"

get shut of   AMERICAN (WEST)
Get out of, get finished with. "He wants to get shut of school as soon as possible."

get the hump   AUSTRALIAN
To be annoyed, offended, get one's back up. "He really got the hump when he wasn't invited."

getting on   BRITISH
Almost, nearly, as in "He's getting on ninety now." Americans would say *going on.*

get up on one's toes   BRITISH
To get one's back up, take offense about something.

get up with the lark   BRITISH
Get up early in the morning. "You have to get up with the lark to outsmart him."

get your skates on   BRITISH
Let's get going fast, hurry up. "Get your skates on, we'll miss the show."

giddy-go-round   BRITISH
Synonym for a *merry-go-round.*

GIGO   AMERICAN
This common U.S. catchphrase (meaning "garbage in, garbage out," or your results are only as good as your data) was coined in the 1960s, when computers were first widely used for data processing.

gin and it   BRITISH
A type of martini, made with Italian vermouth.

ginormous   AUSTRALIAN
A humorous way to describe something extremely large. "He had a ginormous meal."

gippy tummy   BRITISH
Diarrhea. The *gippy* here is a corruption of *Egyptian,* and the complaint was probably so named by visitors to the Middle East. Americans have a similar term: *Aztec two-step,* which generally refers to diarrhea caused by drinking water in Mexico.

girlie barber   MALAYSIAN
A hairdressing salon that is used as a cover for a brothel or a massage parlor.

girl-o   AUSTRALIAN
A girl or a young woman, especially a very attractive one.

girn   SCOTTISH
A grumbling or a snarl, depending on the context.

girt   SCOTTISH
Great; perhaps related to *girt* for "to girdle, encircle."

git   BRITISH
A derogatory term for a man. "He's a stupid old git, isn't he?"

gite   BRITISH
A house rented in France for a vacation, not the whole year. Pronounced to rhyme with *greet*.

to give a wigging   BRITISH
To give someone a severe tongue-lashing, an angry rebuke. The term, first recorded in 1813, may derive from the wigs that British judges wear.

to give heaps   AUSTRALIAN
To annoy someone, give a person a hard time, heaps of trouble. "He's been giving him heaps all year."

give him his cards   BRITISH
To fire a worker, give him his walking papers. "He was late every day, and they finally gave him his cards."

give it a burl   AUSTRALIAN
Slang for give it a try, give it a go. "Give it a burl, you'll get the hang of it."

give it him hot   BRITISH
Beat him up or scold him severely. "Give it him hot and he'll mind his manners!"

to give someone a tinkle   BRITISH
To phone someone, give him or her a ring.

to give the elbow   BRITISH
To end one's friendship with somebody. "We were good friends for years, and then he gave me the elbow."

Gladstone bag   BRITISH

English statesman William Ewart Gladstone (1809–1898) may have never carried the Gladstone bag named after him. Neither did the four-time prime minister *invent* the light, hinged leather bag, but he did do much traveling in his long public career, and the flexible bag was made with the convenience of travelers in mind.

glam up   BRITISH

To dress up glamorously for a major occasion or a big night out.

glare ice   CANADIAN

Smooth, slippery ice. The term is sometimes heard in the United States, too.

glen   IRISH, SCOTTISH

A valley. The word ultimately derives from the Old Irish *glenn,* meaning the same.

glib   AMERICAN (OZARK MOUNTAINS)

Said of brisk, active movements. "He's ninety years old but pretty glib." Does not mean quick of speech, as it does elsewhere.

to glimmer   SCOTTISH

(1) To blink, as if from defective vision. (2) To wink at someone.

gloaming   SCOTTISH

Twilight, the time of day after the sun has set and before it is completely dark.

gloomy Gus   AMERICAN

See *dismal Jimmy.*

to go   SOUTH AFRICAN

To go can mean to do, as in "I plan to go teaching"—that is, "I'm going to become a teacher."

goat meat   AMERICAN (APPALACHIAN MOUNTAINS)

A euphemism highlanders use for venison, when deer are hunted and killed out of legal hunting season.

gob IRISH, AUSTRALIAN, BRITISH

The mouth; perhaps from a Gaelic word.

gobbledygook AMERICAN

Obscure, verbose, bureaucratic language characterized by circumlocution and jargon, and usually refers to the meaningless officialese turned out by government agencies. The late representative Maury Maverick coined the word in 1944 when he was chairman of a congressional committee. He wrote a memo condemning such officialese and labeled it *gobbledygook,* later explaining that he was thinking of the gobbling of turkeys while they strutted pompously.

to go bush AUSTRALIAN

To escape your troubles by leaving "civilization" and heading out for bush country.

God angel BAHAMIAN

A name for a street urchin; from the angelic look on the faces of some urchins.

goddam FRENCH

English-speaking people have been quick on the draw with curses since earliest times. So often did the English in medieval times take the Lord's name in vain, for example, that the French called them *goddams.* Later, in the American Southeast, Native Americans gave the Anglos the same name for the same reason.

God's nightgown! AMERICAN (SOUTH)

A southern exclamation of exasperation or surprise made famous by Margaret Mitchell's heroine Scarlett O'Hara, who used it several times in *Gone With the Wind* (1936).

gofer matches AMERICAN (WEST)

Paper or book matches; because they are unreliable; you strike one, it fails, and you "gofer" another.

gogga SOUTH AFRICAN

Any insect. "A huge storm of goggas attacked the orchards."

goggle box BRITISH

Slang for a TV set, equivalent to the American *boob tube.*

goin' drink till the world looks little   AMERICAN (MOUNTAINS)
Going to get drunk until all my problems seem like nothing at all.

going by shank's mare   BRITISH
This means to go somewhere by walking, to use "Walker's bus," but as far as is known, no horseless Mr. Shank is responsible for this two-hundred-year-old phrase, which is probably Scottish in origin. Neither is there any proof that the expression refers to King Edward I, nicknamed "Long Shanks" because whenever he rode a pony his long legs reached to the ground. The *shank* is the leg, or that part of the leg below the knee, and a mare is usually slower than a stallion. Going by *marrow-bone stage,* a play on the once-real Marylebone (pronounced "Marrybun") stage in London, means the same.

to go into an Irish sulk   CANADIAN (NEWFOUNDLAND)
To sulk or become morose, usually after exhibiting high good spirits.

golden parachute   AMERICAN
A contract guaranteeing a company executive generous benefits, including severance pay, if he loses his job because the company is sold or merged.

golf   POLISH
Poles use the word *golf* to mean the polo shirt that many golfers wear.

gone down the gurgler   AUSTRALIAN
Gone down the drain; spoiled or wasted. In Britain the phrase is often *down the pan* or *down the plughole.*

gone one o'clock   BRITISH
Past one o'clock. "What time is it?" "I don't have my watch on, but it's gone one o'clock."

gone round the bend   BRITISH
To have lost one's mind, gone crazy. "Barry's gone round the bend."

goober   AMERICAN
Goober, for "peanut," was not coined in the southern United States but originated in Africa as the Bantu *nguba* (peanut) and was brought to the

American South by African slaves in about 1834. A southern term for many years, it has achieved wider usage over the past fifty years. *Pinder*, another word for peanut, comes from the Kongo *npinda* and is used chiefly in South Carolina today.

good-belly JAMAICAN
Someone good-natured, kind, good-hearted.

good few BRITISH
A lot, many, a large number. "We have a good few of them."

good on you AUSTRALIAN
"You did a good job." Often said with a thumbs-up.

good show! BRITISH
An exclamation expressing approval or congratulations for something done.

go off one's head BRITISH
To go out of one's mind, go crazy.

goondaism PAKISTANI
Hooliganism. A word formed from the English *goon* and a local language word.

goose pimples AMERICAN
When geese are plucked, the thousands of tiny muscles that pull their feathers erect to form a natural insulation system continue to contract in the cold. The contracted muscles look like bumpy, pimply skin on a bare bird and as far back as the seventeenth century suggested the bumps on human skin caused by cold or fear. However, although the term *goose pimples* was invented in England, the British now use *chicken flesh* in its place. Americans have stuck with *goose pimples;* also *goose bumps.*

gormless BRITISH
Slang for stupid, slow-witted, foolish.

gorry! AMERICAN (NEW ENGLAND)
A common Maine exclamation. "Gorry! What makes you so stupid?"

gotch-eared   AMERICAN (WEST)
An animal such as a horse or a donkey with clipped, drooping ears; from
the Spanish *gaucho* (turned downward). A *gotch-eyed* person is someone
with eyes looking in different directions.

got his kettle on   AMERICAN (WEST)
Angry, boiling mad, planning retribution. "He's got his kettle on for me."

got no patience one   MALAYSIAN
Has no patience. "My wife, she got no patience one." A combination of
Malay and English words is sometimes called Manglish.

go to business   AMERICAN (NEW YORK CITY)
A term still used, mostly by older New Yorkers, for *go to work*—that is, to
a job in an office.

go-to-hell   AMERICAN (NEW ENGLAND)
A go-to-hell is someone who has no concern for what he looks like or what
anyone else thinks of him. The term is rarely applied to a woman.

go to hell across lots   AMERICAN (WEST)
To go straight to hell or the devil. "He thought all non-Mormons were going
to hell across lots."

go troppo   AUSTRALIAN
To go crazy, to become mentally disturbed. *Troppo* may be a shortening
of *tropical,* perhaps in reference to someone stranded on a tropical island.

governor   BRITISH
The British use *governor* (pronounced *guv'nor*) in addressing a boss, as a
title of respect. It can also be used in addressing a customer, although *sir*
is more common today. *Guv'nor* is often shorted to *guv* (q.v.).

go walkabout   AUSTRALIAN
To walk about or wander the countryside, go for a long stroll, wander off
for a long period of time.

go well   SOUTH AFRICAN
A common good-bye or farewell. "Go well, my friend, go well."

go while the play is good   SCOTTISH
A variation on the British *go while the going is good.*

goy   AMERICAN
Goy is Yiddish for Gentile and can be completely innocent or disparaging
in meaning, depending on who is using it and how. Leo Rosten noted that
the word itself is not derogatory, discussing it at length in his excellent
book *The Joys of Yiddish.* The word derives from the Hebrew *goy,*
"nation," and its use in English dates back to at least the nineteenth
century.

gramophone   BRITISH
A phonograph.

grand   AMERICAN, BRITISH
In the United States a grand is slang for a thousand dollars; in Britain it
means a thousand pounds.

grandbaby   AMERICAN (SOUTH)
A common term for a grandchild. "I got three grandbabies so far."

grandma   AMERICAN (APPALACHIAN MOUNTAINS)
To cut down and steal timber from someone else's property; perhaps so
called because an anonymous highlander who stole timber explained that
he got it from "grandma's" place. Another theory has this unusual word
deriving from an old story or joke about a man accused of stealing
another's timber and finally admitting that "Grandmaw might have taken
a few sticks." A *grandmawer* is someone who steals timber.

grand-slam home run   AMERICAN
A baseball home run hit when three runners are on base, scoring four
runs.

Grape   GERMAN
The long-standing German word *die Pampelmuse* for grapefruit has been
supplanted by *der Grape,* a borrowing and adaptation of the word *grapefruit.* See also *Buttondownhemd.*

grass   BRITISH
Slang for an informer, especially a police informer. *To grass* means to
inform. *Squealer* or *snitch* would be the American equivalent.

grasshopper   AUSTRALIAN
A humorous term in the bush for tourists, because like this insect they eat everything in their path. The term is often shortened to *grassie.*

gratters   BRITISH
Slang for congratulations. The nearest American equivalent is the abbreviation *congrats.*

gravy-licker   AMERICAN (WEST)
Someone who takes something for nothing, especially a government dole, instead of working for it; like a cat that hangs around the kitchen licking up gravy instead of hunting for food.

greasy   BRITISH
Slippery, as in "The road's quite greasy this morning."

greasy luck   AMERICAN (NEW ENGLAND)
Good luck. A local Nantucket expression that first arose among whalemen trying out oil from whale blubber on the decks of whaleships. The decks became very slippery at such times, and this was considered lucky because it meant a more prosperous voyage. Well-wishers often wished departing whalemen *greasy luck* when they embarked on a voyage.

greatcoat   BRITISH
An overcoat; rarely heard in the United States.

a great (big) girl's blouse   BRITISH
A weak, cowardly man. "He's a great (big) girl's blouse."

a great impudent oaf   BRITISH
The American version of this phrase would be "a rude slob."

the Great Majority   BRITISH
A humorous term for the dead.

great toe   BRITISH
In America this would be the *big toe.*

green fingers   BRITISH
A green thumb. "He has green fingers," meaning "He is an accomplished gardener."

greenie   SOUTH AFRICAN
In South Africa, a green-colored ten-rand banknote. "He gave me two
greenies for it." In Australia, *greenie* is a disdainful term for an environ-
mentalist.

gridlock   AMERICAN
The halting of vehicular movement in part of a city because key intersec-
tions are blocked by traffic. The word was coined by Sam Schwartz, head
of the New York City Department of Transportation, in 1975.

grinder   AMERICAN (NEW ENGLAND)
Used chiefly in New England, especially Boston, for what is called a *submarine sandwich, hero, hoagie, torpedo, poor boy, Cuban sandwich, wedgy,*
and *Dagwood* in other regions. Made of split loaves of Italian bread, the
sandwich filling consists of meats, cheese, lettuce, and tomato when cold,
but can be filled with hot meatballs and sauce, eggplant parmigiana, and
so on. The sandwiches are called *grinders* because you need a good set of
grinders [teeth] to chew them. See *wedgey* and *hero.*

grisman   NEW GUINEA PIDGIN
Literally meaning "grease man," this word can describe either a fat man
or an unctuous flatterer. This pidgin language is also called *Tok* (talk) *Pisin*
(pidgin).

grog-up   AUSTRALIAN
A *grog-up,* sometimes called a *grog-on,* is a party where plenty of liquor,
or *grog,* is on hand.

grootbek   SOUTH AFRICAN
A boastful big mouth. The Afrikaans *groot* means big, while *bek* means
mouth.

grotty   BRITISH
A synonym for filthy or cruddy, perhaps from the word *grotesque.*

ground floor   BRITISH
In Britain and many other places throughout the world, the street-level
floor of a building is called the *ground floor,* while the next one up is
called the first floor. In America these would be the first and second floors,
respectively.

grouse AUSTRALIAN

Excellent, very good: "He's a grouse swimmer." The word's origin is unknown; it is unrelated to *grouse,* meaning to grumble.

grown NEW ZEALAND

Whole wheat bread. "I'll have grown toast with my eggs."

grue BRITISH, SCOTTISH

A grisly little comic poem with sadistic content and a trick last line. Grues are sometimes called Little Willies in honor of the "hero" of so many, but the name *grue,* coined by Robert Louis Stevenson from "gruesome," is more appropriate. Though their content is never worse than the daily news, most grues are anonymous:

> Willie poisoned father's tea;
> Father died in agony.
> Mother looked extremely vexed;
> "Really, Will," she said, "what next?"

In Scottish *grue* means to shudder. Also heard in northern England.

gubmint catchum fella AUSTRALIAN PIDGIN

A policeman. "Gubmint catchum fella brother belong me." (That policeman is my friend.") For other forms of pidgin see *mary.*

Gude SCOTTISH

(1) God. (2) Good. Both also heard in northern England.

guillotine NEW ZEALAND

Slang for a paper cutter. Also heard in Australia.

guiser SCOTTISH

Someone wearing a disguise such as a mask or a costume.

gully SCOTTISH

Any large knife. Also heard in northern England.

gum BRITISH

Gum, to the British, is glue or mucilage, not c*hewing gum,* which they always call just that.

gunkhole   AMERICAN (NEW ENGLAND)
A mudhole. The word *gunk* is an old Scottish one meaning to hoax or to
fool and is used to mean a mudhole possibly because "some fool once
thought he could walk on mud and it let him down."

gunnysack   AMERICAN (WEST)
The usual word in the West for what is called a *burlap bag* in the North
and a *crocus sack* in the South—that is, a large sack made from loosely
woven coarse material such as burlap. *Gunny* here ultimately derives from
the Sanskrit word *goni* (jute or hemp fiber).

gussuk   AMERICAN
The Eskimo or Inuit word for a white man; said to be patterned on the
Russian word *Cossack*.

gutser   AUSTRALIAN
(1) A fall or a tumble. (2) A downfall or a misfortune.

gutted   BRITISH
Very unhappy. "I was utterly gutted to learn he died in the fire."

guv   BRITISH
A rather dated form of address to a man, especially someone in a position
of authority. Short for *governor* (q.v.). "Need a lift, guv?" Also *guv'nor.*

guy   AMERICAN, BRITISH
A *regular guy* to many in Britain means "a thoroughly grotesque person,"
whereas in America it means "a decent fellow." The difference is not as
pronounced as in the past, but the American meaning still has a strange
ring to British ears, although it is being used more in England every year.
For the British, *guy* owes its origin to the grotesque effigies of Guy Fawkes,
a leader of the infamous Gunpowder Plot, which are carried through the
streets of England and burned in bonfires on November 5, Guy Fawkes
Day. All of the festivities through the years probably mellowed the meaning of the word to include both good and bad guys. But only in America,
far removed from the Gunpowder Plot in distance as well as time, is *guy*
widely used for any "fellow," no ridicule intended. In England to this day
a *guy* remains a ridiculous-looking person. Since the 1970s *guys* in America has been used in referring to women as well as men, especially in mixed
groups of men and women (e.g., "Do you guys want to come over?").

gwine AMERICAN (SOUTH)
Going, going to. "I'm gwine call them boys." Also *gwyne, gine, goan, gorn, gwin, ghy.* It is a pronunciation the South's early aristocrats borrowed from upper-class British speech.

gyp AMERICAN, AUSTRALIAN, BRITISH
Gyp means to cheat in American English, but in Britain and Australia it is slang for pain or trouble. According to popular etymology, *gyp,* for "to cheat," derives from the name of the much-maligned Gypsies, who got their name because sixteenth century Englishmen erroneously assumed that they hailed from Egypt. There is, however, no proof of this derivation.

gypsy cab AMERICAN
A taxi that picks up passengers on the street when it is not licensed to do so.

gypwater AMERICAN (WEST)
Water highly saturated with gypsum and other alkaline salts, which causes a severe upset stomach when drunk in large quantities.

haar SCOTTISH
The name for a local sea mist or fog that can last for days.

haberdashery AMERICAN, BRITISH
A *haberdashery* in the United States is a store selling men's furnishings; in Britain it is a dealer in sewing notions—pins, needles, etc. The word probably comes from the Anglo-Norman *hapertas,* petty wares. A better story, however, has *haberdashery* deriving from immigrant German peddlers in London selling their goods with the cry *"Ich habe das hier"* (I have it here).

hacked off BRITISH
(1) Sad, disappointed. (2) Fed up with. "I'm hacked off with all the paperwork."

had it away BRITISH
Slang for to have had sex with someone. "She had it away with him."

ha-ha

Here is an exclamation that became a word, one of the most peculiar of derivations. A *ha-ha* is "an obstacle interrupting one's way sharply and disagreeably, a ditch behind an opening in a wall at the bottom of an alley or walk." It is used in gardens as a boundary that doesn't interrupt the view from inside, and can't be seen from the outside until you come very close to it; it is in effect a sunken fence, the inner side of the ditch perpendicular to and faced with stone, while the outer side is turfed and sloping. When these ditches, or fosses, were first used extensively in the seventeenth century, people out for a stroll in the country were frequently surprised to find a sudden check to their walk. The exclamations of "ha-ha!," "ah-hah!," or "hah-hah!" in expressing their surprise became the name of the ditch or sunken fence.

hairbag

Slang for a man who doesn't care anymore, who is waiting for retirement, who lets himself go.

hair in the butter

An expression used in Texas to describe a very delicate or sensitive situation. It refers to the difficulty of removing a single hair from a piece of butter.

hairyback

See *crunchy*.

half

When Hawaiians say *half* for *and a half* ("We stay here eight years half, no?") they are imitating a Chinese usage introduced by early Chinese settlers.

half and half

In the United States, a mixture of half milk and half heavy cream, usually sold in pint cartons. In Britain, a mixture of ale and stout sold in pubs.

hammer

Slang for a carpenter.

hanahana man

A plantation worker. *Hana* means work in Hawaiian.

to handbag   BRITISH
To treat a person, idea, etc., ruthlessly or insensitively, especially for a woman politician to do so. The origin of the term, recorded in the *O.E.D.*, is former British prime minister Margaret Thatcher and the handbag she carried, which became "an often-noted symbol of her swaggering power when she was prime minister," according to one news article.

hand go, hand come   JAMAICAN
If you help me, I'll help you; help comes in return for help.

hangman   JAMAICAN
Can mean a Judas goat—that is, an animal that leads other animals to their deaths in a slaughterhouse.

hang in there   AMERICAN
Persevere, do the best you can. In its present sense the phrase dates back to the late nineteenth century.

hap   SCOTTISH
A shelter, a covering. Also heard in northern England.

hapa haoli   HAWAIIAN
A person who is half white. *Hapa* here is the word *half* assimilated phonologically into Hawaiian, with the *l* dropped, the *f* replaced by *p,* and the final vowel added. *Haoli* (pronounced HOW-lee) means white.

ha'porth of difference   BRITISH
No difference at all. "What you say won't make a ha'porth of difference." *Ha'porth* is also an endearing term for someone: "You daft old ha'porth!" *Ha'porth* is a contraction of "halfpenny worth," which is, of course, very little.

happy box   SOUTH AFRICAN
A humorous name for wine sold in a cardboard box with a little spigot.

hard   BRITISH
Can mean stale or dried out. "Who wants this hard bread?"

hard cheddar!   BRITISH
British slang for "tough luck," also heard as *hard cheese!* Cheddar was originally a cheese made only in the village of Cheddar in England's Somerset County.

hard-ears   TRINIDADIAN
Someone who is so stubborn he or she won't even listen.

hard morris   JAMAICAN
A rough, tough street fighter, perhaps from the name of some real Morris
whose identity is unknown today.

hard-pay man   JAMAICAN
A deadbeat, someone who doesn't pay back the money he owes, from
whom it is hard to collect a debt.

hardy   CANADIAN (NEWFOUNDLAND)
Young and active. "When I was a hardy boy I had many a chore to do."

Harley-Davidson   SOUTH AFRICAN
A handlebar mustache; named after the motorcyclists who often ride
Harley-Davidson bikes and who sport such mustaches.

Harley Street   BRITISH
A London street that is the address of many prominent British doctors,
hence a name for the medical profession in general.

Harry Casual   SOUTH AFRICAN
Slang for a lazy or easygoing man or woman, someone without much
ambition.

Harvey Smith   BRITISH
Here is a man whose name means "the finger," or anyway, two fingers,
meaning the same. Harvey Smith, a well-known British show-jumper,
saw his name become better known after he "was alleged to have raised
two fingers" (forefinger and middle) at the judge of a 1971 competition.
A *Harry Smith* came to mean "the obscene gesture," though, of course,
the gesture dates back much farther than Mr. Smith.

Hatton Garden   BRITISH
The street where most of London's diamond merchants are located, hence
the British diamond industry.

haus pepa   NEW GUINEA PIDGIN
Literally "house of paper(s)," which means a business office. This pidgin
language is also called *Tok* (talk) *Pisin* (pidgin).

to have a bag on BRITISH, AMERICAN
In Britain, to be angry, sulky. In America, to be drunk.

to have a bash at BRITISH
To have a go at something, have a try at it. "Let me have a bash at it."
Americans would say *have a try at it.*

to have a bit of kanga AUSTRALIAN
Among *bushies* (q.v.), this means to have some cash. See also *kanga.*

to have a good innings BRITISH
To perform something well, from the game of cricket, where an innings
is the time during which a team or a player is batting.

to have a ticket on oneself AUSTRALIAN
To be in love with oneself, be extremely conceited.

to have a wash BRITISH
To go to the bathroom. "I think I'll have a wash."

to have an eye for the main chance BRITISH
Always alert to use any situation to one's own good. Sometimes heard in
the United States.

to have one's innings BRITISH
To have one's opportunity. In cricket, an innings is a time at bat, because
that player is "in" at bat while the opposition team is "out" on the field.
Other expressions stemming from British cricket include *to keep one's end
up, to catch up,* and *to bowl over.*

havers SCOTTISH
Foolish, nonsensical talk. To *haver* is to talk foolishly, talk nonsense.

to have someone's guts for garters BRITISH
A humorous threat. "I'll have his guts for garters if he's not on time."

to have square eyes BRITISH
Used to describe someone addicted to television.

to have the world by the tail on a downhill pull AMERICAN (WEST)
To have everything going exceedingly well for you.

having someone on BRITISH
Teasing someone, pulling someone's leg. *Putting someone on* is the American equivalent.

headache! AMERICAN
A warning to "watch it!" "heads up!" used by loggers, oilmen, and others in the United States because a heavy object is overhead or coming down: Be careful or you'll get a headache—that is, get hit in the head.

hear, hear! BRITISH
A British cry of affirmation or support often heard in Parliament.

heart-starter AUSTRALIAN
An eye-opener, the first drink of the day, a drink that gets one going.

Heath Robinson BRITISH
A complicated, impractical, but clever and humorous machine or device; similar to the American *Rube Goldberg device,* named after the cartoonist Rube Goldberg.

heavy down BAHAMIAN
Well advanced in pregnancy, big with child. "She heavy down by now."

height of land CANADIAN
An area of high ground forming a watershed.

Heinz hound AMERICAN
A humorous term for a mongrel. From the name of the American Heinz Company, which long advertised fifty-seven varieties of canned food. Also *Heinz dog* and *Heinz.*

hell for leather AMERICAN
To travel, especially to ride, at a very fast pace. "He came by here hell for leather." *Hell bent for breakfast* is a variation on this.

hell-on-wheels AMERICAN (WEST)
Union Pacific Railroad construction gangs in the 1860s lived in boxcars that were pulled along as the line progressed. Traveling and living with

these hard-drinking, often violent men were gamblers, prostitutes, and other unsavory characters. The wild congregation assembled in the boxcars suggested the population of hell to settlers, and the transient town was called *hell-on-wheels*, a colorful term soon applied to any violent, vicious person or lawless place.

to hell or Connaught   BRITISH
During the Commonwealth, under Oliver Cromwell, the native Irish were disposessed of their land in the other provinces and ordered to settle in Connaught or be put to death. This led to the phrase common throughout Ireland, or wherever Irishmen emigrated, of *to hell or Connaught.*

hell with the fires out   AMERICAN (WEST)
A colorful name for the southern desert.

help   BRITISH
A helping, or serving, of food. "He had second helps of everything but water."

hen   SCOTTISH
An endearing form of address to a woman or a girl, as in "I missed you yesterday, hen."

hern   AMERICAN (SOUTH)
Hers. "She's right tall, with them skinny legs of hern."

hero sandwich   AMERICAN
New York City's Italian hero sandwiches, the term first recorded in the 1920s, are named for their heroic size, not for any specific hero. Hero sandwiches are surely among the most numerous-named things in English. Synonyms include *hoagies* (in Philadelphia), *submarines* or *subs* (in Pittsburgh and elsewhere), *torpedoes* (Los Angeles), *wedgies* (Rhode Island), *wedges* (New York State), *bombers* (New York State), *Garibaldis* (Wisconsin), *Cuban sandwiches* (Miami), *Italian sandwiches* (Maine), *Italians* (Midwest), *grinders* (New England), *spuckies* (pronounced spookies; Boston), *rockets* (New York State), *zeps* or *zeppelins* (several states), and *poor boys* (New Orleans), though this last one is made with French instead of Italian bread. Blimpie is a trade name for a similar sandwich, and a Dagwood is any large sandwich—after "Blondie" comic strip character Dagwood Bumstead's midnight snack creations. That's twenty in all—and there must be more!

herself IRISH

An important woman, feminine counterpart of *himself* (q.v.). "Herself wants to see you now."

he wears a two-inch belt and
Big Jim suspenders AMERICAN (TEXAS)

Said in Texas of someone who is very cautious.

Hi! AMERICAN, BRITISH

The most common greeting in the United States, *Hi!* is used in Britain, when it is used at all, to attract someone's attention, as *Hey!* is in America.

higgler JAMAICAN

A peddler, an itinerant huckster selling produce or cheap goods door-to-door or from small market stalls.

high JAMAICAN

The English of an educated person, as opposed to general folk speech.

high blood BAHAMIAN

A common shortening of *high blood pressure.* "She's got high blood."

the high jump BRITISH

Death. "He looked ready for the high jump."

High Street BRITISH

A name often used by the British for the main street in a town or village. Americans commonly use *Main Street.*

hightail it AMERICAN (WEST)

To leave in a hurry, to make a fast getaway. Mustangs, rabbits, and other animals raise their tails high and flee quickly when they sense danger. Trappers in the early American West noticed this, probably while hunting wild horses, and invented the expression.

high tea BRITISH

A light evening meal, often served at about six o'clock in place of supper, that includes cooked dishes as well as tea, scones, etc.

hillbilly AMERICAN

This derogatory name for a hill person is considered insulting at best, and has in the past provoked fights resulting in deaths. It is first recorded in 1904 and implies laziness, ignorance, and stupidity. Highlanders don't mind being called hillbillies by other mountain folk, but they do object to "flatlanders" or "furriners" using the term.

him JAMAICAN

Often used for the feminine *her*, as in "Me see one old woman without him head."

himself IRISH

Frequently used instead of the personal pronoun *he;* can mean the master of the house or anyone of importance. "Himself will be wanting his tea now." Humorously used to describe someone who *thinks* he is important.

hinnie BRITISH

A term of affection for a child commonly heard in northern England.

hip BAHAMIAN

A euphemism for the buttocks. "He fall on his hip."

hippen AMERICAN (SOUTH)

A baby's diaper; the word is used mainly in Tennessee.

hipsters AUSTRALIAN, BRITISH, AMERICAN

Americans would call these tight, low-rise pants *hiphuggers. Hipster* in American English means one who is aware of the latest trends, someone who is with it, especially as concerns jazz.

his elevenses are up CANADIAN (NEWFOUNDLAND)

This saying means a man is dying, because in some old people the two muscles in the back of the neck protrude like two bones resembling the numeral 11.

hoarding BRITISH

A billboard. A *No Hoarding* sign means "no advertisements or notices permitted here."

hobble   CANADIAN (NEWFOUNDLAND)
An odd job, a small piece of work. "I hope I turn up an extra hobble."

hod   SCOTTISH
Hid. "He hod in the closet from the other children."

holdall   BRITISH
A *carryall,* a large bag or case used by travelers. "She found an old holdall
and packed it quickly."

holiday   AUSTRALIAN, BRITISH, IRISH
Time off from work, especially when travel is involved. What Americans
would call a *vacation.*

hols   BRITISH
Short for the holidays. "We're going away for the hols."

home and hosed   AUSTRALIAN
To have successfully finished a job. "As soon as he painted the door he
was home and hosed."

homebrew   CANADIAN
Any pro athlete who plays in the country where he was born and raised.

home, James, and don't spare the horses   BRITISH
Passengers in autos still use this phrase humorously to friends when
given lifts home. The old expression, dating back perhaps to the seventeenth century, was once a common command of nobility to their private
coachmen.

homely   BRITISH, AMERICAN
In Britain, homey, unpretentious, domestic. "It was a homely place, very
warm and comfortable." In America, ugly. "What a homely child!"

home run   AMERICAN, BRITISH
In America, a *home run* is hit over the outfield wall. In Britain, *the home
run* is the final straightaway or homestretch in a horse race.

homework   AMERICAN
A humorous term meaning "lovemaking with one's spouse."

homey   AMERICAN

Originally black English for a friend from your neighborhood (short for homeboy), the term now has some general usage.

honk   BRITISH

To vomit, throw up. "One drink too many and he honked up."

to hook it   BRITISH

To leave. The American slang synonym would be *to take a powder,* get lost for a while, get out of town.

to hook up   AMERICAN

For the past twenty years or so, to hook up has had the meaning of to become sexually or romantically involved.

hoon   AUSTRALIAN

A brutal person, a lout. The word also has limited use in the United States.

hooroo   AUSTRALIAN

Good-bye or so long. Also *hooray!*

hoose   SCOTTISH

Typical Scottish pronunciation and spelling of *house.* "Come doon to my hoose tomorrow."

hoosegow   AMERICAN (WEST)

Jail. The term was coined in the1860s and derives from the Spanish *juzgado* (a court or tribunal), which to Mexicans means "a jail" and was borrowed in this sense by American cowboys. The slang word *jug* for a jail probably also comes from *juzgado* and was recorded half a century or so earlier.

hooter   BRITISH

An automobile horn or siren. Also slang for the nose.

hooters   AMERICAN (SOUTH)

Slang for the female breasts that is becoming nationwide in use.

hoover   BRITISH
A vacuum cleaner. *To hoover* means to vacuum. Named after the American Hoover vacuum cleaner, invented by William Hoover.

Horray Henry   BRITISH
A disparaging term for a big-mouthed, ostentatious member of the "upper classes."

horries   SOUTH AFRICAN
The DTs, or any horrible aftereffects of drinking.

horseback guess   AMERICAN
A rough estimate. "Give me a horseback guess."

horsefeathers!   AMERICAN
A euphemism for *horseshit!* A statement expressing disbelief, this word has been around at least since 1925. It may be related to the term *horsefeathers* once used in carpentry, which were the large feathering strips used in roofing and siding houses. On the other hand, *horsefeathers* may have originated with a saying such as "That's nonsense, that's like saying horses have feathers!"

horses for courses   BRITISH
A mostly British expression urging someone to stick to the thing he knows best. *Horses for courses* comes from the horse-racing world, where it is widely assumed that some horses race better on certain courses—grass, dirt, mud—than on others.

Hotspur   BRITISH
A person with a terrible temper noted for extreme behavior. The word memorializes the nickname of Sir Henry Percy (1364–1403), who led a revolt against English king Henry IV, which resulted in Hotspur's death at the Battle of Shrewsbury. Hotspur's name, however, would probably have never entered the language if Shakespeare had not immortalized him in *Henry IV, Part I,* two centuries later.

Housey-Housey   BRITISH
Roughly the equivalent of the American game Bingo.

housing estate   BRITISH
A housing development or subdivision.

how are you keeping?   BRITISH, IRISH
A common expression meaning how are you doing?, how are you holding up?, etc.

hufty   BRITISH
The British borrowed this word, meaning *look* or *take a look*, from Arabic.

Huli stomach   HAWAIIAN
An upset stomach. The expression stems from the belief that babies suffering from colic had their stomachs turned upside down by a jealous, evil-eyed person known as a Huli.

hull   AMERICAN (WEST)
A synonym for a horse's saddle among cowboys.

hummums   BRITISH
A Turkish bath. A corruption of the Arabic *hammam,* meaning the same, the word came into the language in the late seventeenth century and soon became, in the form of *hummum,* British slang for a brothel, because so many Turkish baths became brothels.

humongous   AMERICAN
Something or someone huge or monstrous. The word has been used, mostly humorously, since the 1960s, and though its origin is obscure it seems to be based, consciously or unconsciously, on words such as *huge, monstrous,* and *mountainous.*

to hump   AUSTRALIAN
To carry something on the back. "He humped the pack over the hill." Originating in Australia, it is now heard in Britain and the United States as well.

hundredweight   BRITISH, AMERICAN
The word is used in both Britain and the United States, but in Britain it means 112 pounds, while in the United States it means 100 pounds.

in the hunt   BRITISH
Said of someone who is in the running, who is very much a candidate for a position or an award.

hunting pink
BRITISH

The famous *hunting pink* jacket is scarlet, not pink. Moreover, it never was pink, taking its name instead from the London tailor named Pink, who designed it for fox hunting in the eighteenth century.

hurl
AUSTRALIAN, SOUTH AFRICAN

To throw up. "He got so sick he had to hurl outside."

hurry-come-up
JAMAICAN

Someone who has achieved success or prominence very quickly. The term sometimes has a negative connotation, as when applied to the *nouveau riche.*

ice
BRITISH, AMERICAN

The usual word in Britain for *ice cream.* In America *ice* means a dessert made with sweetened water and fruit juice.

iced water
BRITISH

Water with ice in it. Americans would always say *ice water.*

ice lolly
AUSTRALIAN

Flavored ice on a stick.

identity disk
BRITISH

A metal disk used to identify servicemen in case of injury. What American servicemen would call a *dog tag.*

idle
CANADIAN (NEWFOUNDLAND)

Thoughtless, mischievous, foolish in behavior, full of tricks. "Those idle boys wrote all over the wall."

if life spare
JAMAICAN

God willing, if God spares me; a promise to do something if one doesn't die before he can. "I'll see you tomorrow if life spare." Also *if life save.*

if you're a mind
AMERICAN (NEW ENGLAND)

If you care to, if you feel like it or want to. "Come on over, if you're a mind."

I gonnies! AMERICAN (OZARK MOUNTAINS)
A euphemistic exclamation, a variation of *My God!* Used only in the Ozarks and southern Appalachians. "I gonnies! He was a big man!"

illey whacker AUSTRALIAN
A confidence man, usually one who works country fairs. The expression's origin is unknown.

the ill place SCOTTISH
A synonym for hell. "When he dies I'm sure he's going straight to the ill place."

imaginary invalid BRITISH
A humorous or euphemistic term for a hypochondriac.

I'm easy about it BRITISH
It's all right with me, it's *O.K.* (q.v.), it's cool. *I'm easy* is heard in American slang and means the same.

imejiappu JAPANESE
The Japanese borrowing of the English words *image up,* to which they have given the meaning "improving one's image." The Japanese call constructions like this "Made in Japan English."

imiji songu JAPANESE
The Japanese borrowing and alteration of the English words *image song,* by which the Japanese mean "a commercial jingle that fits a product's image."

in a bit of a tight AMERICAN (NEW ENGLAND)
Being in trouble. "He helped us when we were in a bit of a tight."

incinerator AMERICAN
See *destructor.*

indaba SOUTH AFRICAN
A meeting or a conference. "The indaba was held in Capetown." The word, which comes from the Zulu language, also has come to mean a problem or a concern, as in "It's not our indaba."

the Industry COLOMBIAN

This English word is used in Colombia to mean kidnapping; there are about eight hundred kidnappings in Colombia annually.

infant school AUSTRALIAN

The grades in school for children ages four to seven. Often called *the Infants.*

in galore CANADIAN (NEWFOUNDLAND)

A phrase meaning "in abundance." "There were fish in galore out there."

ingogo SOUTH AFRICAN

A prostitute who charges half a crown (an *ingogo*), which is twenty-five cents.

in hand AUSTRALIAN, BRITISH

Equivalent to the American *at hand.* "Pay attention to the job in hand."

inheritance powder BRITISH

A humorous term for arsenic, a favorite poison in many British murder mysteries.

in his (her) bad books BRITISH

In trouble with someone, on someone's bad list.

in hospital BRITISH

The British generally drop the article from *in the hospital.* "He's been in hospital since Monday."

ink pen AMERICAN (SOUTH)

A common term for a fountain pen or a ballpoint pen in the American South, where the pronunciation makes it difficult to distinguish pen from pin.

in state NIGERIAN

To be pregnant. "She is in state five months now."

in the basket BRITISH

Rejected, turned down; the basket referred to is the wastepaper basket.

in the nick   AMERICAN, AUSTRALIAN, BRITISH
In Australia, in the nude. "She posed in the nick." In British slang *in the
nick* or *in the good nick* means in good shape or in the pink. In America,
in the nick means "in the nick of time," "just in time."

Inverness   SCOTTISH, BRITISH
Sherlock Holmes wore one of these warm overcoat-cape combinations,
which were named for the Highlands town of Inverness, Scotland, where
they were apparently invented one bone-chilling winter in the 1850s. The
cape is removable from the coat or the cloak.

IQ   THAILAND
In Thailand the English term *IQ*, intelligence quotient, has come to mean
smart or clever.

iron critter   BAHAMIAN
A synonym for an automobile; still used by some older people.

ironmonger's   BRITISH
A shop where tools are sold; similar to the American *hardware store.*

I say!   BRITISH
This exclamation of surprise or astonishment is thought to be typical of
British men by most Americans but is considered rather old-fashioned in
England, though it is still heard there. The expression, never used seri-
ously in America, probably dates back before the late eighteenth century.

isn't   IRISH
Often used in place of *hasn't,* as in "Isn't she come home yet?"

Is your trumpeter dead?   BRITISH
An old insulting term asking someone why he is boasting or blowing his
own horn.

It.   BRITISH
Short for *It*alian vermouth, as in "I'll have a gin and It."

it doesn't go on all fours   AMERICAN
Unlike similar Madison Avenue expressions, this saying, meaning "something isn't quite right," goes back to an ancient Latin proverb, *omnis com-*

paratio claudicat, which literally means "every simile limps," but which British historian Thomas Babington Macaulay translated as "no simile can go on all fours."

it's all double Dutch to me   BRITISH
Means the same as the American "it's all Greek to me," it's unintelligible talk or I can't understand it.

it's porridge   EAST AFRICAN
It's very easy; it's a piece of cake.

it's your shout, mate   AUSTRALIAN
Heard in Australian pubs for "It's your turn to buy the drinks, friend." A *shout* is a round of beers in Australia.

jackanapes   BRITISH
Applied to any pretentious upstart who apes his betters, the British word *jackanapes* probably comes from the nickname of William de la Pole, duke of Suffolk. *Jack* was a common name for a tame male ape in England at the time (attached to the word, as it was to *jackrabbit, jackass,* and others), and Suffolk's coat of arms bore the clog and chain of a trained monkey. When, in 1450, the duke was arrested and beheaded at sea off Dover for alleged treason against Henry VI, de la Pole was derisively styled "the Ape-clogge" and later won the nickname Jack Napes, or Jacknapes. The ending might mean "of Naples," the source of apes brought to England in the early fifteenth century, but there is little doubt that the word earned its popularity and present meaning through Suffolk's nickname, which was even recorded in a satirical song of the day.

jacket potato   BRITISH
A potato baked in its skin; called a *baked potato* in the United States.

Jack Ketch   BRITISH
An executioner. Jack Ketch was generally regarded as a clumsy, barbaric bungler: it took him several strokes to sever William, Lord Russell's head after he moved slightly when the ax was falling. Ketch later apologized for his clumsiness, explaining that that he had been disturbed while taking aim. No one believed him, though, and his name became the name

for a public executioner and a mark of execration long before he died in 1683.

Jack Tar   BRITISH
A sailor. One story has it that the British term arose in the seventeenth century, when sailors wore canvas breeches often spotted with tar from work done on ships. According to another tale, sailors in Lord Nelson's navy wore overalls and broad-brimmed hats made of the tar-impregnated tarpaulin cloth commonly used aboard ship. The hats, and the sailors who wore them, were called *tarpaulins,* which was finally shortened to *tar.*

jader   CANADIAN (NEWFOUNDLAND)
Someone who is disliked, a great nuisance. "Let the jader freeze to death."

jaegers   BRITISH
Though *jaegers* can be any of several rapacious seabirds, in England they are also woolen underwear. The underwear is named for Dr. Gustav Jaeger, whose Dr. Jaeger's Sanitary Woolen System Co. Ltd. manufactured and marketed the various undergarments he designed, beginning in about 1890.

jaislaak!   SOUTH AFRICAN
This exclamation of surprise, disbelief, etc. may be a euphemism for *Jesus!* "Jaislaaik, how did you get here so fast?!"

Jamie Duff   SCOTTISH
There is a story that this Scottish nickname for a professional mourner at a funeral comes from the name of one James Duff, an odd character who attended many funerals in the mid-nineteenth century because "he enjoyed the ride in the mourning coach." More likely the term is from the name of an old firm that supplied mourners for a price.

jammers   SOUTH AFRICAN
Afrikaans for *sorry.* "Jammers, we're not open until five." The word derives from the Dutch word for "pity."

java   AMERICAN
Since about 1850 *java* has been slang for *coffee* in the United States. It obviously derives from the name of the coffee-producing island.

jaw-jaw   BRITISH
Incessant talk. "Jaw-jaw is better than war-war," British prime minister
Harold Macmillan said in a 1958 speech.

jerrican   BRITISH
The Germans developed this five-gallon gas container for the Afrika Korps
during World War II. But the British stole the idea, naming the can the *jerrican,* after the Jerries, or Germans.

I'll be jiggered!   BRITISH
An old British exclamation of surprise, meaning roughly "I'll be damned!,"
once commonly seen in novels and heard in movies.

jiggery-pokery   BRITISH
Secret or dishonest behavior. "Some jiggery-pokery was going on there."

jilleroo   AUSTRALIAN
A young woman worker on an Australian sheep ranch. See also *jockeroo.*

jim-jams   BRITISH
Pajamas, especially when worn by young children.

jinker   CANADIAN (NEWFOUNDLAND)
A Jonah, a person aboard ship who brings bad luck to all his shipmates.

Jnr.   AUSTRALIAN, BRITISH
Used as an abbreviation of *Junior* after a man's name the way Jr. is used
in the U.S.

job   AUSTRALIAN
To punch someone with a heavy blow.

Jock   BRITISH
Slang for a man from Scotland; considered offensive by some people.

jockeroo   AUSTRALIAN
A young man who works on a ranch. His female counterpart is a *jilleroo*
(q.v.).

Joe Bloggs   BRITISH
The British term for the average man, who is called *John Doe* in America.
It also can mean, depending on the context, an average person, or even a
nobody—someone Americans often call a *Joe Doakes* or a *Joe Six-pack*
(q.v.).

Joe Public   BRITISH
The general public; same as the American *John Q. Public.*

Joe Six-pack   AMERICAN
The average guy, who will go home after work and drink a six-pack of
beer.

John Bull   BRITISH
The national nickname for the English. The term comes from John Arbuthnot's satire *The History of John Bull,* first published in 1712.

John Henry   AMERICAN
One's signature. Often called a *John Hancock* as well.

johnny   BRITISH
Slang for a condom. The term's origin is unknown.

Johnny Canuck   CANADIAN
The cartoon character who represents Canada, as *Uncle Sam* represents
the United States and *John Bull* (q.v.) represents England.

John Thomas   BRITISH
The slang term *John Thomas* for the penis is well known but not commonly used in the United States. The origins of *John Thomas* will probably never be established beyond a doubt, but British folklore, running
counter to all known facts, derives the expression from the name of a real
man of prodigious dimensions. According to this tale, the expression "John
Thomas" dates to the Middle Ages, about 1400. At the time there lived in
a Wiltshire village a farmer named John Thomas, whose outlandishly
large member constantly attracted attention even when concealed beneath
his codpiece. But John Thomas succumbed to the sin of pride. Confusing
astonishment with praise, he took to exhibiting himself to anyone who
happened by. Young John was finally tried, hanged, drawn, and quar-
tered—except for the real offender, that is. Puritans being then as they are

still, John Thomas's memorable member was preserved in an economy-size pickle jar, and Barnums of the time toured the countryside exhibiting dead what he had been executed for exhibiting alive. And so, according to the tale, the expression *John Thomas* became part of the language. The trouble is that no etymologist has traced the expression back farther than 1840. All we have is the legend and the expression.

joiner   SOUTH AFRICAN
A traitor. Suggested by those Afrikaners who "joined up" with the British during the Boer War.

jolly good show   BRITISH
A somewhat dated expression said to someone who has performed very well.

jolly, jolly good   BRITISH
Jolly means "very." *Jolly good*, then, is "very good, extremely good." "We had a jolly good time, but it was jolly expensive."

jort   TRINIDADIAN
A snack taken between meals. "Let's have a jort, mon."

joss   BRITISH
Joss is pidgin for a Chinese house idol or cult image, while a *joss house* is a Chinese temple, and a *joss stick* is an incense stick burned before an idol. It seems that early Portuguese explorers were told that these idols were household gods. The Portuguese thus gave them the Portuguese name for God, *Deos*. This sounded like *joss* to the Chinese, and they adopted the word.

judder   AUSTRALIAN, BRITISH
Shudder, shake violently. "The plane began juddering and we thought that was the end."

judy   BRITISH
Slang for a woman, often an unattractive woman.

jugged hare   BRITISH
A popular dish of stewed rabbit. The term is rarely heard in the United States.

juggernaut   BRITISH
The British name for what Americans would call a *tractor-trailer.*

juggins   BRITISH
An idealist. Ernest Benzon, a wealthy playboy, was dubbed "Jubilee Juggins" because he foolishly squandered his entire fortune—a quarter of a million pounds—within two years after beginning to bet at the track during Queen Victoria's Jubilee in 1887. One story claims that the nickname "Silly Juggins" also attached itself to him. *Juggins,* however, was synonymous with "simpleton" long before Jubilee Juggins. Possibly it is a diminutive of *Jug,* a sixteenth-century pet name for Judith, Jane, or Joan. Jugs, Judiths, Janes, or Joans were often maidservants or barmaids at the time, and most servants of the day were considered dull and stupid, at least by their masters.

jumble   BRITISH
A rummage sale; similar to the American *garage sale* or *yard sale.*

jumbuck   AUSTRALIAN
A sheep. "Get those jumbucks in for shearing."

jump-and-jive   JAMAICAN
Shoes or slippers made from old automobile tires. During World War II they were called *Hitler boots.*

jumper   AUSTRALIAN, BRITISH, AMERICAN
In Australia and Britain, a pullover sweater; in the United States, a type of woman's dress.

Juneteenth   AMERICAN
June 19, 1865, the date on which slaves in Texas belatedly learned of their emancipation. (They had been freed by the Emancipation Proclamation in September 1862.) The date is a state holiday in Texas and is widely celebrated by African Americans.

just now   SOUTH AFRICAN
Presently, soon, in a minute. "Don't get out of the car, I'm coming just now."

K

K AMERICAN
(1) Slang for a thousand dollars; from kilo. (2) Baseball scorecard symbol for a strikeout. (3) To strike out: "He K'd four batters in a row."

kabob JAMAICAN
An alteration of *cobweb;* also means the kitchen soot that gathers on cobwebs.

kahuna AMERICAN (HAWAII)
See *big kahuna.*

kanga AUSTRALIAN
Another name, like *'roo,* that is short for the kangaroo. In the bush, *kanga* also means money or cash.

keek SCOTTISH
To peep or look furtively. Also heard in northern England.

keelie SCOTTISH
A tough, a hoodlum. The term derives from the name of the infamous nineteenth-century Keelie Gang of Edinburgh.

keep up one's end BRITISH
Americans would use *hold up one's end,* with the same meaning: to do one's fair share of the work.

keep your eyes skinned BRITISH
Be on the lookout. Means the same as the American *keep your eyes peeled.*

keep your hair on AUSTRALIAN, BRITISH
Equivalent to the American *keep your shirt on,* be patient, be calm.

keep your nose out of the gutter AMERICAN
Don't drink so much that you get drunk and fall down.

keep your pecker up BRITISH
Pecker here refers not to the penis, as many people believe, but to the lip. *Pecker* has been British slang for lip, corresponding as it does to the beak, or pecker, of a bird, since the middle of the nineteenth century, when we

first find this expression meaning "screw up your courage, keep a stiff upper lip." (*Pecker,* for the male organ, has been slang only since the late nineteenth century.) The first recorded use of the phrase is impeccably British: "Keep up your pecker, old fellow" (1853). A more specific explanation is that it refers to a gamecock's bill, the bird's bill or pecker sinking lower toward the ground as he grows more tired and near defeat.

keep yourself to yourself   BRITISH
Mind your own business, keep out of a fight or argument between others.

keep your wool on   BRITISH
Control yourself, don't be impatient. The expression's American counterpart would be *keep your pants on.*

ken   SCOTTISH
(1) To know or have knowledge of a person or a thing. (2) To be acquainted with someone or something. (3) To understand an idea or a situation.

kenant   CANADIAN (NEWFOUNDLAND)
A sneaky, contemptible young person. "I'll have nothing to do with that little kenant." The word's etymology is unknown.

kerb   BRITISH
The edge of a sidewalk. Americans spell it *curb.*

kerb crawling   BRITISH
Slang for riding in a car aside the kerb (curb) on a street and trying to pick up prostitutes.

kerfuffle   BRITISH
Noise, confusion, excitement. "What's all the kerfuffle about?"

ketthers   NORTHERN IRISH
Very badly adjusted people. "And what can you expect from ketthers like that?"

kibitzer   AMERICAN
German card players of the sixteenth century found meddlesome onlookers just as annoying as card players do today. The constant gratuitous

"advice" of these chatterers reminded them of the *Kiebitz* (the lapwing or plover) whose shrill cries frightened game away from approaching hunters. Thus all kibitzers are named for this troublesome bird (also known as the peewit), which inspired the German word *Kiebitzen,* "to look over the shoulder of a card player."

kickshaws   BRITISH
Tidbits of food, trifles of small value. The word, spelled *kickshaws,* was used by Shakespeare in *Henry IV, Part II,* but had formerly been spelled *kickhose.*

kidstakes   AUSTRALIAN
(1) Nonsense or pretense. (2) Small stakes, a small amount of money.

kill-devil   AMERICAN (MOUNTAINS)
Potent moonshine so powerful and poorly made that it could kill the devil himself.

kill-me-quick   SOUTH AFRICAN
A humorous term for any strong liquor.

kill oneself out   BAHAMIAN
To work until you are exhausted. "He kill himself out on the job."

kill one's neck   HAWAIIAN
To break one's neck. "He fell into the hole and kill his neck." Still occasionally heard in Hawaii.

kindie   NEW ZEALAND
Kindergarten, for children ages three to five. Sometimes heard in Australia.

King's English   BRITISH
Proper English, English as it should be spoken. Several English kings didn't speak English, but this term has nevertheless been in use since the mid-sixteenth century. It was used by Shakespeare in *The Merry Wives of Windsor* (1600), and three centuries earlier Chaucer wrote "God save the king, that is lord of this language."

kin teet   JAMAICAN
From *skin* plus *teeth.* To draw back the lips and reveal the teeth, or to grin
or laugh with pleasure.

kiosk   BRITISH
Newsstand is the common American term, though *kiosk* is sometimes
used in the United States for the structure itself.

kip   BRITISH
Slang for a bed, a room in a rooming house, a sleep, or to sleep. *To kip
down* means to turn in for the night.

kirby grip   BRITISH
A hairpin or a bobby pin. Also called a *hair grip.*

kirk   SCOTTISH
(1) A church. (2) *The Kirk* is the name of the official church of Scotland
(Presbyterian). (3) *Kirk* also can be a verb meaning to attend church.

the kiss-my-arse latitudes   BRITISH
The *kiss-my-arse latitudes* is used mostly in the British merchant marine
for the "homestretch," when a ship is close to port and the crew cares
about nothing but getting ashore and tends to ignore orders—especially
if the crew has already been paid.

kiss my back cheeks   AMERICAN (NEW ENGLAND)
A Maine euphemism for *kiss my ass* that is sometimes heard in other
areas of New England as well.

kiss of life   BRITISH
A colorful term, based on *kiss of death,* for the life-saving method of
mouth-to-mouth resuscitation.

kiss out   SOUTH AFRICAN
To pass out, usually from too much drink. "He made a lot of noise and
then suddenly kissed out."

kist   SCOTTISH
Can mean a chest or a box. Also heard in northern England.

kittle   SCOTTISH
(1) To tickle with the fingers. (2) To excite a person by flattery. (3) To rouse a person with strong words. As an adjective, *kittle* means ticklish.

klondike   CANADIAN (NEWFOUNDLAND)
A period of plenty when everyone is doing very well economically, as in "It's a klondike here this year." The term derives from the Klondike gold rush in the early twentieth century, when great fortunes were made.

klutz   AMERICAN
Originally a Yiddish term, deriving from the German *Klotz,* "a log or a block of wood." *Klutz* describes a clumsy, graceless person; a bungler; a fool. A *klutz,* however, can be an intelligent person, just someone badly coordinated.

knackered   BRITISH
Slang for very tired. "I'm too knackered to work anymore."

knickers   BRITISH, AMERICAN
In Britain, women's underwear; in America, they are a type of short men's pants worn today mainly by golfers.

to knock acock   BRITISH
To greatly surprise someone by doing something unexpected.

knockers   AMERICAN
Either a woman's breasts or a man's testicles in American slang.

knock galley west   BRITISH
To knock into smithereens. No one has been able to explain why a ship's galley or the compass point west have anything to do with this expression. They may not. The words may be a corruption of the dialect term *collyweston,* which in turn derived from the town of Colly Weston in Northamptonshire, a town reportedly given to excessive violence. Colly Weston itself may have been named for a local, violent troublemaker of the same name.

to knock up   BRITISH, AMERICAN
In Britain *to knock up* simply means to rouse someone, to wake someone up by knocking on his or her door, to visit. In America, it is well-known slang for to make a woman pregnant.

the knowledge
BRITISH

The location of the streets in London, which a taxi driver must learn to obtain his license.

know one's cans
AMERICAN (WEST)

Cowboys on the range in the nineteenth century were usually starved for reading matter and often read the labels on the cook's tin cans, learning them by heart. A tenderfoot could always be distinguished because he didn't *know his cans*.

kokua
HAWAIIAN

A loanword from the Hawaiian language meaning help, or to help. "Your kokua is really appreciated."

kosher
AMERICAN

In *The Joys of Yiddish* (1968) Leo Rosten calls *kosher* "the most resourceful Yiddish word in the language." It derives from the Hebrew *kasher*, "fit, appropriate," and strictly means fit to eat according to Jewish dietary laws, but by extension it can mean authentic, trustworthy, or legal, among various other shades of meaning. It is often heard in expressions such as "that's not kosher," that's not right or legal.

kraal
SOUTH AFRICAN

A corral or enclosure for livestock, or a cluster of huts surrounded by a stockade.

krag
SOUTH AFRICAN

Energy, power, strength; from the Dutch *kracht* meaning the same.

krans athlete
SOUTH AFRICAN

An offensive slang term that roughly means a "big baboon."

kriminal
CZECH

A borrowing and slight alteration of the English word *criminal*. However, *kriminal* means a jail in Czech. Similarly, *angina* (from the English *angina*) has come to mean "tonsillitis," of all things.

kvetch
AMERICAN

Very common as both a noun, for a chronic complainer, someone who complains about the smallest things, and a verb meaning to complain incessantly about such things ("Stop your kvetching, will you?"). Originally from the German *quetschen,* "to squeeze, pinch." Pronounced k'VETCH.

kye SCOTTISH
Cows. "Move the kyes to the next pasture."

kyle SCOTTISH
A narrow channel of water, usually between two islands.

kylie AUSTRALIAN
(1) A boomerang. From the Aborigine word *karli,* meaning the same. (2) An offensive word for a black person. (3) Australian slang for an immigrant who doesn't speak English.

lab HAWAIIAN
A bathroom, the word deriving from a confusion of *lab*oratory and *lav*atory.

labrish JAMAICAN
A workhorse word that means gossip, jokes, memories, songs, or tall tales, among other things.

ladder BRITISH
What Americans would call a *run* in a stocking or in pantyhose.

laddie book BRITISH
A macho men's magazine, with photos of nude or seminude women, fast cars, etc.

ladies' fingers AMERICAN, AUSTRALIAN, BRITISH
The usual term for the vegetable generally called *okra* in the United States. In America, the term *ladyfinger* is used for a small, narrow sponge cake. In Australia *ladyfingers* are a variety of short banana.

ladybird BRITISH
The *lady* refers to "Our Lady," the Virgin Mary, in whose honor the beneficial insect was named. These brightly colored beetles of the family

Coccinellidae, which feed on aphids and other destructive garden pests, are known in America as ladybugs but in Britain as *ladybirds,* due to a British aversion to the word *bug,* which is strongly associated there with buggery, or sodomy. Some American Southerners favor the British version of the word.

lager lout   BRITISH
A member of a group of young men given to loud, unruly behavior after drinking too much beer (lager).

lah   SINGAPOREAN, MALAYSIAN
An expression similar to the American *like* or *you know,* used mainly in conversation. Where an American might say "She's, like, very tall," a Singaporean speaking might say "She's lah, very tall." *Lah* is said to come from a Chinese dialect, but its use is considered to be a sure way to identify a Singaporean or a Malaysian.

lallies   BRITISH
Slang for a woman's legs.

lamp belong Jesus   SOUTH SEAS PIDGIN
The sun, this expression owing much to Christian missionaries in the South Seas.

land element   CANADIAN
The ground troops or army of the Canadian Armed Forces.

land sakes alive!   AMERICAN
An old-fashioned euphemistic exclamation of surprise. Often heard as *lands sake alive* or just *land sakes.*

lang   SCOTTISH
The typical pronunciation and spelling of *long.* "It's a lang way hame (home)."

lang hame   SCOTTISH
The long home; that is, one's grave in the earth.

lang-shankit   SCOTTISH
Used to describe someone long-shanked or long-legged.

lappie   SOUTH AFRICAN
A rag or cloth used for housework such as dusting. From the Afrikaans
lap, rag.

larder   BRITISH
The pantry or food closet. Americans rarely if ever use this common British
expression.

larrikin   AUSTRALIAN
A young street hoodlum. Said to derive from *Larry,* a pet name for
Lawrence, but no one seems to know why. It might also come from *lar-
rup,* to beat or thrash.

lashings   BRITISH
A humorous term for lots of food and drink. "There were lashings of good
food on the buffet."

lash out   AUSTRALIAN
To spend a lot of money wastefully. "He lashed out five thousand pounds
for it." Also used by the British.

lass   SCOTTISH
A common term for a girl or a young woman. *Lassie* is also frequently
used.

last but one   AUSTRALIAN, BRITISH
The next to the last. "This is the last but one of them."

late   SOUTH AFRICAN
Deceased. *Late* in its sense of deceased is generally used only attribu-
tively (e.g., "My late father"). But in South African townships, where
English is usually a second language, *late* (for deceased) is usually heard
in the predicative (e.g., "My father is late.")

later   AMERICAN
A shortening of "see you later" that probably originated among surfers
but is now widely used. "Later, man." *Lates* and *late* are used in the same
way.

law agent SCOTTISH
A lawyer or a solicitor in Scotland.

lawed AMERICAN (OZARK MOUNTAINS)
Litigated, went to court to establish rights, sued. "He lawed fer that piece of land."

lawyer AMERICAN
An attorney; there are no solicitors and barristers performing separate functions in the United States, as there are in Great Britain.

lay-by BRITISH
What in America would be called a *rest area* or *a rest stop;* a roadside parking area off a highway.

lazabout IRISH
A lazy person who stays home, doesn't go out to find work. "The no-good lazabout spongin' cheat!"

lazy as Lawrence BRITISH
The Romans burned the Christian martyr St. Lawrence alive on a gridiron over a slow fire, and legend has it that he addressed his torturers ironically with the words "I am roasted enough on this side. Turn me around, and eat." Over the years the legend has become more British, and St. Lawrence's words are now "Turn me around; for this side is quite done," which is supposed to signify that the martyr was too lazy to move in the flames. More probably the expression *lazy as Lawrence* has something to do with the heat of St. Lawrence Day, August 10.

lazy as Ludlam's dog BRITISH
Legend has it that old Mrs. Ludlam, a sorceress, had a dog who lived with her for many years in her cottage in Surrey near Farnham. So lazy was her dog that when strangers approached he always lay down or leaned up against a wall to bark, or didn't bother to bark at all. There are several versions of the tale, all of them responsible for the proverbial British expression *lazy as Ludlam's dog.*

lazy Susan AMERICAN
See *dumbwaiter.*

lead   AUSTRALIAN, BRITISH
A leash. "All dogs should be kept on a lead in the street."

leader   BRITISH
What would be called an *editorial* in American newspapers and magazines.

leather breeches   AMERICAN (MOUNTAINS)
Beans dried in the pod, then boiled "hull and all."

leave well alone   BRITISH
A more succinct variation on the American *leave well enough alone.* "Don't
bother him now. Leave well alone." *Let well alone* is also used.

left carrying the can   BRITISH
In the United States this would be *left holding the bag*—that is, to be left
responsible for something, to be the fall guy after the others involved in
a scheme have protected themselves from prosecution or absconded.

left holding the baby   BRITISH
The same as *left carrying the can* (q.v.).

lefty   BRITISH, AMERICAN
In Britain, a *lefty* is a political leftist; in America, a left-handed person.

legless   AUSTRALIAN, BRITISH
So drunk one can't walk, or can barely walk.

lemonade   AMERICAN, AUSTRALIAN, BRITISH, NEW ZEALAND
In the United States, a drink made of lemon juice, water, and sugar. In
Australia, Britain, and New Zealand, a clear soda pop such as the trade-
marked Sprite or 7-Up.

let it abee   SCOTTISH
Let alone; don't mention it. "Let it abee, laddie, or you'll be sorry."

let's talk turkey   AMERICAN
Let's get down to real business. According to an old story, back in Colonial days a white New England hunter unevenly divided the spoils of a
day's hunt with his Native American companion. Of the four crows and

four wild turkeys they had bagged, the hunter handed a crow to the Native American and took a turkey for himself, then handed a second crow to the Native American and put still another turkey in his own bag. All the while he kept saying "You may take this crow and I will take this turkey," or something similar, but the Native American wasn't as gullible as the hunter thought. When he had finished dividing the kill, the Native American protested "You talk all turkey for you. You never once talk turkey for me! Now I talk turkey to you." He then proceeded to take his fair share. Many scholars believe that from this apocryphal tale, first printed in 1830, comes the expression *let's talk turkey.*

let the side down BRITISH
To embarrass friends or family by one's actions. "You've let the side down, Reggie."

levenses BRITISH
A morning snack or a coffee break, usually of coffee and biscuits. The word is a shortening of *elevenses,* which refers to the time it is usually served.

library ticket BRITISH
A card allowing one to borrow books from a library. Americans would call this a *library card.*

license plate AMERICAN
See *number plate.*

lido BRITISH
A public, open-air swimming pool, from the famous Lido resort in Venice.

lifesaver AUSTRALIAN, AMERICAN
In Australia, a *lifeguard,* someone who watches over swimmers at a beach or a swimming pool; in America, a ring-shaped life preserver.

lift BRITISH
In America, an *elevator.*

light come, light go BRITISH
Means the same as the American English *easy come, easy go.*

lightie   SOUTH AFRICAN
Slang for a child or a young boy. "They've two lighties at home."

lightning strike   AUSTRALIAN, BRITISH
A sudden strike by workers without warning and without union approval, what Americans would call a *wildcat strike.*

the light shines out of him (her)   BRITISH
An expression of great love or admiration. Similar to the southern American dialect phrase "She (he) thinks she (he) hung the moon and stars."

like a curate's egg   BRITISH
Something satisfactory in some ways but not in others: "The play was rather like a curate's egg." The expression originated with a story in a British magazine in which a timid curate had been served a bad egg while dining at the home of an important parishioner. He is asked how the egg tastes and, not wishing to offend his host, says that parts of it are excellent.

like a shag on a rock   AUSTRALIAN
Utterly alone; suggested by the large Australian seabird called a *shag* sitting alone on a rock.

like peas   BAHAMIAN
In abundance. "He got girlfriend like peas."

limb   BRITISH
An affectionate name for a *little devil,* a mischievous child; short for *limb of the devil.*

lime   TRINIDADIAN
To hang around, hang out, loiter.

lint   AMERICAN, BRITISH
In Britain, a surgical dressing. In America, bits of fiber and fluff that cling to clothing (called *fleck* by the British).

lintie   AUSTRALIAN
A sprite; possibly from the Scottish *lintie,* a linnet, which is a small European finch.

liquor store   AMERICAN
A place where bottles of liquor and wine are sold. In Britain these are called wine merchants. See also *package store.*

little most   JAMAICAN
Almost; nearly. "She little most lovely as her sister Sarah."

the little people   IRISH
Leprechauns and other imaginary creatures. Also called *the little folk.*

a little red bit   SCOTTISH
A baby; a newborn infant. "He's a wee one—a little red bit, all kicken' and cryin' and yawnin' at the same time."

live   CANADIAN (NEWFOUNDLAND)
Something real or actual, as in "Nobody had any live cash." Is also applied to something homemade, such as "live jam" or "live bread."

live by the olden days time   BAHAMIAN
To follow old customs and methods; to live as one's ancestors did.

to live short   AMERICAN (NEW ENGLAND)
To live in poor circumstances, to live in an undesirable place. "Often somebody from Maine who is living short in a far place will come back home."

living room   AMERICAN
See *lounge room.*

the local   BRITISH
Short for the local pub. "I'll be down at the local."

loch   IRISH, SCOTTISH
A lake, or an arm of the sea similar to a fjord. The word can be traced back to Old Irish. A small lake is called a *lochen.*

locker room   AMERICAN
See *changing room.*

lockfast   SCOTTISH
A strongbox equipped with a lock. "His money is all in a lockfast."

lollipop man or woman   BRITISH
A traffic crossing guard for schoolchildren. So called because of the STOP
sign mounted on a stick that such guards carry.

lolly   BRITISH
(1) Money. (2) Ice cream or an ice on a stick.

lolly water   AUSTRALIAN
A soft drink. *Lolly* means "candy" in Australian English.

Lombard Street   BRITISH
The name of this London Street, where many banks and other financial
institutions are located, is sometimes used to mean the financial community in general, the way Americans would use *Wall Street.*

lone parent   BRITISH
In America, a *single parent.*

lonesome water   AMERICAN (MOUNTAINS)
Sweet water from a source close to one's first home. "Once you come home
and get a drink of lonesome water you always stay home."

long belly   JAMAICAN
A greedy man or woman. Also *long gut.* "That long belly eat all day."

long drop   SOUTH AFRICAN
A humorous term for a privy dug deep into the earth; some have sides
and a back but no roof or front.

long-headed   BRITISH
Shrewd or very wise.

long pockets and short arms   BRITISH
Used to describe a miser, someone who won't part with a penny of his or
her full pockets.

long-sighted   BRITISH
Farsighted. "He's so long-sighted he needs glasses for everything up close." Britons use *short-sighted* for a nearsighted person.

loo   BRITISH
Loo, a slang word for "toilet" and British in origin, may be a mispronunciation of *le lieu*, French for "the place," but no one is sure. It also could be a shortening of *gardy loo*, a warning cry housewives made when they emptied chamber pails out the windows into the street, *gardy loo* being a corruption of the French *gardez l'eau*, "watch out for the water." It is said that a man traditionally walks on the outside of a woman in the street because chamber pots were emptied out the window in Elizabethan times; in those days a man was expected to take the greater risk of walking near the curb and protecting his lady by shielding her with his body as well.

lookahere   AMERICAN (OZARK MOUNTAINS)
Look here. "Lookahere, it's the parson comin'."

to look fit for butchering   BRITISH
To look fit and healthy. "Well, you look fit for butchering today."

look-through window   BRITISH
A large window. What Americans would call a *picture window* or a *bay window*.

loopy   BRITISH
Slang for loony or crazy. "He's one loopy character."

Lord Hawhaw   BRITISH
Someone who makes propaganda for the enemy. William Joyce (1906–1946) earned the sobriquet for his mocking broadcasts from Berlin during World War II. The American-born British fascist was captured after the war, adjudged a British subject because he held a British passport, and hanged for his crimes.

lorry   BRITISH
A large motor vehicle for hauling goods. What Americans would call a *truck*.

lose the train   BRITISH
Americans would use the phrase *miss the train*. "We lost the train and had to wait another hour."

lossie   SOUTH AFRICAN
A floozie or a fast woman. "All the lossies hang out at that bar." Rhymes with *floozie*.

a lot of keys   BRITISH
A set of keys, as in "I locked myself out, but luckily I had a second lot of keys."

loudhailer   AUSTRALIAN, BRITISH
A megaphone or bullhorn. The British also use this expression, but it is unknown in the United States.

lounge room   AUSTRALIAN
Americans would call this the *living room* of a house; Britons would call it a *sitting room*.

love, luv   BRITISH
A common way of addressing a member of the opposite sex. "I'll have it for you by tomorrow, luv."

love hole   AMERICAN (OZARK MOUNTAINS)
Heard in the Ozarks for a gully, ditch, or depression along a road. Such a gully often caused a female passenger in a buggy or a car to bump up against the male driver or jolted the two riders into one another's arms.

luau   AMERICAN (HAWAII), AUSTRALIA
A party or a celebration. The word is now commonly used in the mainland United States and in Australia as well.

lube   AMERICAN (ALASKA)
To have sexual intercourse, as in "They were lubing all night."

luck penny   BRITISH
A good-luck penny; also called *luck money*.

lucky dip   BRITISH
Items drawn without being seen. A *grab bag* in American English. "Each of us fished in the lucky dip."

lumber room   BRITISH
A storage room for old furniture and junk. *Lumber room* has no currency in the United States. What Americans call *lumber,* wood used in building something, is called *timber* in Britain. One possible explanation for the difference is that American homesteaders, in clearing their land for farming, left many discarded trees lying around; this clutter, or lumber, was later cut or split into the wooden planks that Americans know as lumber today.

lurgy   AUSTRALIAN, BRITISH
A humorous term for a minor illness of little consequence. "He's taken to bed with some little lurgy." Also *lurge.*

lurk merchant   AUSTRALIAN
A shrewd, shady merchant or operator of any kind. *To lurk* means to act suspiciously in Australian.

m

mac   BRITISH
A raincoat; short for *mackintosh,* named for its nineteenth-century British inventor, Charles Macintosh (1766–1843), who in 1823 became the first person to produce a practical waterproof cloth. Macintosh's raincoats won popularity overnight, but his name was spelled wrong from the very beginning. Properly, the *mackintosh,* as it is sometimes called, should be *macintosh,* although the other spelling prevails.

macked out   AMERICAN
An African American expression meaning all dressed up. The word could possibly derive from the French word *maquereau,* meaning "pimp."

maggies   JAMAICAN
Slang for a pair of handcuffs; the origin of the term is unknown.

maggoty drunk   IRISH
Very drunk, so drunk one is filthy from lying or crawling around on the ground.

mahosker   AMERICAN (NEW YORK CITY)
Money, pay, paychecks. "I had the idea, he put up the mahosker."

mail   AMERICAN (HAWAII)
In most of America, letters, packages, etc., delivered by the post office. In Hawaii, a letter. "Did I get a mail today from anyone at home?" In Britain, the comparable term is *post*. "Has today's post arrived?"

maize cob   BRITISH
What in America would be called *corn on the cob*.

makari   SCOTTISH
Makari are poets, the term deriving from the rare word *makar* (a variant of "maker"), an archaic Scottish term for a poet.

to make a balls-up of it   BRITISH
To attempt something and fail utterly, make a mess of it.

make big   SOUTH AFRICAN
To raise a child to adulthood. "She made him big, gave him every advantage, but he never comes to see her."

make die-dead   HAWAIIAN
An expression used by children in games such as cops and robbers, when one child "shoots" another.

make four eyes   JAMAICAN
Said of two people trying to stare each other down.

make free with yourself   SAINT HELENA
Take risks, don't play it safe.

make like   AMERICAN (NEW YORK CITY)
To imitate. "Gimme a bat and I'll make like Mickey Mantle."

to make old bones   BRITISH
To live to a very old age. "We all hope to make old bones."

make soft   HAWAIIAN
Be careful, as in "Make soft with the eggs in that package."

mama-man   JAMAICAN
A derogatory term for someone considered an unmanly man, or a man who does "women's work." Also *maama-man.*

mammy   IRISH
Mother. *Mam* is a British regional term meaning the same. *Mammy* was once commonly used in the American South to mean a black woman who cared for white children but is considered a derogatory expression today.

man-hands   AMERICAN
Unfeminine hands. Used to describe a beautiful woman whose overly masculine hands are her only flaw. "She's gorgeous, except for those man-hands of hers." Coined on the television comedy series *Seinfeld.*

Manhattan clam chowder   AMERICAN
New England clam chowder is a soup made with clams, vegetables, and milk—never with a tomato base. Manhattan clam chowder, however, is always made with tomatoes. This great American gastronomic controversy became national news in 1939 when Assemblyman James Suder introduced a bill into the Maine legislature making the use of tomatoes in clam chowder illegal in that state. The punishment his unenacted bill specified: Make any offender harvest two bushels of clams at high tide. See also *New England chowder.*

manky   BRITISH, IRISH
Dirty, revolting. "He took out his manky handkerchief and blew his nose." "That's really manky." Also *manky-dirty.*

mannish   JAMAICAN
A word applied to both men and women that means impertinent, forward. "You too mannish for me, sir."

manse   SCOTTISH
The living quarters of a Presbyterian minister, usually attached to the church. The term is also used in the United States.

Mansions   BRITISH
Used by the British in the names of buildings containing flats, or apartments. "His address is 10 Bristol Mansions."

maple-head
Eponymous words and phrases often derive from the names of obscure people. This unusual old term from the Ozarks means "a very small head." It is said to come from a pioneer family named Maples noted for their small heads.

maquiladora city
Cities in Mexico on the U.S. border that have *maquiladora programs* set up by the Mexican government. Under these programs, parts are shipped by, say, an American manufacturer in El Paso to a company in the nearby Mexican city of Juárez that assembles the parts, the finished products exported back to the United States duty-free except for the value added in Mexico. The idea was born in about 1964. *Maquiladora* derives from the Spanish *maquila* (the portion received by a miller for milling someone's grain).

marmalade
The Danes use the English word marmalade to mean any jam, whereas in English it means a clear, jellylike preserve made from the pulp and rind of fruits, such as orange marmalade.

marrow
Marrow is a British term that is sometimes used in America. It means "a long, green squash," often zucchini, and has its origins in the use of *marrow* as the term for the pulp of a fruit, which dates back to at least the tenth century. Squash was often called *marrow-squash* in eighteenth-century America.

mary
In this form of pidgin, a jargon spoken in the southern Pacific, the word *mary* means "a woman," as in "That fella man him catch'm money belong mary." (That man took the woman's money.) Melanesian Pidgin is also called Neo-Melanesian and *beche-de-mer*. Other examples of this pidgin include *long way big bit* (very far), *sing-sing* (a song or dance), *pigeon* (a bird of any kind), *finish altogether* (die), *belly* (any part of the body below the neck), and *gammon* (to lie). There are hundreds more.

mash
Slang for mashed potatoes. *Bangers* (sausages) *and mash* is a popular dish.

mass   SOUTH AFRICAN
A synonym for weight. Someone overweight could be called *overmass.*

mass action   SOUTH AFRICAN
Any large demonstration, including a strike, a sit-in, a march, etc.

master   AMERICAN (NEW ENGLAND)
Excellent. "He did a master job building his house."

mate   AUSTRALIAN, BRITISH
Buddy, chum, comrade, partner. The term dates back to the late fourteenth
century in England and is still common there. It has, however, become a
hallmark of Australian speech and is usually associated with that nation.
The Aussies even apply *mate* to people they barely know. Americans use
the word mainly for a spouse.

matey   AUSTRALIAN, BRITISH
Very friendly. "They've been matey now for a year or so."

maths   BRITISH
An abbreviation of *mathematics.* "He studies maths." In America the
abbreviation is *math.*

maxie   SCOTTISH
A big error, a serious maximum mistake. "Horror of horrors—a maxie!"
Mainly a historical term, little used today.

mazel tov   AMERICAN
Although the literal meaning is "good luck," this widely known Yiddish
expression means "congratulations" or "best wishes" on one's success or
good fortune; it is not said to a person when wishing him or her luck.

me   IRISH
Frequently used instead of *my,* as in "She made me lose me temper," or
"Me telly is broken."

mealie   SOUTH AFRICAN
(1) Corn or maize. (2) An ear of corn. Sometimes called *mealies.* The
word derives from the Portuguese *milho* meaning the same.

meanwhile, back at the ranch   AMERICAN
An expression that originated as a movie caption in the silent film era at the beginning of the twentieth century, these words are used humorously today when someone wants to get back to a story after going off on a tangent.

memsahib; sahib   BRITISH, INDIAN
Indians used to address British women as *memsahib* in the days when the sun never set on the empire. The word is simply a feminine form of the Urdu *sahib*, "sire" or "master," *mem* representing the "ma'am." The respectful title is first recorded in 1857, *sahib* attested to as far back as 1696. The terms are still used in India, but aren't exclusively applied to the British anymore.

men   THAILAND
One of many words adopted by the Thais that are borrowed from English but have been given different meanings than they have in English. In this case *men* is a shortening of *menstruate*.

meneer   SOUTH AFRICAN
A word from the Afrikaans meaning "sir" or "mister." Also *mynheer*.

mere   BRITISH
A lake or a pond. The word is never used in America by itself but is found in place names such as Edgemere, Broadmere, etc.

meshuga   AMERICAN
Crazy, insane; from the Hebrew and Yiddish for the same. "He's meshuga, she's meshuga, they're both meshuga."

meteorological office   BRITISH
The office that tracks and forecasts the weather. Americans would always use "weather bureau" instead.

mews   BRITISH
Any large former horse barn that has been converted into a house or flats (apartments).

Mexican toothache   AMERICAN
See *Montezuma's revenge*.

to mezzle AUSTRALIAN
Slang for *to complain.* "He's always mezzling."

mickle SCOTTISH
An adjective that can mean great, big, large, much, or abundant.

middy AUSTRALIAN
What Aussies call for when they order a medium (nine-ounce) glass of beer.

might could AMERICAN (SOUTH)
A reduction of "might be able to." "He might could tell you all about it."

mighty small poatoes and few in a hill AMERICAN
An old saying meaning something or someone of little consequence. "He's mighty small potatoes and few in a hill."

milk-and-manure belt SOUTH AFRICAN
Any affluent area outside of a large South African city.

milk bar AUSTRALIAN
In Australia a *milk bar* isn't a bar serving milk but a local convenience store.

milk-ice CANADIAN
Patches of thin ice formed in depressions in a field or a meadow.

milko AUSTRALIAN
Slang for a milkman. "The milko made a lot of noise during his delivery this morning."

milkshake AMERICAN
In most of America a milkshake is a thick, sweet drink made of milk, ice cream, and syrup. An exception is Rhode Island and eastern Massachusetts, where such a drink is called a *cabinet,* after the wooden cabinet in which the mixer used to be encased; a *milkshake* in Rhode Island is just milk and syrup shaken up together. In northern New England the drink most Americans call a *milkshake* is called a *velvet* or a *frappé* (pronounced *frap*).

milliard   BRITISH
Milliard is the British word for the American "billion," or one thousand million. The term is also used in Russia and Germany. The American *trillion* is equivalent to the British *billion.*

minder   BRITISH
If you have a *minder* in Britain you have a personal bodyguard.

mineral   BRITISH
Not mineral water, but what Americans would usually call a soft drink.

mi no manki bilong you   NEW GUINEA PIDGIN
Literally "me no monkey belong you," which means, "I'm not your servant (or slave)." This pidgin language is also called *Tok* (talk) *Pisin* (pidgin).

miserable   CANADIAN (NEWFOUNDLAND)
Can be used to mean "very," as in "It's a miserable fine day."

mister   ITALIAN
The Italians have borrowed the English word *mister* and put it to a totally different use, making *un mister* mean "a (sports) coach."

miz   BRITISH, AMERICAN (SOUTH)
Depressed, down, the word a shortening of *miserable.* A British mystery novel might be titled *The Case of the Miz Ms.* In the American South *Miz,* meaning "Mrs.," is a title of respect for a married woman.

moaning minnie   BRITISH
A whiner, a complainer, male or female, who annoys other people.

mocks   BRITISH
Practice tests used to prepare students for real exams later on. "When do you take your mocks?"

moggy   AUSTRALIAN, BRITISH
In Australia, an ordinary cat that is unkempt, ungroomed. "I've had my moggy now for three years." Also *moggie.* The British use the word, which derives from *mongrel,* to describe a cat of undetermined breed.

moider   BRITISH
In America *moider* is a dialect pronunciation of murder, but in northern
England *moider* means to confuse, worry, perplex. *To be moidered* there
means to be bothered.

moke   AUSTRALIAN
A poor horse, an old nag. "Why did he ever buy a moke like that?"

molly man   IRISH
A homosexual, an effeminate man.

mom-and-pop store   AMERICAN
A small retail business run by a married couple, or any small U.S. business with a few employees. Mom-and-pop stores are an old American
institution; there were, for example, thousands of candy stores run by hus-
band-and-wife teams in New York City from the 1920s through the 1950s.
But the term *mom-and-pop store* is first recorded in 1951.

monkey nuts   BRITISH
A common term for peanuts rarely heard in the United States, but common in Britain.

monkey's wedding   SOUTH AFRICAN
Rain and sunshine coming at the same time. Possibly the translation of a
Zulu phrase meaning the same, though its origins are unknown.

Montezuma's revenge   AMERICAN
A euphemism for diarrhea named after the Aztec emperor who lost his
empire to the conquistadors. Usually caused by impure water, the debili-
tating illness also goes by the names of the *Curse of Montezuma,* the *Mexican two-step* or *fox trot,* the *Aztec Hop,* and the *Mexican toothache.* In
other parts of the world it is known as the *Tokyo trots,* the *Rangoon runs,*
and the *Delhi belly.*

mooch   AMERICAN, BRITISH
In American English *mooch* means to borrow, usually with no intention
of paying back, as in "He's always mooching cigarettes off me." In British
English the word means to walk about slowly and carelessly without any
purpose, or, more currently, to "hang out."

mooncussers   AMERICAN
Mooncussers were so called because they cursed (cussed) the moon and
the light that it brought, robbing them of their livelihood. During the early
nineteenth century, these lowlifes lured merchant ships to shore on dark
nights by waving lanterns that were mistaken for the lights of other ves-
sels. When the ships were destroyed on rocks, their cargo was collected
by the mooncussers as salvage.

moose milk   CANADIAN
A humorous term for any strong liquor. See also *wolf juice.*

mopoke   AUSTRALIAN, NEW ZEALAND
The name of a small owl whose call sounds like *mopoke, mopoke.* It also
has become the name for a stupid person, or for someone who seems
very unhappy.

moral certainty   AUSTRALIAN
Aussies alone use this expression to mean "a sure thing," as in "It's a moral
certainty."

more better   HAWAIIAN
Better, as in "It's more better to eat before you do big drinking."

moreish   AUSTRALIAN
Describes something so good to eat that you want to eat more of it. "Those
were moreish biscuits she made for breakfast."

morning-morning   BAHAMIAN
A common reply to someone greeting you with a "Good morning."

mortise lock   BRITISH
See *dead bolt lock.*

Mothering Sunday   BRITISH
Another name in Britain for what is always called Mother's Day in the
United States. It falls on the fourth Sunday in Lent.

mouse potato   AMERICAN
An amusing new coinage based on *couch potato* (someone who spends
too much of his or her time sprawled out on the couch sleeping, eating,

or watching TV). A mouse potato spends too much of his or her time on the computer.

mouti mouti
A gossip, someone who won't stop talking, a motormouth. *Mouti* here is a pronunciation of *mouthy.*

movies
Movies is still the most popular word for the motion pictures in America. There are, however, several synonyms. In Chicago, for example, *show* is mainly used ("Let's go to the show"). *Films, flicks,* and even *cinema* (rarely) also are heard, though these are primarily British terms.

moxie
Courage, nerve, or guts. The expression derives from Moxie, a bitter-tasting New England soda pop. In the nineteenth century it was marketed as a nerve tonic, which led to its association with courage.

mozzie
Slang for a mosquito.

Mr. Fraid
A ghost. "Watch out or Mr. Fraid will get you sure."

much
Often used in place of "many," as in "I don't get much days off."

muck about
Muck means *mess* in British, and to *muck about* is to *mess around,* as Americans would put it. "Stop mucking about with those glasses before you break them."

muddie
A large, delicious crab native to the wetlands of New South Wales.

mud room
A small room or lobby in a house where muddy boots, shoes, or clothing are removed.

muggins BRITISH

A humorous name for a stupid or foolish person. "That muggins will have to look after the shop."

mug lair AUSTRALIAN

A vulgar, stupid person who is often a show-off as well. "That mug lair's no mate of mine."

mug up CANADIAN (NEWFOUNDLAND)

To have a cup or a mug of tea, usually along with a snack, between meals. "His men were always mugging up."

mukluk CANADIAN

A warm, sturdy boot made from seal fur that Eskimos wear, or a similar boot. The word derives from the Inuit for "large seal." Also spelled *muckluck.* The expression *muckluk telegraph* means word of mouth.

mulligrubs AMERICAN (OZARK MOUNTAINS)

(1) Ill temper, surliness, colic. (2) The blues, sadness. "I knowed in reason she'd have the mulligrubs over him."

mum BRITISH

The short form of *mother;* rarely heard in the United States. *Mummy* is also used. The U.S. equivalent is Mom or Mommy.

mumsy BRITISH

Old-fashioned and unattractive in appearance. "Look at that mumsy dress she's wearing."

musical ride CANADIAN

A *Mountie* (q.v.) performance on horses with musical accompaniment.

muskeg CANADIAN

A very marshy area, especially in the North. Sometimes called a *keg.*

mus mus JAMAICAN

The term is used to mean either a mouse or a small rat.

musquash CANADIAN

A name for the muskrat that is commonly used in the Canadian North.

muti   SOUTH AFRICAN
The borrowing of a Zulu word meaning "medicine." "That muti the doctor prescribed is too strong for me."

mutton dressed as lamb   BRITISH
An old expression describing old (or middle-aged) people trying to dress as if they were younger. The words seem to be eighteenth-century-British in origin, like *muttonhead,* which meant adulthood a century ago.

my old dutch   BRITISH
My dear old wife; *dutch* here may be a corruption of *duchess.*

naai   SOUTH AFRICAN
A whore or a prostitute. "She called the other woman a naai." As a verb, *naaien* means to engage in sexual intercourse. The word derives from the Afrikaans *naaien,* meaning the same.

naff   BRITISH
Slang for someone or something unfashionable, unattractive. To *naff off* means to go away, get lost, as in "Naff off, will you?"

namba wan time   NEW GUINEA PIDGIN
Literally "number-one time," which means "the first time." This pidgin language is also called *Tok* (talk) *Pisin* (pidgin).

nana   AUSTRALIAN
Head, as in the expression "He's off his nana"—that is, crazy.

nance   BRITISH
Short for *nancy,* a derogatory term for a male homosexual.

napkin   AMERICAN
See *serviette.*

nappy   AUSTRALIAN, BRITISH
A diaper. "He's still in nappies." The American English *diaper rash* is *nappy rash* in Australia and Britain.

nark   AMERICAN, BRITISH, AUSTRALIAN
An American federal *narcotics* agent is called a *nark* in underworld slang.
The British use the term, said to derive from a Gypsy word, for a police
informer, a stool pigeon. A *nark* in Australian slang is a spiteful person.

narrow at the equator   AMERICAN (WEST)
Very hungry, belt tightened to the last notch. "I got to get me some grub;
I'm gettin' narrow at the equator."

nation of shopkeepers   BRITISH
Though Napoleon applied this term contemptuously to the British, he
didn't invent it. Apparently he read it in Adam Smith's *Wealth of Nations*
(1776) or quoted the phrase of a contemporary. Smith wrote in full: "To
found a great empire for the sole purpose of raising up a people of customers, may at first sight appear a project altogether unfit for a nation that
is governed by shopkeepers." Thirteen years before him Josiah Tucker, a
religious leader in Gloucester, had written: "A Shop-keeper will never get
the more Custom by beating his Customers; and what is true of a Shop-
keeper, is true of a Shop-keeping nation."

natter   BRITISH
To talk on and on while saying nothing of any consequence, as in "He nat-
tered away for an hour." A *natter* also means a chat. In both meanings,
the word is not widely used in the United States.

navvy   BRITISH
This manual laborer or ditchdigger may take his name from the esteemed
navigator aboard a ship. *Navvy* for such an occupation may have been
suggested, in about 1825, by a joke about Britsh canal diggers being direc-
tors or navigators of ships (the ships could only sail in the directions they
dug). The British also use the expression *work like a navvy,* q.v.

nearly never killed a bird yet   WEST INDIAN
An old hunting saying meaning a miss is as good as a mile, or near misses
don't count.

near to   BRITISH
Near. "He lived near to me." Americans would say "He lived near me."

nebby   SCOTTISH
Nosy, curious, a busybody or gossip. Also heard in northern England.

neck BRITISH, AMERICAN

In Britain, slang for a police station, and impudence, nerve, cheek. In America, slang for kissing and for sexual foreplay.

necklace SOUTH AFRICAN

A tire filled with gasoline placed around the neck of someone thought to be a police informer and set on fire.

need the toilet SCOTTISH

A Scottish euphemism for "have to go to the bathroom." "'I need the toilet,' the old lady told them."

nervy BRITISH, AMERICAN

Among the British *nervy* means nervous or jumpy ("I was all nervy meeting him"), while to Americans it usually means rude and pushy ("What a nervy thing to say").

never-done food BAHAMIAN

Food that will never be finished cooking while uninvited guests hoping for an invitation to eat remain in the house.

never grab with both hands, just grab with one AMERICAN

A maxim instructing a person not to be greedy and grasping but not to be too altruistic either, especially in business dealings.

New England chowder AMERICAN

Breton fishermen who settled the Maritime Provinces of Canada contributed the word *chowder* to the language. The soup called a *chowder* or *clam chowder* is made with milk in Maine and Massachusetts, this being the famous *New England clam chowder.* But in Rhode Island and farther south, it often is made with water and tomatoes. The two schools are not at all tolerant of each other. One Maine state legislator, in fact, introduced a bill making it *illegal* to add tomatoes to chowder within the state of Maine, the penalty being that the offender must harvest two bushels of clams at high tide. See also *Manhattan clam chowder.*

new fella AUSTRALIAN PIDGIN

A stranger. "New fella shotum, killum boss." For other forms of pidgin see *mary.*

Newgate Calendar   BRITISH
Often used today to mean a Who's Who of crime and notorious criminals
everywhere, the *Newgate Calendar* was begun in 1773 as a biographical
record of the most notorious criminals confined at England's famed Newgate Prison.

newsreader   BRITISH, AUSTRALIAN
A newscaster on British or Australian radio or television news programs.
Also called a *reader.*

New York minute   AMERICAN
A very short time. "He had it done in a New York minute."

next day but one   BRITISH
Two days, the day after tomorrow. "I'll see you next day but one, Harry."

nib   BRITISH
The point of a fountain pen. Americans almost always use "pen point"
for the *nib* of a fountain pen, though the British word is occasionally used
in America.

nice bit of crumpet   BRITISH
An attractive woman, a *real dish* in American slang. *Nice bit of skirt* is
also heard in Britain.

nice guys finish last   AMERICAN
A cynical proverb that has been attributed to former Brooklyn Dodgers
manager Leo Durocher, who wrote a book using it as the title. Back in the
1940s Durocher was sitting on the bench before a game with the New
York Giants and saw opposing manager Mel Ott across the field. "Look at
Ott," he said to a group of sportswriters. "He's such a nice guy and they'll
finish last for him." One of the writers probably coined the phrase *nice
guys finish last* from this remark, but the credit for it still goes to Leo the
Lip. It is one of several baseball expressions that have become proverbial
outside the sport.

nick   BRITISH
(1) To steal something. (2) To nab or catch someone committing a crime.
(3) *The nick* means prison, jail, or the "slammer," as American slang
has it.

nickel   CANADIAN (NEWFOUNDLAND)
A movie, as in "It's a great nickel." After a well-known movie theater
named the Nickel (a nickelodeon) in St. John's, Newfoundland.

niks   SOUTH AFRICAN
Nothing. "I couldn't hear niks with that music playing so loud."

nil   BRITISH
Zero. Unlike Americans, the British use *nil* in the scores of games. American speakers would say "The score was three to nothing (or three-zero,
or three-zip)," while the British would say "Three to nil (or nought)."

niminy-piminy   BRITISH
Affectedly delicate or refined. Apparently the rhyming compound was
coined by (General) John (Gentleman Johnny) Burgoyne in his novel *The
Heiress* (1786), when Lady Emily instructs the vulgar Miss Alscrip to stand
in front of a mirror and keep pronouncing *niminy-piminy* to give a pretty
form to the lips. In *Little Dorrit* (1855–1857) Dickens had Amy do the same
with *papa, potatoes, poultry, prunes,* and *prism.*

nineteen bites to a bilberry   BRITISH
An old British expression that means to make a major production of an
inconsequential act, just as it would be to take nineteen bites of a berry
(Vaccinium myrtillus) no more than one-quarter inch in diameter.

to nip straws   SOUTH AFRICAN
A saying of unknown origin that means to be afraid. "He nipped straws
before the test."

n.n.   BRITISH
The expression *n.g.* has been an abbreviation for "no good" since at least
1839 in America. The term *n.n.* is a British one dating back to the beginning of the twentieth century and means "a necessary nuisance," especially a husband.

no   SCOTTISH
Can mean *not,* as in "Will y' no come here?"

nob   BRITISH
A humorous term, sometimes derogatory, for a rich or socially prominent
person. *Nob* probably derives from *noble.*

nobble   AUSTRALIAN, BRITISH
(1) To catch, corner, or buttonhole someone to get that person to listen.
(2) To drug a horse so it can't win a race.

no be   SCOTTISH
Won't be, as in "He no be comin'."

no bura   JAPANESE
The Japanese borrowing and alteration of the words *no bra,* which the
Japanese use to mean braless (as in the *braless look*).

nocaut   SPANISH
A Spanish borrowing and alteration of the word *knockout* (in boxing).

no-hoper   AUSTRALIAN
A fool, an ineffectual person, someone there is no hope for, what Americans would call a *loser.*

no ka dé   JAPANESE
The Japanizing of the words *no car day.* In Japan *no ka de* (no car day)
is the day of the month on which certain drivers are not allowed to use
their cars. To help curb air pollution every driver is assigned a certain no
car day.

nokku auto   JAPANESE
The Japanese borrowing and alteration of the word *knockout* (in a boxing match).

no more too much strong   AUSTRALIAN PIDGIN
A poetic way of saying someone is old or is getting old. "Him no more too
much strong." For other forms of pidgin see *mary.*

no oil painting   BRITISH
Said of someone not beautiful or handsome in appearance. "She's no oil
painting, but everyone likes her."

nong   AUSTRALIAN
A complete fool, a silly person. Also heard as *nong-nong.* The word is
probably from an Aboriginal language.

no-see-um   AMERICAN (NEW ENGLAND)
A small stinging fly of the Maine woods. The word is possibly Penobscot
Indian in origin or is simply a humorous name for the small fly.

nose paint   AMERICAN (WEST)
Whiskey, because drinking a lot of it often turns the nose red.

Nosey Parker   BRITISH
A nosey person. Matthew Parker, who became archbishop of Canterbury
in 1559, acquired a reputation for poking his nose into other people's business. His reputation is largely undeserved, but Catholics and Puritans alike
resented his good works, taking advantage of his rather long nose and
dubbing him *Nosey Parker,* which has meant an unduly inquisitive person ever since. The above, at least, is the most popular folk etymology for
Nosey Parker. But other candidates have been proposed. Richard Parker,
leader of the Sheerness Mutiny in 1797, is one strong contender. This
Parker poked his nose so deeply into what the military thought their
exclusive bailiwick that he wound up hanged from the yardarm of HMS
Sandwich.

no slow fuckin'!   AMERICAN (SOUTH)
Slang for work faster, no malingering. A prison guard might say to chain
gang convicts "Move it along. No slow fuckin'!"

no tacchi   JAPANESE
The Japanizing of the Englilsh words *no touch.* The Japanese use *no touch*
to mean "have nothing to do with something."

not a man   JAMAICAN
No one. "Not a man get any of this food tonight."

not a skerek left   AUSTRALIAN
There's no more left to eat. *Skerek* means a small fragment and also is
spelled *skerrik.*

notch   AMERICAN
A mountain pass mostly used in place names such as Franconia Notch in
New England's White Mountains.

not cricket

A well-known term meaning not fair; in allusion to the sport of cricket, with its tradition of fair play.

not easy

Describes someone alert, on the ball, successful. "He's not too easy, he scored three goals."

not in the same league with

Not comparable with, nowhere near as good as someone or something else. The expression probably comes from the sport of baseball, in which someone in the major leagues is generally a far better player than someone in the minor leagues. See also *not in the same street with*.

No Through Road

In the United States this British traffic sign would read *Dead End*.

not in the same street with

Americans would say *not in the same league with* (q.v.), nowhere near equal to.

not on your nelly

An old humorous saying meaning never, impossible, no way. "Will I go there? Not on your nelly." The expression probably derives from Cockney rhyming slang.

not short a bob or two

Someone who is rich or well-to-do. A *bob* is a rather dated term for a shilling, a British coin used in the past that was worth twelve pence.

not worth a brass razo

Not worth anything, to be broke. A *razo* is an imaginary coin worth nothing. Pronounced *razz-o*.

nought

Often used to mean *zero*. Not much used in American English today, though the first decade of the twenty-first century may be called "the oughts."

noughts and crosses   BRITISH
The game Americans call *ticktacktoe.*

nous   AUSTRALIAN, BRITISH
Good sense, judgment, shrewdness, general ability. "He had good business nous." Pronounced "noose."

now-now girl   ZIMBABWEAN
An up-to-date, modern young woman.

no worries   AUSTRALIAN
A term Australians use to mean no problem, no big deal, it doesn't matter: "No worries, mate, pay me tomorrow."

nudge nudge   AUSTRALIAN, BRITISH
An expression used to suggest that something with a sexual meaning has been said by a person in a group. Also *wink wink.*

nudo   JAPANESE
The Japanizing of the word *nude. Oru nudo* means all nude, stark naked, while a *nudo show* is a striptease show.

number plate   AUSTRALIAN, BRITISH
What Americans would call a car's *license plate.* "The police traced the car's number plate."

nunch   CANADIAN (NEWFOUNDLAND)
A snack taken before any meal. "You kids stop your nunching."

nutter   BRITISH
Someone eccentric or crazy, what Americans would call a *nut.* "He's a real nutter, all right."

nylon   SOUTH AFRICAN
A slang term for a woman, or for an easy woman. Perhaps from the nylon stockings women commonly wore at one time, or from police vans with nylon like wire-mesh sides.

O'   IRISH

The *O'* common in Irish names such as O'Connor, O'Reilly, etc., derives from the Gaelic *ogha* or the Irish *oa*, both meaning "a descendant of." Denis O'Connor strictly means "Denis, a descendant of Connor." According to a good story, in the past the *O* was taken away from the name of any family that didn't wholly support the Irish Republican cause, leaving us with Connor instead of O'Connor, etc.

ocky   CANADIAN (NEWFOUNDLAND)

A polite word, or a word used by children, for excrement.

odd done by   BRITISH

To be treated badly. "He felt odd done by when nobody answered his letters or returned his calls."

odd-man   BRITISH

This expression has nothing to do with peculiar, strange, or crazy. In Britain, *odd-man* simply means a handyman, someone who does odd jobs around the premises for a price.

odds and sods   AUSTRALIAN

Humorous slang for *odds and ends,* diverse, small items of little value.

O'Donohue's white horses   IRISH

Whitecaps on a body of water. Every seventh May Day the Irish chieftain O'Donohue returns to the Lakes of Killarney riding his great white steed, gliding over the waters to sweet unearthly music, a host of fairies preceding him and strewing his path with spring flowers. Foaming waves on a windy day are thus known as *O'Donohue's white horses.* Legend has it that more than one beautiful young girl believed so strongly in O'Donohue that she threw herself into the water so he would carry her off to be his bride.

o rai   JAPANESE

Japanizing of the words *all right.* Frequently used instead of *O.K.* (q.v.).

off license   BRITISH
The British name for what Americans would call a liquor store or a package store.

off one's nana   AUSTRALIAN
To be crazy or to lose one's temper. "He's off his nana." *Nana* is slang for the head.

off-sider   AUSTRALIAN
A partner, an assistant, someone who helps. "I need another off-sider around here."

off the boil   BRITISH
Under control, not a crisis anymore. "That issue is finally off the boil."

of the same kidney   BRITISH
Of the same sort or disposition. This expression was British slang in the early eighteenth century, its use deplored by Jonathan Swift along with words such as *banter* and *bamboozle*. All have since become standard. The expression has its origins in the ancient belief that the kidneys were "the seat of the affections" and thus largely determined one's personality or temperament.

o gaats!   SOUTH AFRICAN
A common exclamation of surprise or disappointment; *gaats* apparently derives from the Afrikaans *gat*, "hole" or "anus."

oh, crumbs!   BRITISH
An exclamation meaning roughly "That's tough" in America.

oik   BRITISH
An uneducated, offensive, piggish oaf who respects no one, has no manners.

to oil   CANADIAN (NEWFOUNDLAND)
To beat up someone badly. "You'll get well oiled if you fight him."

oil of angels   BRITISH
Money or gold, particularly money used as a bribe. The *angel* here refers to a fifteenth-century coin bearing the visage of Michael the Archangel.

O Jesus, Mary, and Joseph!   IRISH
A common exclamation expressing several emotions, especially surprise at bad news. Also just "Jesus, Mary, and Joseph!"

O.K.   AMERICAN
H. L. Mencken called *O.K.* "the most shining and successful Americanism ever invented," an Americanism used the world over. Most word authorities believe that *O.K.* comes from the nickname of Martin Van Buren (1782–1862), who rose from potboy in a tavern to president of the United States. Van Buren was elected president in 1836. He became an eponym during the campaign of 1840, when he ran for reelection in a tight race against "Tippecanoe and Tyler, too," General William Henry Harrison, legendary hero who fought against the Indians at Tippecanoe, and Virginian John Tyler. The election of 1840 had brought with it the first modern political campaign. Harrison's followers, trying to identify Van Buren with the aristocracy, christened the general the "log cabin and hard cider candidate" and tagged Van Buren "Little Van, the Used Up Man," "King Martin the First," the "Little Magician," and several other of the derogatory nicknames he had earned over the years. But "Old Kinderhook," a title bestowed upon the president from the name of his birthplace in Kinderhook, New York, sounded better to his supporters. To stem the tide somewhat, a group in New York formed the Democratic O.K. Club, taking their initials from "Old Kinderhook." These initials, appealing to man's love of being on the inside of events, became a sort of rallying cry for the Democrats. The battle cry, mysterious to most people, spread rapidly and soon acquired the meaning "all right, correct," probably because "Old Kinderhook," or O.K., was all right to his supporters, even though he eventually lost the election. See also *A-O.K.*

O.K. by me   AMERICAN
In use for at least half a century or so, this expression is a Yiddish one given wider currency by the media. The *by me* in the phrase comes from the Yiddish *bei mir.*

oke   JAPANESE
The Japanese borrowing and alteration of the word *orchestra.*

old bads   JAMAICAN
Ragged old clothing. "He's wearing his old bads." Also *old broke.*

old bean   BRITISH
This affectionate form of address for a friend or acquaintance isn't heard much anymore but once commonly issued from the mouths of stage and movie men.

Old Bill   BRITISH
Slang for the cops, the police. "Quiet, here comes Old Bill."

old buba   JAMAICAN
An old man who embarrasses himself and family by trying to appear young. "She live with that old buba."

old cock   BRITISH
A form of address to an old friend. "How have you been, old cock?"

olde worlde   BRITISH
A derogatory term for something artificially old, such as a reconstructed village from another century that is not authentically old.

old gaffer   BRITISH
An old geezer, an old duffer. *Gaffer* itself means an old man, so *old gaffer* is somewhat redundant, but that is how the expression is mostly used. *Gaffer* is thought to be a contraction of either *grandfather* or *godfather*. An *old gammer*, for "an old woman," derives from either *grandmother* or *godmother* and is rarely heard outside rural England.

old geezer   BRITISH, AMERICAN
This expression is something of a redundancy, because *geezer* itself means an eccentric old man. *Geezer* is a British dialect word for a mummer or masquerader who wore a disguise in parades and often acted eccentrically.

old josser   IRISH
An old man. "The old josser couldn't keep up with them."

old man   AUSTRALIAN
Used to mean a male kangaroo that has grown to full size.

old man of the sea   BRITISH
A tenacious person, like the character in the tale of Sinbad the Sailor in the *Arabian Nights.* In this tale the old man clung to Sinbad's shoulders for many days and nights until Sinbad got him drunk and threw him off.

old mosshorn   AMERICAN (WEST)
An old person, often one set in his ways, like an old cow with moss on his horns. "'He's one of those old mosshorns who thinks he knows it all.'"

old top   BRITISH
A form of address once used in addressing a man but rarely heard anymore.

old unspeakables   CANADIAN
A colorful name for the silent films of the early movies.

Old Year's Night   SOUTH AFRICAN
A common name for New Year's Eve. Also called *Old Year's Evening.*

once in a way   BRITISH
Occasionally. Americans would say *once in a while.* "Once in a way we drive down there."

one   HAWAIIAN
Used in place of *a,* as in "He drink jus' like one horse." Derived from Chinese pidgin, due probably to the absence of an indefinite article in Chinese.

one fella moon   AUSTRALIAN PIDGIN
A month. "Him come back one fella moon." (He'll return in a month.) For other forms of pidgin see *mary.*

one-horse town   AMERICAN
A very small town. The term, dating back to the late nineteenth century, was originally *one-horse outfit,* this referring at first to a small ranch and then to a small business.

one on his (her) own   BRITISH
A unique person, rare, one of a kind. "He's one on his own, all right."

one-eyed village   BRITISH
A very small village, what might be called a *one-horse town* in America.

one-way ticket   AMERICAN
A ticket good for travel only in one direction, with no return, the opposite of a round-trip ticket. The British and Australians call these tickets a *single ticket* (q.v.) and a *return ticket,* respectively.

on it   AUSTRALIAN
A popular phrase meaning a person is drinking beer or liquor. "He's always on it these days."

on lunch   SOUTH AFRICAN
Often used instead of *at lunch.* "He's on lunch with the boss today."

ono   AUSTRALIAN, BRITISH
An abbreviation for "or nearest offer" used in advertisements for sales of personal possessions: "Will sell for ten pounds, ono."

ono-looking   HAWAIIAN
Ono means delicious in Hawaiian; hence the Hawaiian *ono-looking* means "good-looking."

on the arm   AMERICAN
Slang for something free of charge; often used by police. "His meals were always on the arm."

on the brew   BRITISH
Another way to say *on the dole*—that is, *on welfare* or *public assistance.*

on the fang   AUSTRALIAN
To be eating. "I'm on the fang right now. Call me later."

on the go   BRITISH
In the works, in progress. "He has a new play on the go."

on the job   BRITISH
A slang expression meaning to be having sex. "He was on the job when the telephone rang."

on the pig's back   CANADIAN (NEWFOUNDLAND)
To be well-to-do, prosperous. "He's been on the pig's back since he got promoted."

on the tea cart   BRITISH
See *on the wagon.*

on the up and up   AUSTRALIAN, BRITISH, AMERICAN
In Australia and Britain, continually improving, as in "His career has been
on the up and up since he moved to London." In America, a person *on
the up and up* is honest and trustworthy.

on the wagon   AMERICAN
During the late ninteenth century, water carts drawn by horses wet down
dusty roads in the summer. At the height of the Prohibition crusade in the
1890s men who vowed to stop drinking would say that they were thirsty
indeed but would rather climb the water cart or wagon than break their
pledges. From this sentiment came the expression "I'm on the wagon, I'm
trying to stop drinking." The British use the term *on the tea cart.*

on tick   BRITISH
Tick here is just an abbreviation for *ticket.* First recorded as early as 1648,
on tick originally meant a written IOU or "ticket," then came to mean "on
credit."

on your nerves   SOUTH AFRICAN
Nervous, anxious, edgy. "Calm down. You've been on your nerves all
morning."

oof   BRITISH
Slang for dough, money. Said to be an abbreviation of the Yiddish word
oofish, meaning the same.

oog   SOUTH AFRICAN
The source or eye of a river or a stream. "It's oog is up in the mountains."
From the Afrikaans *oog, eye.*

oolet   SHETLAND ISLANDS
A brat. "Dey oolets baith." (Both of them are brats.)

oom   SOUTH AFRICAN
Uncle, a respectful name often used to address uncles who are relations
or any older man.

oor SCOTTISH
The typical pronunciation and spelling of *our*. "Oor Jamey came hame (home)."

oot SCOTTISH
Typical Scottish pronunciation and spelling of *out*. "She'll be right oot."

op AUSTRALIAN, BRITISH
Short for a medical operation. "I had a serious op last month."

operating theatre BRITISH
What Americans would call a hospital operating room.

orange squash BRITISH
A drink that would be called *orangeade* in America; a blend of water and orange juice.

Oreo AMERICAN (BLACK ENGLISH)
A derisive name for a black person whose values are believed to be too much like those of whites. An *Oreo* is a chocolate cookie with white filling. See *Apple.*

orts AMERICAN (NEW ENGLAND)
Leavings or refuse—from table scraps and inedible hay to cattle droppings and fish entrails. This Old English word meaning "spoiled hay" survives in New England speech, chiefly in Maine.

Oscar Asche AUSTRALIAN
Money. Australian musical comedy star Oscar Asche (1872–1936) made a tidy fortune on the stage and saw his full name become Australian rhyming slang for cash. "*Oscar Asche* for cash" was eventually shortened to *Oscar*, making him the only man whose prenomen means "money" in a generic sense.

ought BRITISH
Zero. The term is also occasionally heard among older speakers in the United States, as in "He was born in nineteen ought eight."

oupa SOUTH AFRICAN
A respectful term used to address a grandfather or any elderly man.

our BRITISH
Often used to precede the name of a family member or someone known well to the speaker. "And how are you feeling, our Martin?"

ourie SCOTTISH
(1) Shabby, ragged, dirty. (2) Sad, melancholy.

out all about AUSTRALIAN PIDGIN
Everywhere. "White fella him go out all about." For other forms of pidgin see *mary*.

outback AUSTRALIAN
The desert, far removed from populous cities, especially in Australia's Northern Territory, one of the biggest of the country's states and territories.

outhouse AMERICAN, BRITISH
Though exclusively an outside privy in America, an *outhouse* is any building on the grounds of a main dwelling in Britain.

outie SOUTH AFRICAN
Someone homeless, down-and-out, but not a hobo or a tramp.

outlander AMERICAN (MOUNTAINS)
A foreigner or a stranger, someone who lives in another place. "We don't want no outlander here."

outside child BAHAMIAN
A euphemism for an illegitimate child. An *inside child* is the opposite. Also called an *outside brother, outside sister,* and *outside.*

over the moon BRITISH, IRISH
Overjoyed. "He was over the moon about his promotion."

over to AMERICAN (NEW ENGLAND)
Over at. "He says it's raining over to his place."

owl-gal JAMAICAN
A girl or a woman who prowls in the night looking for men.

oxter
A dialect word for armpit, from the Latin *axilla*. The word is used (as a play on *Oxford*) in the title of *The Oxter Dictionary* (1984), a compilation of uncommon words that gives several recent citations.

oy!
"Oy is not a word," Leo Rosten writes in *The Joys of Yiddish* (1968). "It is a vocabulary. It is uttered in as many ways as the utterer's histrionic ability permits. It is a lament, a protest, a cry of dismay, a reflex of delight. But however sighed, cried, howled or moaned, *oy!* is the most expressive and ubiquitous exclamation in Yiddish." *Oy vay,* a shortening of *oy vay iz mir,* is also used as an "all-purpose ejaculation," Rosten notes. He doesn't list *oy gevald,* which Henry Roth used as "a cry of alarm, concern or amazement" in *From Bondage* (1996). But Rosten does list *gevalt* or *gevald* alone as the same kind of cry and cites the folk proverb "Man comes into the word with an *Oy!*—and leaves with a *gevalt.*" I have heard *oy!,* and *oy vay!,* for that matter, uttered by New Yorkers of many religions, races, and nationalities. *Gevalt* also.

pacifier
A rubber or plastic nipple for a baby to suck on. The British call this a *dummy.*

package
A bag. "He put all the groceries in one brown paper package."

package store
A term used in some parts of the United States for a *liquor store* (q.v.).

pack of cards
Americans would always call these a *deck of cards.*

pally
Often heard, especially in Boston, for *pal, friend, buddy.* "Keep yah shirt on, pally. We'll get there on time."

pan
A toilet bowl. "Don't forget to flush the pan." See also *down the pan.*

pants   BRITISH
Pants does not mean trousers in Britain, as in the United States, but men's underpants.

pantyhose   AMERICAN
See *tights.*

papamama   NEW GUINEA PIDGIN
A clever term meaning "parents." This pidgin language is also called *Tok* (talk) *Pisin* (pidgin).

paper talk   AUSTRALIAN PIDGIN
A letter. "Him catchum (gettum) paper talk." For other forms of pidgin see *mary.*

paraffin   SOUTH AFRICAN
(1) A light rain. "We've had only paraffin for two months now." (2) Kerosene. (3) A cheap gin.

paralytic   AUSTRALIAN
Slang for someone so drunk that he can't move, is paralyzed in place.

parking lot   AMERICAN
An outdoor area for parking cars. The British use the term *car park.*

parliamentary language   BRITISH
Language that is restrained, like the language generally heard in the British Parliament; a civil and courteous way of speaking or arguing.

parping the hooter   BRITISH
British slang for honking a car's horn loudly.

parson's nose   BRITISH
A Victorian with a sense of humor so named this walnut-sized protuberance on the rear end of a turkey or other fowl that is actually the bird's tail (minus the feathers). It is also jocularly called "the part that went over the fence last," this term heard in the United States as well.

pas op South African

Watch out, take care. "Pas op or they'll arrest you." An Afrikaans expression from the Dutch *oppassen,* to be alert, be on guard. Pronounced *pass-awp* (rhymes with *yawp*).

pass degree British, Australian

In Britain, a college degree given to students who pass their courses but don't earn honors. In Australia, a degree completed in three years instead of the usual four years.

passel American (South)

A group, many; the word is a corruption of "parcel." "A passel of infantry marched through town."

passion gap South African

The gap in the gums left when the four top middle teeth are missing. Some Africans believe this increases erotic appeal when kissing and have these teeth pulled by dentists. Also called the *love gap*.

pater British

An old term for *father* that is used only humorously today. *Pater* is the Latin for father.

patience British

The British name for the card game Americans call *solitaire*.

pato Japanese

The Japanizing and alteration of the words *part*-time, which the Japanese use to mean a part-time job.

patza American (New York City)

A casual, amateurish chess player, often one who plays chess in city parks. The term, which has only been traced back to about 1955, derives ultimately from the German *patzer,* "bungler," and is quite common in New York City.

Paul Pry British

A meddling idler with no business of his own except everybody else's is called a *Paul Pry,* after the character of that name in British playwright John Poole's comedy *Paul Pry* (1825).

pawk   SCOTTISH
A humorous trick. *Pawky* means tricky, sly, cunning. "He is a pawky businessman."

pay the earth   BRITISH
To pay a great deal for, to pay an arm and a leg for. "He paid the earth for that old car."

peaceful place   AMERICAN (WEST)
Heaven. "He's gone to the peaceful place."

pearly   BRITISH
A pushcart vendor of fruit and vegetables. Named after the colorful costumes decorated with mother-of-pearl buttons that such vendors have worn for a century on British holidays.

peckerwood   AMERICAN (SOUTH)
A derogatory term for a poor white person (though the word's earliest meaning was "woodpecker").

Pecksniff   BRITISH
An arch hypocrite who cants moral homilies even while acting immorally. Every *Pecksniff* takes his name from Mr. Pecksniff, the hypocrite architect in Dickens's *Martin Chuzzlewit*.

peeler   IRISH
A policeman. See also *bobby*.

peely-wally   SCOTTISH
Describes someone feeling under the weather, weak and sickly. "I'm feeling peely-wally today."

peepy-eyed   JAMAICAN
Someone with hooded eyes, eyes that always seem partly closed.

peever   SCOTTISH
(1) The stone used in playing hopscotch. (2) The game of hopscotch itself.

pelican crossing   BRITISH
A marked place on the street where cars must stop to let people cross. The *pelican* in the word is a rough abbreviation of pedestrian (*pe*) light (*li*) controlled (*con*) crossing.

penny dreadful   BRITISH
What Americans called a *dime novel*, any inexpensive thrilling tale of war, romance, etc. The penny dreadfuls and dime novels of yesteryear were replaced by pulp novels, which were themselves replaced by cheap paperbacks and television.

pennyline   SOUTH AFRICAN
A term used in black slang to mean a cheap prostitute. "She nothing but a pennyline."

perishing   AUSTRALIAN, BRITISH
Very cold weather. "It's perishing there in the winter."

perk up   AUSTRALIAN
To vomit, throw up. "He perked up his lunch after drinking so much."

perp walk   AMERICAN (NEW YORK CITY)
A term, short for *perpetrator walk,* used for more than fifty years by New York City police and newspaper photographers, that describes the moment when a criminal suspect is walked out of a station house. The exit was designed to allow the police to display their latest catch and to shame the suspect.

peter   AMERICAN (OZARK MOUNTAINS)
A euphemism for the penis. Etymologist Vance Randolph wrote that "Very few natives of the Ozarks will consider naming a boy Peter" because of this significance. "An evangelist from the North shouted something about the Church being founded on the rock of St. Peter," Randolph noted, "and he was puzzled by the flushed cheeks of the young women and the ill-suppressed amusement of the ungodly. Mountain folk don't even like to pronounce common names like *Hitchcock* or *Cock.*"

Peter ain't better than Paul   BAHAMIAN
Another way to say "You are no better than I am." Probably a biblical reference.

petrol   BRITISH, IRISH, AUSTRALIAN
Gasoline.

pharmacy   AMERICAN
See *chemist.*

pianolo   HAWAIIAN
A cowboy. In 1832 King Kamehameha III hired three Mexican cowboys to
manage a herd of longhorns. The name of these *españoles* (Spaniards)
became corrupted to *pianolos* and is still used to describe all the cowboys
riding Hawaii's ranges today.

piazza   AMERICAN (NEW ENGLAND)
A name still used for a porch, especially by older New Englanders. "It's
nice to count the stars while sitting out on the piazza in the evening."

pibroch   SCOTTISH
A music piece for the bagpipes, usually martial in character but sometimes
a dirge.

pickin' a cherry   AMERICAN
Slang for running a red light.

pickney   JAMAICAN
Children. "Some pickney good, some bad."

to pick up weight   SOUTH AFRICAN
To put on weight. "Sally picked up weight eating all that rich food."

piece of skirt   BRITISH
Slang for a sexually attractive woman. The expression is not heard in the
United States, where a *piece* is the equivalent term.

a piece of the lolly   BRITISH
Some of the loot, gravy, dough, or money. "He wanted a bigger piece of
the lolly for planning the job." See also *lolly.*

a pig (to do)   BRITISH
Something that is very difficult to do, as in "That's a pig to do." Americans would say "That's a bitch to do."

pikin   CAMEROON PIDGIN
Children. "Dem very bad pikin dey hab."

pills   AMERICAN
See *tablets.*

pimp   AMERICAN, BRITISH, SOUTH AFRICAN
A pimp is a procurer for prostitutes in America, but in Britain it is a bundle of kindling, used to get a fire started. A pimping shed is simply a woodshed. In South Africa a *pimp* is black slang for any spy or informer, in or out of prison.

pine   HAWAIIAN
Hawaiians often call a pineapple a *pine* because the first name for the fruit in the islands was the Spanish *pino,* which was anglicized to *pine.*

pio the light   HAWAIIAN
Put out the light, turn off the light. *Pio* is Hawaiian for to extinguish, put out.

pipped at the post   BRITISH
To be beaten in any race, usually by a slim margin. *Pip* means to beat in British slang.

pirate taxi   SOUTH AFRICAN
An unlicensed taxicab, what would be called a *gypsy cab* (q.v.) in the United States.

pissed   AMERICAN, BRITISH, IRISH
Americans sometimes use this British slang term for "very drunk," but generally *pissed (or pissed off)* means "very angry" in the United States.

piss off   AUSTRALIAN, BRITISH, AMERICAN
Get out of here, go away. To *piss off* also means to anger in Australian, British, and American slang.

pistol   AMERICAN
(1) The word among Maine lobstermen for a lobster with only one claw or none. (2) A name for pastrami in New York delis, where a waiter might convey your order to a counterman or short-order cook as "A pistol on rye."

pit   BRITISH, AMERICAN
In England this is the main floor of a theater behind the stalls or front section seats. In America the pit is the section below the stage where the musicians sit and is also called the *orchestra pit.*

play it small   AMERICAN
To feign humility. "Don't play it small, we know you're good."

play whaley   AMERICAN (OZARK MOUNTAINS)
To make a stupid mistake, blunder badly. "I sure played whaley when I joined the army." An old-fashioned term said to derive from a stupid (perhaps fictional) family named Whaley.

pleasure!   BRITISH
Pleasure!, a shortening of "It's my pleasure!," is often used by the British in place of "You're welcome!," or "No problem," or "Don't mention it!"

plonk   BRITISH
Any cheap wine of poor quality, the term said to be a humorous play on the French words *vin blanc,* which World War I British soldiers called *blink-blonk,* then *blonk,* and finally *plonk.*

pluck   BAHAMIAN
An obvious euphemism for *fuck,* to have sexual intercourse with.

plummy   BRITISH
A word the British use to describe a low-speaking voice with long-held vowels that is thought to be typical of the upper classes. "He had a plummy accent."

plushed to the scuppers   BRITISH
To get "plushed to the scuppers" is to get very drunk, but the expression is recorded in no slang dictionary. It apparently derives from the British slang *plushed,* for "drunk," first recorded in the late nineteenth century. Perhaps the phrase is a nautical one. *Scupper* is a drain at the edge of the deck that allows accumulated water to run off into the sea or the bilge. So anyone *plushed to the scuppers* would be drunk to overflowing.

po-faced AUSTRALIAN, BRITISH

Someone or something that is too serious and negative. It also can mean expressionless. "He remained po-faced while everyone else laughed at the jokes." The origin of the term is unknown.

pogonip AMERICAN (WEST)

An icy winter fog that forms in western mountain valleys, especially in Nevada, the heavy fog often blocking the sun for days and appearing like a fine snow; the Shoshonean Indian word *pogonip* has been translated as "white death," the fog thought to cause pneumonia.

poke AMERICAN (NEW ENGLAND)

A synonym for *stomach.* "My poke's all filled up." *Poke* means a paper bag in other U.S. regions.

policy SCOTTISH

The extensive private grounds surrounding a great country house in Scotland.

pollie AUSTRALIAN

A politician. "What do you expect? He's a bloody pollie." *Pol* is the U.S. equivalent.

ponce AUSTRALIAN, BRITISH

In addition to its meaning of "pimp," a *ponce* is also a derogatory term for "a campily effeminate man," as one dictionary puts it.

pong AUSTRALIAN, BRITISH

A very unpleasant smell. "What a pong his place has."

pooh-bah BRITISH

A politician who holds several offices, or a pompous, self-important person. In Gilbert and Sullivan's operetta *The Mikado* (1885), Pooh-Bah is the personal name of the arrogant Lord High Everything Else, this being the source of the word.

poof AUSTRALIAN, BRITISH

An offensive slang term for a homosexual that has little or no currency in the United States.

pool hall AMERICAN
A commercial establishment where pool tables are rented for the playing of pool and billiards. Also called a poolroom, a billiard parlor, and, by the British, a billiard saloon. See also *snooker hall.*

poontang AMERICAN (SOUTH)
Thomas Wolfe used this word for the vagina in *Look Homeward, Angel.* The expression probably comes from the French *putain* (prostitute) by way of New Orleans.

poor boy AMERICAN
See *hero sandwich.*

poor me boy JAMAICAN
An exclamation of self-pity like *poor me* or *woe is me.* "Poor me boy, I wish I'd never been born." Also *poor me girl.*

poortith SCOTTISH
A synonym for poverty or the condition of being impoverished. Also heard in northern England dialect.

poor white trash AMERICAN (SOUTH)
A derogatory term for lower-class white people. Other such objectionable slur names are *poor white redneck* and *peckerwood.*

pop AMERICAN
Mob talk meaning to kill, as in "I'd like to pop him for what he done." More generally, to hit someone.

poppet AUSTRALIAN, BRITISH
A beloved, adorable child. Often used as a term of endearment, as in "How's my little poppet?"

popskull whiskey AMERICAN (APPALACHIAN MOUNTAINS)
Cheap, potent moonshine, so named because it seems to pop things inside your skull.

porridge BRITISH
Americans eat their oatmeal or other hot cereal in the morning, rarely calling it *porridge,* as the British do.

possie   AUSTRALIAN
A position or spot, as in "It's a good possie for surfing this morning."

postal ballot   BRITISH
In U.S. and Australian elections this would be called an absentee ballot
(q.v.). The British also use the term *postal vote* for it.

postal code   AUSTRALIAN, BRITISH
What Americans would call a *zip code.* "You didn't put the postal code on
your letter."

poste restante   BRITISH
Equivalent to the U.S. *general delivery department* in a post office, a
department that receives letters and parcels and holds them for people
who are traveling. The term is borrowed from French.

postie   AUSTRALIAN
A mail carrier or a postman. "The postie brought three letters today."

pot   SCOTTISH
A shorter version of what Americans would call a *pothole* in the road.

pot head   AMERICAN (MAINE), CANADIAN (NEWFOUNDLAND)
(1) In Maine this term has nothing to do with habitual users of marijuana,
meaning instead someone of very limited intelligence, with a head like an
empty pot. (2) In Canadian Newfoundland *pot head* is a name for the
northern pilot whale, with its prominent bulbous head.

pot plant   BRITISH
What Americans would call a *houseplant.* "Be sure you water my pot
plants."

potted book   BRITISH
A potted book is a condensed book, one that has been made shorter and
easier to understand.

poxy   BRITISH
Something inconsequential, of little value or importance. "That's a poxy
little house he lives in."

prairie gold   CANADIAN
A term used for wheat in the Prairie Provinces (Manitoba, Alberta, and Saskatchewan) because of the grain's great economic importance.

prairie oysters   AMERICAN
A euphemistic menu term for a bull's testicles; synonyms are *mountain oysters, Rocky Mountain oysters,* and *Spanish kidneys.* Any supposed aphrodisiacal effect is probably psychological.

pram   BRITISH
A baby carriage, short for *perambulator.*

prang   AUSTRALIAN
An auto or airplane accident. "That was some bloody prang he was in."

prawn   BRITISH, AUSTRALIAN
In Britain, the name for a type of crustacean resembling a shrimp. In Australia, slang for a fool.

premmie   AUSTRALIAN
A premature baby. The equivalent American term is *preemie.*

pressies   AUSTRALIAN
Presents, gifts. "She got lots of Chrissie (Christmas) pressies." Also *prezzies.*

press-up   BRITISH
Both Americans and Australians call this exercise a *push-up.* "Give me twenty press-ups."

private address   BRITISH
One's home address as opposed to a business address. "Send it to my private address."

prompt to time   BRITISH
Punctual, right on time. "He wasn't late or early; he was prompt to time."

proper hot inside head   AUSTRALIAN PIDGIN
Very angry, incensed. "Him proper hot inside head." For other forms of pidgin see *mary.*

province CANADIAN
Roughly the Canadian equivalent of a U.S. state. Canada has ten provinces with *provincial* governments, including legislative bodies. Any park in one of the provinces is called a *provincial park.*

pruning shears AMERICAN
See *secateurs.*

pseud BRITISH
A poseur, fake, phony, a pseudo-intellectual. "She talks like she knows something, but she's just another pseud."

pub AUSTRALIAN, BRITISH, IRISH
The term *pub* for a bar or a tavern, used in England and much less frequently in America, is an abbreviation of *public house.* The word isn't recorded until about 1865, *public* being the contraction used before that. Canadians generally use the term *bar.*

publican AUSTRALIAN, BRITISH
The person in charge of a pub or a bar. Also called the *pub-keeper* or *landlord.*

puff puff train BRITISH
American children would call this a *choo-choo train.*

pukka BRITISH, INDIAN
Rhyming with luck-a, *pukka* derives from the Hindu word *pokka,* meaning "cooked, ripe, mature." The British brought it home from India in the late seventeenth century, and the word has since become a workhorse adjective meaning genuine, good, real, substantial, permanent, reliable, and conventional, as in "He's a pukka player." Among Indians a *pukka sahib* is a genuine gentleman. The word is also spelled *pucka.*

pull down HAWAIIAN
To lose weight: "Didn't you pull down some since last year?"

pull up your socks BRITISH
A warning for someone to do better. "If you don't pull up your socks you'll be out of a job."

pull your head in   AUSTRALIAN
Don't butt in, keep out of it; mind your own business. "Pull your head in and let him play the fool himself."

to punce   SCOTTISH
To kick or to punch. A *punce* is a kick, punch, or blow.

Punch's advice   BRITISH
A warning not to do something. *Punch's advice* derives from the most historically famous joke of the British humor magazine *Punch*. The magazine announced that it would send advice to those about to marry. The advice turned out to be: "Don't."

puncture   BRITISH
In Britain one has *a tire with a puncture;* in the United States one has a *flat tire.*

pundas   SOUTH AFRICAN
Backside, buttocks. "He gave him a kick in the pundas." The word derives from the Xhosa *impundu,* meaning the same.

punter   AUSTRALIAN, BRITISH
Any bettor at a racetrack or elsewhere; a stock market speculator. To a prostitute, however, a punter is a customer—a *trick* or a *John.*

push along off   BRITISH
Leave. "Well, I must push along off now." An American might say, "Well, I'd better take off."

push-pin   BRITISH
In the United States this is a *thumbtack.*

push-up   AMERICAN
See *press-up.*

pussel gutted; puzzle-gutted   AMERICAN (SOUTH)
Potbellied. The word perhaps derives from *purse* or from the dialect term *puscle,* suggesting a swollen gut. "That pussel-gutted sheriff come prowling around here." Also *pus-gutted, pussy-gutted, pustle-gutted.*

pussy   AMERICAN (OZARK MOUNTAINS)
Rustic, awkward. "He's very pussy, comes from back in the woods."

put a cat among the pigeons   BRITISH
To stir up trouble in a group, to cause controversy. "He's really put a cat
among the pigeons with that proposal."

put a quart in a pint pot   BRITISH
To try to do something impossible; not even worth a try.

put foot inside a shoe   BRITISH
Lived or was born, as in "You're the most sensible person that ever put
foot inside a shoe."

put in the fangs   AUSTRALIAN
To ask someone to loan money. "He put in the fangs the minute he saw
me." Patterned after an animal biting (putting the bite on) someone.

put it about   BRITISH
To have sexual relations with many people. "He's been putting it about
for as long as I can remember."

put the black on someone   BRITISH
To blackmail someone. "She put the black on him at the end of their affair."

putz   AMERICAN
Putz is Yiddish for "penis" and also has come to mean a fool, a jerk, an
obnoxious person. Synonyms from Yiddish are a *schmekel,* a *schmuck,* a
schlong, and a *shvantz,* all of which mean penis as well as jerk or obnoxious person.

to quarm   BAHAMIAN
To show off, or to walk in an affected way, especially by a woman. "Here
she come quarmin' down the street."

quarter days   SCOTTISH, IRISH, BRITISH
In Scotland the four days that mark the quarter of the year (*Candlemas,*
Whitsunday, Lammas, and *Martinmas.*) In Ireland, Wales, and England,
the four quarter days are *Lady Day, Midsummer Day, Michaelmas,* and
Christmas.

quat   CANADIAN (NEWFOUNDLAND)
To squat down, head bowed, as if trying to hide. "Quat down there and they won't see you."

the Queen's (or King's) peace   BRITISH
The *Queen's peace* is the peace or protection of all law-abiding British subjects, though in past times it applied only to those in the royal employ. The term is used in *Blackstone's Commentaries.*

queen's tears   SOUTH AFRICAN
Any powerful drink, especially gin. One story has it that the term refers to Queen Victoria's crying after the Zulus defeated the British at Isandhlwana.

Queen's weather   BRITISH
Fine weather. Queen Victoria supposedly was fortunate in having good weather most of the time she appeared in public. Her good luck led to the British expression *Queen's weather,* for "a fine day for a public occasion, an outing, a party, etc."

queer as Dick's headband   BRITISH
Oliver Cromwell's son Richard (1626–1712), who ineffectually ruled England as Protector after his father, was widely called Queen Dick for his effeminate ways. Whether he was a homosexual isn't known, but homosexuality certainly isn't alluded to in the expression *as queer as Dick's hatband.* This means "as strange as Dick's crown," a crown on the head of such a weak, ineffectual person seeming incongruous or ridiculous to most of his subjects. Though several writers have associated "queer" with homosexual in the phrase, the slang *queer* for homosexual isn't recorded until the 1920s.

quiff   BRITISH
A hairstyle for men that is called a pompadour in the United States.

qui-hy   INDIAN, BRITISH
The Hindi *Koi hai,* meaning "Is anyone there?," is a cry used in India to summon a servant. These words, in the form of *qui-hy,* were used by the British when they occupied India to mean an Anglo-Indian, especially one living in Bengal. It also had some British military use in the sense of a summons to a servant.

quin BRITISH
The American shortening of quintuplet is *quint,* but the British say *quin,* as in "The quins are doing well."

R **rabbit food** AMERICAN
Raw vegetables, or a salad of raw vegetables. Often used in a derogatory way.

Rachmanism BRITISH
An eponymous word, named after a London landlord, that means the exploitation of poor tenants.

raining pitchforks and bull yearlings AMERICAN (TEXAS)
A term used in Texas for a very heavy rain, a downpour.

raise billy hell AMERICAN (WEST)
Make a big fuss or a commotion. "She raised all billy hell about the ruined curtains."

raise hob BRITISH
Hob was the nickname of Robin Goodfellow, a mischievous household spirit of folklore. *To raise hob* has for centuries meant to act devilishly like him, to be mischievous.

ramstam SCOTTISH
A person who is stubborn, obstinate. Also heard in northern England.

randy AUSTRALIAN, BRITISH
Sexually excited, horny. This slang word is also heard, infrequently, in the United States.

ranny AMERICAN (WESTERN)
A top cowhand, short for *ranahan,* which means the same.

rare steak AMERICAN
See *underdone steak.*

rasher of bacon

The *rasher* in this British term, rarely heard in America, means a slice and probably didn't get its name because it is cooked *rashly* or "quickly." *Rasher* here is more likely a corruption of *rasure*, "a thin slice or shaving."

ratbag

(1) An eccentric person. (2) A troublemaker. *Ratbagging* is a display of eccentricity. *To get the rats* is to be crazy, as is to be *ratty*.

rather!

An exclamation meaning yes, most certainly. "Do you like her?" "Rather!"

rat rhyme

Doggeral, crudely or irregularly fashioned verse; pronounced *rat-rim*.

raver

A stunning woman; the word is possibly short for a *raving beauty*.

rave up

A wild party or a wild time. "That was some rave up they had last night."

readies

Slang for money. "Have you got the readies to start up the business?"

reason hard

In the Rasta talk or Dread Talk of the Rastafarians, this means to argue.

rebel yell; Texas yell

Some experts believe that the *rebel yell*, or *yalo*, originally used in combat in the Civil War and intended to strike terror into the hearts of the enemy, came from the Creek Indians, loosely combining "the turkey gobbler's cry with a series of yelps." The high-pitched, blood-chilling yell may have been borrowed by Texans and adopted for their *Texas yell*, but others say the Texans got their yell from the Comanche Indians. In any case, everyone agrees that the "Yah-hoo" or "Yaaaaaheee" of fiction writers sounds nothing like the rebel yell; several experts believe it is a corruption of the old fox-hunting cry *tallyho* (q.v.).

red-handed AMERICAN
In the act of committing a crime, as in "We caught him red-handed." A British speaker would say "We caught him dead to rights."

red-assed AMERICAN (WEST)
Cowboy slang for being in a bad mood. "He's real red-assed today."

redcoat CANADIAN
A member of the Royal Canadian Mounted Police, after their scarlet jackets.

redeye gravy AMERICAN (SOUTH)
A favorite southern gravy made from the frying pan juice of country ham, thickened with flour and frequently containing a little coffee for color and flavor.

red Indian BRITISH
A Native American, or American Indian; the term is not used in the United States, where it is considered offensive by many.

redneck AMERICAN (SOUTH)
A poor, white, working-class, often rowdy Southerner, usually one from a rural area. The word, which is often derogatory, has its origins in the sunburned necks of farmers and outdoor laborers and originally meant a poor farmer.

reggae JAMAICAN
This style of Jamaican music, combining blues, calypso, and rock 'n 'roll, was named in 1968 after Frederick "Toots" Hibbert's song "Do the Reggay." The word *reggay* in the song comes from the Jamaican *rege* or *strege* for a raggedy or dowdy fellow.

resit MALAYSIAN
A Malaysian borrowing and alteration of the word *receipt*.

a rest AUSTRALIAN
Humorous slang for a year in jail. "All he got was a rest."

retiral SCOTTISH
A retirement from work or business. "The staff celebrated their boss's retiral."

Reuben AMERICAN (NEW YORK CITY)
This grilled sandwich of corned beef, Swiss cheese, sauerkraut, and dressing on rye bread was possibly invented in the early 1900s at Manhattan's Reuben's Delicatessen. But no one is sure of this, even though the Reuben has long been associated with New York City.

rez AMERICAN
A word many Native Americans use as a short form for reservation, a tract of land owned by an Indian tribe.

rhino BRITISH
Another of the many slang terms for money (*lolly, brass,* etc.). This term may derive from the high cost of rhinoceros horn, which the Chinese believe is an aphrodisiac.

rhyme JAMAICAN
Besides its usual meaning, *rhyme* can mean a joke or an amusing story.

to rick BRITISH
To sprain, strain, or twist. "He ricked his ankle just before the big race."

to ride backwards up Holburn Hill BRITISH
To go to one's own hanging. Up until 1784, the year of the last execution at Tyburn in London, condemned men would go to the gallows riding backwards on a horse all the way up Holburn Hill, which rose steeply from Newgate Prison to the gallows at Tyburn. This was probably done to prevent the condemned from being shocked with a distant view of the gallows.

to ride close herd on AMERICAN (WEST)
To close herd literally means to keep cattle close together, compact; thus *to ride close herd on something* is to pay close attention to it, not to let it get far out of your sight or out of hand. "He rode close herd on that plan from the start."

right-o BRITISH
A well-known expression meaning *O.K.* (q.v.), all right.

right on your drag AMERICAN (WEST)
The two men riding at the rear end of a herd are called the drag by cowboys. From this term came the expression *he's right on your drag,* meaning someone is hot on your trail, either the law or a creditor.

right smart   AMERICAN (SOUTH)
(1) A great deal or large number; very large or great; very much or many.
"There was right smart of water in the ditch." (2) A good idea; also *right smart idea.*

right stuff   AMERICAN, BRITISH
The British were using this phrase a century ago to describe good soldiers,
mainly in the form of "the right sort of stuff." American author Tom Wolfe
made it popular again with his book *The Right Stuff* (1979), which described
the character, intelligence, courage, etc., needed by U.S. astronauts.

to ring   BRITISH, IRISH
Call on the telephone. "Why didn't they ring?" Rarely heard in the United
States, where the sentence would be "Why didn't they call?"

to ring in   AUSTRALIAN
To substitute something fraudulently, especially in gambling on horserac-
ing when a *ringer* is used.

ringing the changes   BRITISH
A *change* in the ancient art of bell ringing is the order in which a series
of bells are rung. Theoretically it would be possible to ring 479,001,600
changes with twelve church bells without repeating their ringing order—
although it would take nearly thirty-eight years to do so. *Ringing the
changes* has long been a competitive sport among bell ringers, and the
present champions are eight ringers and their conductor, who rang a
peal, all the possible changes on a series of bells, on eight bells in 1963.
The peal consisted of 40,320 changes and took two minutes short of
eighteen hours. Past feats like this inspired the expression *to ring the
changes,* to try every possible way of doing something, to state something again and again in different ways, or even to work something to
death.

ring road   BRITISH
What Americans would call a *beltway* or *a belt parkway.*

rink rat   CANADIAN
Slang for a person who does odd jobs at a skating rink in exchange for
free admission to hockey games and free time to skate on the ice.

ripper
AUSTRALIAN

Excellent, great, terrific. "She had a ripper of a holiday at the shore."

risin'
AMERICAN (OZARK MOUNTAINS)

A boil. "I've got a risin' in my ear that's about to kill me."

rising beauties
AMERICAN (SOUTH)

Slang for women's breasts, the expression made famous in American literature by Erskine Caldwell in *God's Little Acre* (1933): "There ain't a man alive who's ever seen a finer-looking pair of rising beauties as she's got."

riz
IRISH

Commonly used instead of *raised,* as in "She riz six kids all by herself."

roadkill
AMERICAN

An animal that is killed by a car or a truck and, often, flattened by traffic.

Robin Hood's barn
BRITISH

To *go all around Robin Hood's barn* means to wander in a roundabout way, finally arriving at the right conclusion. Robin Hood, of course, had no barn, living in Sherwood Forest, and trying to get around a barn that wasn't there was an apt description for early travelers lost in the woods.

robin run
CANADIAN

The first and richest run from maple trees in the spring, which makes the finest maple syrup.

rockmelon
AUSTRALIAN

A cantaloupe, because it resembles a large, round rock.

rode hard and put up wet
AMERICAN (WEST)

To have been treated badly, abused. "I feel like I been rode hard and put up wet." The analogy is to a horse that is sweaty from having been worked hard and is not properly cared for.

romance boy
JAMAICAN

A man who chases women; a skirt-chaser. "She foolin' with that romance boy."

'roo bar AUSTRALIAN

Not a "kangaroo bar," where drinks with a big kick are served; simply a bar device attached to cars in bush country to help protect them from damage should a kangaroo collide with them.

ropeable AUSTRALIAN

Frantic with rage, angry, quick-tempered. The expression was suggested by wild cattle being roped or lassoed and fighting with all their might.

rope of sand BRITISH

Expressing futility, ties that neither bind nor hold, *rope of sand* is an old expression that may well be proverbial. It is rarely heard in the United States.

ropey AUSTRALIAN, BRITISH

Something of poor quality or in poor condition. "Get that ropey chair out of here."

rort AUSTRALIAN

A racket, scheme, trick, any fraudulent act. A *rorter* is a professional swindler.

rough as a cob AMERICAN (WEST)

Very rough and tough, like a coarse corncob. "He looked rough as a cob and no one messed with him."

roughie AUSTRALIAN

(1) A swindler, a cheat. (2) Any uncouth person. "You don't want to play cards with that roughie."

round BRITISH

A sandwich. *Half round* means half a sandwich.

round-trip ticket AMERICAN

See *one-way ticket, single ticket.*

roup SCOTTISH

Another word for an auction. *To roup* is to sell at auction.

rozzer IRISH
A policeman. "Three rozzers came after them."

rubber AMERICAN, BRITISH
Rubber is common slang for a condom in America, but in England it means an eraser.

rubbernecking AMERICAN
See *curiosity delay.*

rubbish BRITISH, IRISH
Generally used instead of *garbage* or *trash.* "He put out the rubbish." The word is not as widely used in this sense in the United States.

rubbish tip BRITISH
A local garbage dump or garbage heap for household garbage, etc.

rubby-dubber CANADIAN
Canadian slang for an old man, often an alcoholic, who follows a carnival, supporting himself with odd jobs there and spending most of his pay on drink.

ruck BRITISH
(1) A crowd, multitude, throng. (2) In rugby, a huddle of players around the ball.

ruddy BRITISH
Used as an intensive, as in "He's a ruddy liar!" or "She's a ruddy great baby!"

rude parts BRITISH
A euphemism for the genitals, male or female.

ruggerbugger SOUTH AFRICAN
A sports fanatic, someone whose life revolves around rugby and other sports.

rum boy BAHAMIAN
A derogatory name for a drunkard, an alcoholic vagrant.

run around like a headless chook   AUSTRALIAN

To run around like a chicken with its head chopped off, to be extremely excited, dysfunctional. A *chook* is a chicken.

run a sandy   AMERICAN (OZARK MOUNTAINS)

To play a trick on someone, to bluff someone. "That's the last time he'll run a sandy on me."

rundale   IRISH

Land that is jointly occupied or jointly owned by two people.

to run for office   AMERICAN

See *to stand for election.*

to run in   AUSTRALIAN, BRITISH

To break in. "He has to run in the car before he races it."

runners   BRITISH

String beans; they are often called *runner beans* as well.

running flush   BRITISH

What American poker players would call a *straight flush.*

S

sad and sorry   BRITISH

A humorous term for an installment plan purchase. "I bought it on the sad and sorry."

saddler of Bawtry   BRITISH

Someone in too much of a hurry. "Like the saddler of Bawtry, who was hanged for leaving his liquor," says this Yorkshire proverb. It seems that the real saddler of Bawtry was on his way to the gallows and adamantly refused to stop with his guards for a last drink, as was the custom in York in the eighteenth century. Passing the tavern by, he hurried to the gallows, where *Jack Ketch* (q.v.) quickly accommodated him. His pardon from the king arrived only a few minutes later.

Sally Army   AUSTRALIAN

A humorous name for the Salvation Army.

saloon car   BRITISH
An automobile that an American would call a sedan.

saltings   BRITISH
A salt marsh or tideland near the sea. "Specially adapted plants grow in the saltings."

same like   JAMAICAN
The same as, just like. "He cheap, same like his brother."

samey   AUSTRALIAN, BRITISH
A disparaging term meaning not distinctive or original. "All his books are somewhat samey."

sango   AUSTRALIAN
Slang for a sandwich, which is also called a *sanger.*

sand shoes   AUSTRALIAN
Australian slang for tennis shoes.

sannup   AMERICAN (NEW ENGLAND)
A mischievous boy always getting into trouble. The term derives from a Maine Abnaki Indian word for young boy. "Get out of that tree, you little sannup."

sark   SCOTTISH, BRITISH
A long, shirtlike garment worn as a nightshirt or a chemise. Also heard in northern England.

Sassenach   IRISH, SCOTTISH
A derogatory name for an English person. The word derives from the Gaelic for Saxon.

saut   SCOTTISH
Typical Scottish pronunciation and spelling of *salt.*

sayer   SCOTTISH
An old term for a poet that has some literary use today.

says I   IRISH
An expression frequently used in recounting a conversation, as is *says he, says she,* etc. "'I'm going to town,' says I. 'No, you're not,' says she."

to scarper   AUSTRALIAN, BRITISH
To leave in a hurry, especially to evade the law. "Here they come. Let's scarper!"

scat!   AMERICAN (SOUTH, SOUTHWEST)
Said after someone sneezes instead of *God bless you!* or *gesundheit!* by many Americans in the South and the Southwest.

scatty   AUSTRALIAN, BRITISH
Forgetful, scatterbrained, silly. "This job is driving me scatty."

schlep   AMERICAN
A Yiddish word that has become part of the American vocabulary, meaning (1) to carry or lug: "He schlepped the package all the way from the Bronx." (2) To move in a slow, awkward, or tedious manner.

schmuck   AMERICAN
Judging by its common use by New Yorkers, one wouldn't think *schmuck* was an obscene word. *Schmuck* is Yiddish for penis, deriving somehow from a German word meaning "ornament," and has come to mean a stupid, obnoxious person, of whom there are apparently so many that *schmuck* is one of the best-known Yiddish expressions.

schnook   AMERICAN
A timid, ineffectual person, one pitied rather than disliked; in fact, a *schnook* can be quite likable. This Yiddish expression comes from the German *schnucke,* "little sheep."

schnorrer   AMERICAN
An impudent beggar, moocher, or sponger who acts like it's one's duty to give him money; a haggler or a habitual bargain hunter; a cheapskate; a chisler. *Schnorrer* can mean all these things and more. The word is a Yiddish one, probably deriving from the German verb for to beg.

schoolie   AUSTRALIAN
Like *chalkie* (q.v.), this is a slang name for a schoolteacher.

school leaving   SOUTH AFRICAN
Graduation from a school. "Her school leaving was held in June."

a Scotch breakfast   SCOTTISH
A substantial breakfast with a variety of delicious dishes.

Scratch   AMERICAN (NEW ENGLAND)
A name for the devil, especially in New England. "Better be good or you'll be seeing old Mr. Scratch one day."

screech   CANADIAN (NEWFOUNDLAND)
Any cheap rum, presumably because it makes one screech; one brand is marketed as "Screech."

screed   SCOTTISH
(1) A drinking bout. (2) A rip or a tear in a piece of cloth.

script   AUSTRALIAN
A written prescription from a doctor. "Dr. Gold wrote me a script."

scruff   BRITISH
A dirty, disheveled person. "How could you bring that scruff in here?"

scrum   BRITISH
Short for scrummage. A play in rugby when a group of attacking players from each of the two teams come together, heads down, and push against each other, trying to win control of the ball.

scrummy   BRITISH
Scrumptious. "Bring home some more of those scrummy cookies."

to scunner   SCOTTISH
To loathe or to feel disgust about someone or something. "I took a scunner to him."

to scutter   SCOTTISH
To scurry, a variation of *scuttle*. "They scuttered out of the room in a hurry."

sea cow   SOUTH AFRICAN
Another name for the hippopotamus, primarily used in days past but
remembered now in place names such as Sea Cow Valley.

secateurs   BRITISH
The British name for what Americans call garden *pruning shears*. Pronounced *sek-ah-tours*.

sedan   AMERICAN
See *saloon car*.

see-me-no-more   BAHAMIAN
A humorous name for a cemetery. "Soon I be in the see-me-no-more."

see you later, alligator   AMERICAN
A common good-bye, still heard occasionally, that was taken from the title
of a Bill Haley song in 1957. The reply was often "In a while, crocodile."

selectman   AMERICAN (NEW ENGLAND)
A member of a board of town officers chosen each year in New England
towns to manage local affairs. The term has been in use for several hundred years.

to sell the pass   IRISH
To be a traitor. Irish legend holds that when a regiment of Crotha, Lord of
Atha, was holding a pass against the invading army of Trathal, the "King
of Cael," one of Crotha's soldiers betrayed the pass for money, the invaders
were victorious, and Trathal became King of Ireland. This inspired the
ancient Irish expression *selling the pass*, "betraying one's own for money
or other gain."

send to Coventry   BRITISH
To ostracize. The historic city of Coventry in England may have been built
near and taken its name from *Cofa's tree*, in which case the otherwise
anonymous Cofa family name is remembered in at least three words or
phrases. The most common of these means boycotting a person by refusing to associate or have dealings with him, which is called *sending him
to Coventry*. This phrase is of uncertain origin, arising either because Roy-
alist prisoners were sent to the staunchly Puritan town during the Great
Rebellion, or due to the fact that Coventry was at one time so antimilitary

that any soldier posted there found himself cut off from all social intercourse, the townspeople even refusing to talk to the troops. The Germans with their devastating bombings laid waste to much of Coventry in World War II, destroying seventy thousand homes, all but the great spire of the fourteenth-century Cathedral of St. Michael, and many other historic sites, which led to the term *to coventrate*—to attempt to bomb a city out of existence.

send up the river AMERICAN

To send to prison. The river referred to is the Hudson, up which, at Ossining, New York, is the prison popularly known as Sing Sing, founded in 1830.

sent down BRITISH

Expelled: "He was sent down from Cambridge."

serviette BRITISH

A table napkin. A *napkin* in Britain is a child's diaper. "Don't forget to place serviettes by the sides of the plates when setting the table for dinner."

set fire, you! AMERICAN (NEW ENGLAND)

Pay attention. "Set fire, you, or you're not going to graduate."

set the Thames on fire BRITISH

To *set the Thames on fire* is an old expression, said of the Rhine and other rivers as well, meaning to do something marvelous, to work wonders, to almost set the world on fire. However, one persistent story claims that the *Thames* in the phrase is not the famous river, but a misspelling of *temse,* a word for a corn sieve in the eighteenth century. According to this theory, a joke about a farm laborer who worked his temse so hard that it caught fire probably led to this expression for "to do something remarkable." As with so many word derivations, the truth will probably never be known.

seven-sided son of a bitch AMERICAN (WEST)

The western U.S. variant of the expression *seven-sided animal.* Both mean a one-eyed man or woman, "each having a right side and a left side, a fore side and a back side, an inside and an outside, and a blind side."

sexing BAHAMIAN

Having sexual intercourse. "They been sexing in that shack house."

shag   AUSTRALIAN, BRITISH
Slang for to copulate, have sex with. The expression is heard more frequently in the United States today. *Shagged out*, slang for very tired,
hasn't yet made it to America. The title of the film *The Spy Who Shagged
Me* (2000) caused no concern in the United States, where few people knew
what it meant.

le shake hand   FRENCH
A French borrowing and alteration of the British English *handshake*.

shambolic   BRITISH
Poorly organized, confused. "He's the most shambolic person I've ever
met."

shandy   AUSTRALIAN
A popular drink consisting mainly of beer with a bit of clear soda pop
(called lemonade) added. See *lemonade*.

shanghai   AUSTRALIAN
In Australia *shanghai* means a slingshot, not to force or trick a man to
serve as a crew member aboard a ship.

sharkspotter   AUSTRALIAN
The name given to any helicopter that flies along a coast to spot sharks
in or near swimming areas.

sharp   AMERICAN, BRITISH
In America sharp can mean bright, intelligent, quick-witted; but in England
it is far from a compliment, referring to a sneaky, unprincipled person.

shaw   SCOTTISH, AMERICAN
In Scotland, the stalks and leaves of potato plants and other root plants,
including turnips and parsnips. In the midwestern United States a *shaw*
is a thicket or a small woods.

Shawinigan handshake   CANADIAN
To give someone a Shawinigan handshake means to strangle him. Here's
one that hasn't made any dictionary yet. It is named after the mill town
of Shawinigan in Québec, Canadian prime minister Jean Crétien's home-

town. It seems that the prime minister once "literally wrung the neck of a protester who got close to him at a Flag Day rally in Ottawa" (*New York Times,* October 28, 1998), and Canadians took to calling any such throttling a *Shawinigan handshake.*

shebeen   IRISH, SCOTTISH, SOUTH AFRICAN

An unlicensed drinking establishment. *Shebeen* derives from the Gaelic *sibin,* bad ale. See also *shebeen queen.*

shebeen queen   SOUTH AFRICAN

A derogatory term for an elderly black woman who sells liquor illegally, a *shebeen* being a kind of speakeasy where such liquor is sold. See also *shebeen.*

sheep station   AUSTRALIAN

A huge Australian farm where sheep are raised.

sheila   AUSTRALIAN, NEW ZEALAND

A girl or a young woman. The term dates back to the late nineteenth century and probably derives from the personal name Sheila. It is one of the best known of Australianisms. Also used for a female kangaroo.

sherbet   AMERICAN, BRITISH, AUSTRALIAN

In the United States this is strictly a frozen dessert made of fruit juice, sugar, water, milk, egg white, or gelatin. In Britain it is a beverage made of sweetened fruit juice. But in Australia it means any alcoholic beverage, especially beer.

shilpit   SCOTTTISH

Weak or puny, timid. "He's just a shilpit of a man."

shingle   BRITISH

A pebbly or rocky beach. The term is rarely used in this sense in the United States.

a shingle short   AUSTRALIAN

Said of someone stupid or not very intelligent. "Jodie's always been a shingle short."

shit belong-um fire   PIDGIN ENGLISH

This apt bit of pidgin English was used by Lascar seamen employed as stokers on nineteenth-century British steamers. It means ashes.

shivoo   AUSTRALIAN
A party, a celebration. "We're having a shivoo out at our place tonight."

shocker   JAMAICAN
Not a shocking book, or film, or story, but simply an electrician.

shonky   AUSTRALIAN
Something or somebody of poor quality, shoddy. "That's a shonky jacket he's wearing."

sho 'nuff   AMERICAN (SOUTH)
(1) Sure enough, a pronunciation known to millions nationally from thousands of comedy routines. (2) Really, actually (in a question). "Are you that old, sho 'nuff?"

shoot   BRITISH
A hunting expedition on which small game such as birds and rabbits are shot. When an Englishman goes after foxes and deer, however, he goes on a fox or deer *hunt*. British wit Oscar Wilde defined a fox hunt as "The unspeakable in full pursuit of the uneatable."

shooter   BRITISH
British underworld slang for any handgun. "Shall I carry a shooter for the job?"

to shoot the cat   BRITISH
British slang meaning to vomit, throw up, be sick. The expression, similar to the American slang *shoot (or toss) one's cookies,* has been traced back to the early nineteenth century, but the use of *cat* in it has never been satisfactorily explained.

to shoot the moon   BRITISH
To move out from a residence at night without paying back rent. In American slang, to *shoot for the moon* means to try for the very best.

short   AMERICAN (NEW ENGLAND)
A lobster under the legal size requirements for keeping one, the opposite of a *keeper.*

short list   BRITISH
To be put on a list of people most likely to be chosen for something, a list that has been winnowed from a longer one. For example, several novels

are short-listed each year for Britain's prestigious Booker Prize, and from this short list a winner is selected. The expression is not a new one, dating back about seventy-five years, and is becoming familiar in the United States.

shortsweetening   AMERICAN (OZARK MOUNTAINS)
Sugar. "I like lots of shortsweetening in my coffee."

shoulder   AMERICAN
See *verge.*

shoulder candy   AMERICAN
Candy for a sexy young woman dates to about 1968, when the word possibly originated in New York City. *Shoulder candy,* meaning the same, but generally applied to fashion models, has only been recorded in the past few years, as has *arm candy.*

show   AMERICAN
See *movies.*

showerproof   AUSTRALIAN, BRITISH
What Americans would call *water-repellent.* "He wore a showerproof coat."

shower tea   AUSTRALIAN
A party for a woman soon to be married. This would simply be called a *shower* in the United States.

shuftee   BRITISH
An Arabic word adopted by the British meaning "a quick look," as in "Let us have a shuftee at it."

sick as a cat   BRITISH
Americans would say *sick as a dog* to mean the same—that is, very sick.

sickie   AUSTRALIAN
Slang for a sick day, an absence from one's job. "He took a sickie and went to the game."

side

Slang for "arrogance," excessive pride. "He's a decent chap, has no side to him at all."

sidewinder

A dangerous, treacherous man, from the sidewinder rattlesnake, so named for its lateral locomotion.

silvertail

An elderly, rich, influential person; also someone who puts on airs. The word was perhaps originally suggested by the Silver-Tailed Dandies, the nickname of an old British regiment whose officers had elaborate silver embroidery on the tails of their coats.

since Adam was a lad

A long time. "I've been going there since Adam was a lad, before he met Eve."

since the hogs et my brother up

Heard in the mountains as a humorous way of saying "a long time." "Haven't seen you since the hogs et my brother up."

since when

A newly rich man or woman. The expression possibly derives from a phrase such as "Since when did he get money?"

singlet

A man's T-shirt or undershirt, often without sleeves. *To have [something] up one's singlet,* however, means to have something up one's sleeve.

single ticket

A *one-way ticket* (q.v.), not a *round-trip ticket,* which in Britain and Australia is a *return ticket.*

to sit above the salt

To sit in a place of honor. In ancient times salt was highly valued, so much so that spilling salt became an unlucky omen among the Romans. Roman soldiers were in fact paid in salt *(sal)* at one time, this the origin of our word *salary.* Through the centuries a number of expressions reflected the importance of this precious seasoning and preservative. "Not worth his salt" referred to the salary the Romans paid their soldiers; *to sit above the salt* was to sit in a place of distinction, above the saler, or saltcellar, at a medieval table. The last expression is still used in Britain, as is its opposite. *Below the Salt* is the title of a historical novel by Thomas Costain.

sitting room   BRITISH
See *lounge room.*

six sixes in an over   BRITISH
A cricket term. One journalist has written that it "is best explained to Americans as the equivalent of six home runs off six consecutive pitches . . . a godlike effort that has only been accomplished twice in the history of the sport."

Sjambok rule   SOUTH AFRICAN
Sjambok, for "a rhino-hide whip," is said to come from the Malay language. The word, however, is associated with the Boers of South Africa, *sjambok rule* meaning a repressive, tyrannical rule of whips and violence. The word is an international one, recorded in the dictionaries of many languages. It seems to have come into English in the first quarter of the nineteenth century.

skelly-eyed   SCOTTISH
An old slang word used to describe a squint-eyed person.

to skelp   SCOTTISH
To slap. A *skelp* can be a slap or the sound of a slap.

skerrick   AUSTRALIAN, BRITISH
A small fragment or amount. "There's not a skerrick of meat left."

skerry   SCOTTISH
The name for a small, rocky island or a very rocky coastline.

skip   IRISH, AUSTRALIAN, BRITISH
(1) A servant at Dublin's Trinity College and other colleges. (2) In British and Australian English, a *skip* is a Dumpster.

skirl   SHETLAND ISLANDS
Shriek. "Dey skirl lack (like) donkeys."

skite   AUSTRALIAN, SCOTTISH
(1) A quick stroke or chopping blow. (2) A joke, prank. (3) A person who
is the butt of a joke, someone held in low esteem. In Australia, a *skite* is
a boaster or braggart, the word here a shortening of the British *blather-
skate* meaning the same.

skreich of day   SCOTTISH
A poetic term for the time of day when the cock crows, daybreak. *Skreich*
means screech.

skrik   SOUTH AFRICAN
Sudden fright or panic. *Skrik* derives from the Dutch *schrik* for fright.

skylark   BRITISH
A lark, something done for fun that might be wrong but not seriously so.

slag   BRITISH
A derogatory slang term for a low-class, loose woman. *To slag,* however,
means to criticize someone.

slainte   IRISH
A drinking toast familiar to Irishmen everywhere, *slainte* (pronounced
s-lawn-cheh) is simply Gaelic for *cheers* (q.v.).

slaister   SCOTTISH
To make a mess, create confusion about something.

slam   AMERICAN
A prison or a jail. Also called the *slammer.*

to slang   AUSTRALIAN, BRITISH
To curse someone angrily. "They were slanging each other in the middle
of the street."

slangs   HAWAIIAN
Slang words. "We don't like to use slangs here."

slap-up job   BRITISH
Excellent work. "He did a slap-up job building that house." In the United
States a *slap-up job* or *slapdash job* means just the opposite.

to slash
AUSTRALIAN, BRITISH

Slang for "to urinate," a term used only by men. "I took a good slash."

slate
AUSTRALIAN, BRITISH

To attack critically, to trash, as in "His book was slated by the reviewers."

slavey
BRITISH

A maid who does general housekeeping. "I'm not your slavey around here anymore."

slee
SCOTTISH

Sly. "They are slee wee diels (devils)."

sleekit
SCOTTISH

An adjective meaning, among other things, slick, smooth, sly, sneaky, deceitful.

sleeping policemen
TRINIDAD

Humps in the road to slow traffic. In the United States these would be called, less colorfully, *speed bumps, road bumps,* or *safety bumps.*

sleep on a clothesline
BRITISH

The expression "I'm so tired I could sleep on a clothesline," with much more British than American use today, dates back to eighteenth-century England, when people unable to afford a bed in boardinghouses were charged two pennies to sit on a communal bench through the night, leaning on a clothesline stretched tightly in front of them. The taut "two-penny rope" was cut in the morning, the sleepers jolted into reality again.

sleepy dust
CANADIAN (NEWFOUNDLAND)

The matter found in the corners of the eyes after sleeping. "Sand" or "sleep" in American English.

slider
SCOTTISH

A common name for what Americans would call an ice cream sandwich.

Slim
EAST AFRICAN

A name given by East Africans to the AIDS disease, which has ravaged the African continent and often reduces those it attacks to living skeletons.

sling   AUSTRALIAN
A bribe. "He took a sling and they found out about it." The word also can be used to mean a tip for services rendered.

sling off   AUSTRALIAN, BRITISH
To speak abusively or impertinently, to ridicule. "Don't sling off on him like that."

slingshot   AMERICAN
See *catapult*.

lo slip   ITALIAN
For some reason the English word *slip* is used by the Italians to mean male swim trunks or undershorts (briefs). Other more literal Italian borrowings, among hundreds, include *il poster, la pop art, il play, lo script, il camerman, il drink, il weekend, il party, lo shopping, il supermarket,* and *il luncheonette.*

to slip on your guava   SOUTH AFRICAN
To make a complete fool of yourself. *Guava* means "backside" in Afrikaans, so the term literally means "to slip on your ass."

slipper   GERMAN
A German borrowing of the English word *slipper,* though the Germans use *slipper* to mean any slip-on shoe, such as loafers.

slip-slops   SOUTH AFRICAN
The sandals that Americans often call flip-flops.

slob   IRISH
Very muddy ground. "We walked a mile through the slob."

slob ice   CANADIAN
Chunks of thick ice that are melting in a body of water.

slogger   BRITISH
A boxer who punches hard, or a cricket player who often hits the ball a long way. In American baseball and boxing such a powerful man would be called a *slugger* (q.v.).

slop　　　　　　　　　　　　　　　　　　BRITISH
This word, meaning a cop, is shortened and slightly altered backslang, deriving from *ecilop—police* spelled backward.

un slow　　　　　　　　　　　　　　　　　FRENCH
A French invention, from the English word *slow,* for an American blues song.

slowcoach　　　　　　　　　　　　　　　　BRITISH
A slow, lazy person, what Americans would call a *slowpoke.*

slugger　　　　　　　　　　　　　　　　AMERICAN
(1) In baseball a powerful distance hitter who hits a lot of long home runs. (2) In boxing a powerful, hard-hitting puncher, as opposed to a more highly skilled boxer. See also *slogger.*

slut　　　　　　　　　　CANADIAN (NEWFOUNDLAND)
Not a promiscuous woman, but a large tin kettle used for boiling water over an open fire.

slut's wool　　　　　　　　　　　　　　　BRITISH
Americans might call these *dust bunnies* or *dust balls*—dust found under the bed and in other places difficult to reach.

slygrog　　　　　　　　　　　　　　　AUSTRALIAN
A humorous name for illegally sold liquor. *Slygrogging* among the Aussies is illegal or underage drinking.

small-little　　　　　　　　　　　　　　HAWAIIAN
Sometimes used in place of *small.* "When I was small-little I lived here."

smalls　　　　　　　　　　　　　　　　　BRITISH
(1) A humorous old term for underwear. (2) Two- or three-line ads in newspapers or magazines.

smashing　　　　　　　　　　　　　　　　BRITISH
This well-known Briticism means "terrific" and is often applied to a strikingly beautiful woman.

smir SCOTTISH
A fine, misty rain. "A smir came in over the Highlands."

smoking FRENCH
The French term for a tuxedo.

smoko AUSTRALIAN, NEW ZEALAND
A coffee break or a tea break. "Let's take our smoko, mate."

smoodger AUSTRALIAN
Slang for a habitual flatterer. "That bloke's such a smoodger, telling me I'm pretty all the time."

snag AUSTRALIAN
A sausage. "We slipped a few snags on the barbie." The word also can mean a worthy, formidable opponent.

snail mail AMERICAN
A disparaging term for the U.S. Postal Service coined by Internet e-mail users.

snake fella AUSTRALIAN PIDGIN
A bad man, someone sneaky and dangerous. *Snake* also can mean nasty. For other forms of pidgin see *mary.*

snaky AUSTRALIAN
Irritable, angry, touchy. "Calm down, don't get snaky about it." The word may derive from the British *snarky,* meaning the same. See also *snitchy.*

sneck SCOTTISH
A door latch or its lever. "Be sure you lock the sneck on the gate."

sneesh SCOTTISH
The tobacco preparation snuff. Also used in northern England.

snib SCOTTISH
The bolt on a door or a window.

snig   AUSTRALIAN, NEW ZEALAND
To drag a log over the ground by a chain attached to it. "He snigged three logs over here."

snitcher   NEW ZEALAND
A remarkably good-looking or attractive person. The term's origin is unknown; it is no relation to the snitcher who is an informer.

snitchy   AUSTRALIAN
Bad-tempered, cross. "What's he so snitchy about?" See also *snaky.*

snob   AUSTRALIAN
A shoemaker or a cobbler. The word comes from a Scottish word meaning the same, being no relation to the *snob* meaning a haughty person.

snobare   ITALIAN
The Italians, who have adopted many English words in the past fifty years, in this case borrowed the word *snob* and made out of it the verb *snobare,* to snub.

snogging   AUSTRALIAN
Slang for smooching, making out, making love. Its origins are obscure.

snooker hall   SCOTTISH
In the United States this would be called a *pool hall* (q.v.) or a *billiard parlor.*

snorter   BRITISH
Slang for something really good, excellent, outstanding. "A real snorter, that car he bought."

to snout   AUSTRALIAN
To bear a grudge against someone. *Snout,* as a noun, means a grudge.

snye   CANADIAN
(1) A part of a stream that runs off from the main stream and later rejoins it. (2) A channel joining two rivers. (3) A backwater.

soapstone son of a bitch AMERICAN (WEST)

Soapstone has a greasy, slippery feel to it and thus is an appropriate name for an unctuous character, just as *Soapy Sam* (q.v.) was in Britain more than a century ago.

Soapy Sam BRITISH

A slippery person. The first Soapy Sam, Samuel Wilberforce, bishop of Oxford and later Winchester, was a noncomformist and controversial clergyman if ever there was one. Although he was a devout man in his personal life, this position forced him to develop a suave, unctuous manner of speaking, persuasive but expedient almost to a fault. By 1860 he had earned the nickname Soapy Sam, which has since been applied to any slippery, unctuous speaker who can talk his way out of anything. The coining was perhaps given an assist by the initials "S.O.A.P." on the floral decorations above the stall where he preached—these standing for the names Sam Oxon and Alfred Port. See also *soapstone son of a bitch.*

sod BRITISH

Short for *sodomite.* (1) Slang used to describe somebody or something thoroughly unpleasant. "Get out of here, you stupid sod!" (2) Also can be used to show sympathy, as in "The poor old sod never had a chance." (3) A common curse, as in "Sod this damn car!" or "Sod it!"

sod all BRITISH

Nothing. "I haven't done sod all for a week or so."

Sod's law BRITISH

Another name for Murphy's law—anything that can go wrong, will go wrong.

soft fruit BRITISH

Strawberries, raspberries, or any other fruit without pits.

soft top BRITISH

In the United States a soft top would be called a *convertible* (car).

solicitor BRITISH

In Britain a *solicitor* handles the preliminaries of law cases, while a *barrister* (q.v.) is a lawyer admitted to plead at the bar in superior courts.

solitaire   AMERICAN
See *patience.*

Solwara he stret olgeta   NEW GUINEA PIDGIN
Literally "Salt water he straight altogether," which means "The ocean is
calm." This pidgin language is also called *Tok* (talk) *Pisin* (pidgin).

son-of-a-bitch stew   AMERICAN (WEST)
You use everything but "the hair, horns, and holler," according to one
recipe for *son-of-a-bitch stew,* commonly made on chuck wagons in the
Old West. All the innards of a steer, including heart, brains, and kidneys,
had to be included in the stew, but the most indispensable ingredient was
guts (tripe). This inspired the old saying "A son of a bitch might not have
any brains and no heart, but if he ain't got guts he ain't a son of a bitch."

son of a whore   AMERICAN (NEW ENGLAND)
This commonly used epithet is not taken too seriously in northern New
England, where it is heard most frequently. It does yeoman service in
describing everything from a beloved friend ("How are you, you old son
of a whore?") to an avowed enemy, and is applied to situations of good
luck as well as bad luck, even to women as well as men. This is not to
say, however, that someone might not take extreme exception to the term.

sonsy   SCOTTISH
Used to describe a good-looking, buxom woman. Also can mean plump,
cheerful, robust.

son-wife   JAMAICAN
A daughter-in-law; a shortening of *son's wife.* "She his son-wife."

sook   AUSTRALIAN
Any very timid person; a crybaby, a coward. The word may derive from
suck, suggesting an adult still sucking at his mother's breast.

sooner   AMERICAN (APPALACHIAN MOUNTAINS)
A child born fewer than nine months after his or her parents were married; one who came sooner than he or she should have.

sort   SCOTTISH
To mend something. "He used old nails to sort the fence."

souter SCOTTISH
Another name for a shoemaker. Pronounced *sue-ter.*

south of the border AMERICAN, SCOTTISH
South of the border to Americans is "down Mexico way," across the Rio Grande. In Scotland it refers to England, the *border* being the one between Scotland and England.

spanging AMERICAN
Slang for begging or panhandling; used by young street beggars and said to be the result of a slurred and shortened "spare any change?"

spanner BRITISH
An adjustable wrench; a monkey wrench.

lo speaker ITALIAN
The English word *speaker* here is used to mean *announcer* on radio or television.

special election AMERICAN
See *by-election.*

spend a penny BRITISH
A British euphemism for "go to the bathroom." A penny used to be the nominal fee to use a public restroom.

spieler AMERICAN, AUSTRALIAN
(1) In Australia, a gambler or a swindler. (2) In the United States, a carnival barker.

spine-bashing AUSTRALIAN
Loafing or resting. To *spine-bash* means to loaf or to lay around.

spirtle SCOTTISH
A stick used for stirring porridge. Also called a *spurtle.*

to spit chips AUSTRALIAN
To become very angry; the *chips* referred to are French fried potatoes, which an angry person could spit or splutter out while eating them.

to spit the dummy   AUSTRALIAN
To lose your temper. The expression's origin is unknown.

spitting a bit   BRITISH
Used to describe a light rain. "Oh, it's just spitting a bit."

splendacious   JAMAICAN
Splendid, ornate, glamorous. "She is all dressed up splendacious."

split   BRITISH
Slang for someone who acts as a police informer. To *split on* someone is
to inform on him or her.

a spot of bother   BRITISH
A spot of bother is a bit of trouble.

sprog   AUSTRALIAN, BRITISH
(1) Slang for to give birth. "Has she sprogged yet?" (2) A baby.

spruiker   AUSTRALIAN
A slang term for a carnival barker or a *spieler* (q.v.). Pronounced *spru-iker.*

spunk   AUSTRALIAN
A good-looking, sexually attractive man; a hunk. "She thinks he's a spunk,
I think he's a punk."

spun sugar   BRITISH
A term for what is called *cotton candy* in the United States.

spyhole   AUSTRALIAN, BRITISH
A peephole—a small hole in a door through which one can see without
being seen.

square dance   AMERICAN
A dance for four couples arranged in a square form. Usually featured at
country hoedowns.

squat   BRITISH
Slang for an apartment. "I'm all settled down in my new squat." See also
flat.

squattocracy   AUSTRALIAN
Rich owners of large, costly, countryside landholdings.

squill candy   AUSTRALIAN
A child's lollipop or sucker.

squire   BRITISH
A term once used for a man who owned most of the land in a village.
Infrequently used now as a light, friendly greeting.

sri   BRITISH
A slurring word in Cockney dialect speech that means "that's right." "It
was two years ago, wasn't it, Fred?" "Sri," Fred replied.

stag   AUSTRALIAN, BRITISH
A financial term meaning a person who buys a company's stock intend-
ing to sell it immediately for a profit. The process is called *stagging.*

stag party   BRITISH
What would be termed a *bachelor party* in the United States. Also called
a *stag night* by the British and *bucks party* (q.v.) in Australia. Americans
use *stag* in the term *stag films,* pornographic films once shown only at
male gatherings.

stalls   BRITISH
Seats in the orchestra, on the main floor of a theater or cinema.

standard   SOUTH AFRICAN
A grade in school. "She's in the fourth standard this year."

to stand for election   AUSTRALIAN, BRITISH
To run for election, as Americans would put it. "He is standing for election this year."

stand play   JAPANESE
The Japanese borrowing and shortening of the English words *grandstand
play,* meaning to play to the grandstand seats, to perform ostentatiously
to impress an audience.

starkers   BRITISH
Without any clothes, buck naked. "He ran starkers across the stage."

starve the lizards!   AUSTRALIAN
An exclamation of disgust, dismay, or surprise. See also *stone the crows.*

sterling   BRITISH
British money. In medieval England a sterling was a coin worth about a penny and took its name from the star *(steorra)* embossed upon it. The *pound sterling* began life as a hundred of the smaller sterlings, and its value, of course, has risen and fallen over the years.

sticket   SCOTTISH
(1) A person unsuccessful in his or her chosen profession. (2) Imperfect or ruined.

sticky beak   AUSTRALIAN
Australian slang for a busybody, someone whose nose is always stuck in someone else's business. The word also can be a verb: "She only came to sticky beak."

sticky tape   AUSTRALIAN
A transparent adhesive tape generally made of cellophane.

sticky wicket   BRITISH
A *sticky wicket* is a difficult or awkward situation that calls for delicate handling. This 1920s British expression comes from the phrase *bat at a sticky wicket,* meaning to contend with great difficulties, which has its origins in cricket. In cricket a sticky wicket (goal) literally means that the ground around a wicket is soggy because of recent, heavy rain. This condition doesn't allow the ball to bounce well, making things difficult for the players trying to field it.

still have some snap left in one's garters   AMERICAN (SOUTH)
A southern expression dating back to the late nineteenth century and meaning "still energetic, not yet worn out." "I really think," Senator Russell B. Long of Louisiana told the press on March 17, 1985, "that it's better to retire on Uncle Earl's terms, when you still have some snap left in your garters." Mr. Long was referring to his legendary uncle, former Louisiana governor Earl Long.

stirrer   AUSTRALIAN
A troublemaker, someone who likes to stir things up.

stitch up   BRITISH
To cover up a crime. "The authorities stitched up the whole affair for
more than a year."

stompie   SOUTH AFRICAN
A cigarette butt. "The fire was started by a stompie someone dropped."
Also *stumpy*.

stone   BRITISH, IRISH, AUSTRALIAN, NEW ZEALAND
A weight measure equal to 14 pounds, or 6.35 kilograms, that has been
used less frequently since the introduction of the metric system. The term
never had currency in the United States, but was common in other English-speaking countries such as Australia and New Zealand. "He weighs
about ten stone."

stone the crows   BRITISH
A mild exclamation of surprise or delight. "Well, stone the crows if it's not
old Henry."

stonker   AUSTRALIAN
Slang for to defeat, to baffle, to put out of action. "We stonkered them,
mates."

stopping   BRITISH
What Americans would call a *filling* in a tooth. "He put a stopping in this
molar."

stop-up   AUSTRALIAN
A person who likes the nightlife; also one who likes to sit up instead of
going to bed.

to stot   SCOTTISH
To run with long leaps and bounds, like a deer or an antelope.

straight flush   AMERICAN
See *running flush*.

the straight wire   AUSTRALIAN
The real, genuine thing, especially news that is authentic. "That's the
straight wire."

strangler   BRITISH
Slang for a necktie.

strath   SCOTTISH
A wide valley or a large plain beside a river.

to stravage   IRISH, SCOTTISH
To wander aimlessly, to stroll or saunter. Also *stravang.*

streets ahead   BRITISH
Far better or superior. "Our team is streets ahead of theirs."

strewth!   BRITISH
Said when one is surprised. Similar to the American *gee!* or *gee whiz!*

strides   AUSTRALIAN
Slang for men's trousers. "He bought a new pair of strides."

strongpala pepa   NEW GUINEA PIDGIN
Literally "strong-fellow paper," which means "cardboard." This pidgin
language is also called *Tok* (talk) *Pisin* (pidgin).

strop   AUSTRALIAN, BRITISH
A bad, unpleasant mood. "Dad's been in a real strop since this morning."

stubby   AUSTRALIAN
A popular small bottle of beer. "Gimme a stubby, mate."

to stuff   BRITISH
Slang for to have sex with a woman, as in "He stuffed her."

stunned mullet   AUSTRALIAN
A person who is or seems dazed and completely out of it. "He looks like
a bloody stunned mullet." A mullet is a gray, stout-bodied, edible fish.

submarine sandwich   AMERICAN
See *hero sandwich.*

suburbio   SPANISH
Suburb. An example of an English word borrowed for another language
but given a completely opposite meaning. A *suburbio* (from *suburb*) in
Spain is a slum quarter or shantytown in a city.

suck the hind tit   AMERICAN
Get the worst of something, have the worst position, because hindmost
teats are thought to have the least milk. "These workers here been sucking the hind tit for years now."

sufferer   RASTAFARIAN
In the Rasta talk or Dread Talk language of Rastafarians a *sufferer* is someone who lives in a ghetto.

suit   AMERICAN
The word *suit,* now used to describe all business executives, was first used
in Hollywood for studio executives.

sull up   AMERICAN (SOUTH)
Grow sullen, sad. "She sulled up and cried."

sunbaker   AUSTRALIAN
A sunbather, a sun-worshiper, a person who loves to soak up the sun, or
as Cockney speakers put it, *to take the sun.*

sun blind   AUSTRALIAN
An awning or shade to protect one from the sun.

sundowner   AUSTRALIAN, BRITISH, SOUTH AFRICAN
A tramp, vagrant, or migrant worker to Australians. An Australian tramp
is so called because he shows up at sundown, too late to work but just in
time for supper. In Britain and South Africa a *sundowner* is an alcoholic
drink taken at sunset. See also *swaggie.*

sun him go sleep   AUSTRALIAN PIDGIN
A way of saying night is upon us. *Close up sun go* means evening. For other
forms of pidgin see *mary.*

sun-hot   JAMAICAN
Noontime, midday. "Sometime he come at sun-hot."

sunnies   AUSTRALIAN
Sunglasses. "I forgot my sunnies when I went to the beach."

super   KOREAN
Borrowed from English by the Koreans but used only to mean *super-market*.

supergrass   BRITISH (COCKNEY)
In Cockney rhyming slang, a *grasshopper* is a *copper* or a policeman. This rhyming slang is the source of the word *grass* for a police informant or squealer and its latest variation, a *supergrass*.

sure   IRISH
A very common interjection characteristic of Irish speech, as in "Sure, and he's not too old."

sus   BRITISH, IRISH, AUSTRALIAN
(1) Short for suspect. (2) To check out. (3) Used as an adjective meaning suspicious. The Australians spell the word suss. "His actions seemed suss to the inspector."

swacked   SCOTTISH
Thoroughly drunk, tight. "He was sure swacked last night."

swaggie   AUSTRALIAN
A tramp or a migrant worker. Also called a *swagman* and a *sundowner* in Australia.

swanning around   AUSTRALIAN, BRITISH
Not working, wasting time. "She's been swanning around here all day."

swede   BRITISH
A root vegetable Americans usually call rutabaga.

sweet   AUSTRALIAN, BRITISH
(1) Candy. (2) Dessert such as cake, pie, or ice cream. "I'll have two sweets with my tea." Also called *sweetie*.

sweet Fanny Adams   BRITISH
Something with no value. Fanny Adams was murdered and mutilated in
1812, her body cut into pieces and thrown into a river. Her murderer, Fred
Baker, was publicly hanged. Young Fanny Adams's name, given wide currency, was adopted by sailors to indicate a particularly distasteful meal,
since Fanny Adams had been disposed of in a kettle. In fact, when kettles
came into use in the British Navy they were dubbed Fannys, as were tins
(cans) of meat. There is no doubt that Fanny Adams is also the basis for
the military expression *sweet Fanny Adams,* meaning something worthless or nothing at all.

sweet mouth   AMERICAN (SOUTH), JAMAICAN
Smooth, unctuous flattery designed to win over a person. There is no firm
proof of it, but this expression possibly comes from Krio, an English-
based Creole of Sierra Leone, specifically from the expression *swit mot*
(sweet-mouth) for "flattery." To *sweet-mouth* someone is the opposite of
to *bad-mouth* him or her.

sweetshop   BRITISH
What Americans would call a *candy store* (q.v.). "Run round to the sweetshop and bring back some taffy."

swimmers   AUSTRALIAN
A bathing suit. "I put on my swimmers and went into the water."

swot   AUSTRALIAN, BRITISH
To study long and hard for an exam. "I've been swotting for this exam all
week."

sybie   SCOTTISH
A thin spring onion, a scallion. Also called a *syboe.*

sympathetic   POLISH
Borrowed as is from the English word but used to mean friendly or likable.

T

ta   AUSTRALIAN, BRITISH, IRISH
An exclamation meaning thank you. "Ta ever so much."

ta, ta   AUSTRALIAN, BRITISH
Short for "good-bye," "so long."

tablets   BRITISH
Pills. "Did you take your tablets today?"

Taffy   BRITISH
A nickname, sometimes disparaging, for a Welshman. Also *Taf.*

tail of the eye   BRITISH
The corner of the eye. "She watched him from the tail of her eye."

take a captain cook   AUSTRALIAN
Rhyming slang for "take a look."

take against   BRITISH
To come to dislike a person. "They've taken against her recently."

takeaway food   BRITISH
What Americans would call *takeout food,* or simply *takeout* (q.v.).

take it gently   BRITISH
Americans would usually say *take it easy*—that is, don't work too hard.

takeout   AMERICAN
See *takeaway food.*

to take the gilt off the gingerbread   BRITISH
To spoil or ruin something that would have been enjoyable or more enjoyable.

to take the mick   AUSTRALIAN, BRITISH
To make people laugh at a person by mimicking that person. "He's always
taking the mick on someone." Also *take the mickey* and *take the mickey
out of.*

talk dollars   PHILIPPINE
To speak English, which is the language of government, education, and
business in the Philippines and is spoken by sixty-five million Filipinos.

talk moonlight   AMERICAN (OZARK MOUNTAINS)
To talk nonsense, foolishness, as if you were a little crazy.

tall hair   JAMAICAN
Used to describe long hair, not an Afro.

tallyho   BRITISH
The cry *tallyho* originated on British fox hunts in the nineteenth century, where it was, and still is, the cry of a hunter on first sighting the fox. The term is said to have its roots in the French hunter's cry of *tayau*. *Tallyho* is used humorously today in the sense of "we're off."

tam   SCOTTISH
The eponymous hero of Robert Burns's poem "Tam O'Shanter's Ride" (1791) wore a cap similar to this traditional woolen cap with the pompon that is worn by the Scots today and called a *tam,* or *tam-o'-shanter.*

tamago head   HAWAIIAN
Tamago, introduced by Japanese settlers in Hawaii, means "egg." Thus *tamago head* means an "egghead," a stupid person. The term has no connotation of "intellectual," as *egghead* does in the mainland United States.

tamasha   BRITISH
An Arabic word adopted by the British that means a big show, an exciting event. The word has no currency in the United States.

tapsalteerie   SCOTTISH
Topsy-turvy, upside-down. Also *tapsieteerie.*

to tap someone's claret   BRITISH
To give someone a bloody nose. Claret is a prize-fighting term meaning "blood."

ta-ra   BRITISH
So long, good-bye. "Ta-ra, see you tomorrow."

tar seal   NEW ZEALAND
A road's asphalt surface. The *Tar Seal* is the nickname for the main highway.

tart up BRITISH
To dress or doll something up, usually in a gaudy, excessive way. *Tart* is slang for a prostitute.

tass SCOTTISH
(1) A small ornamental cup or goblet. (2) The drink in such a cup or goblet.

tattie bogle SCOTTISH
A scarecrow. *Tattie* means ragged, shabby.

tattie howker SCOTTISH
A poor potato picker or other agricultural worker in ragged clothes.

tawie SCOTTISH
Docile, easy to manage. Pronounced *tow-ee;* rhymes with *Chloe.* See also *taws.*

taws SCOTTISH
A leather whip divided into strips used to punish schoolchildren.

tea caddy BRITISH
A small box for storing tea. The term derives from the Malayan *kati,* "a weight of about twenty-one ounces," perhaps because tea used to be packed in twenty-one-ounce boxes.

teapoy BRITISH
Because it is used for serving tea, this small, often three-legged table is thought to take its name from the drink. But the table's name has nothing to do with tea. Brought back from India by the British, the little table is named from the Hindi *teen,* three, and the Persian *pae,* foot(ed).

tearaway BRITISH
A young troublemaker. "He's been a tearaway since he started school."

tea towel BRITISH
In American English this would be a *dish towel.*

telephone booth AMERICAN
See *call box.*

telephone want you   JAMAICAN
Sometimes heard in hotels, offices, etc., for "You are wanted on the telephone," or "You have a call."

tell me about it   AMERICAN (NEW YORK CITY)
I know exactly what you mean, perhaps better than you do. "I hate the damn rush hour." "Tell me about it."

telly   BRITISH
A television set, or television in general. Americans never use the word, preferring *TV* or *tube.*

ten-gallon hat   AMERICAN (WEST)
Although the name is usually thought to be an indication of its liquid-holding capacity, the Americanism *ten-gallon hat* has its origin in the Spanish word for braid, *galon*—the wide-brimmed hats worn by cowboys were originally decorated with a number of braids at the base of the crown. Vaqueros, in fact, called the hat the *sombrero galon.*

thank-ye-ma'am   AMERICAN (NEW ENGLAND)
An American courtship term that dates back to nineteenth-century New England. Roads at the time had diagonal earthen ridges running across them that channeled off rainwater from the high to the low side and prevented washouts. Rural Casanovas driving their carriages along these rude roads made sure that they hit these ridges hard so that their female companions would bounce up in the air and bump into them. With the head of his sweetheart so close, the gentleman could steal a kiss, and usually expressed his gratitude with a *thank-ye-ma'am,* that expression becoming synonymous with a quick kiss or any hole in the road that caused riders to bump up and down. Preceded by *wham* (or *slam*), *bam,* the term also means a quick act of coitus. Both meanings date back to the end of the nineteenth century.

that dog don't hunt   AMERICAN (SOUTH)
That idea or theory isn't logical, doesn't wash; popularized in the movie *J.F.K.* (1991), set in New Orleans and Texas.

that horse won't start   BRITISH
That plan or idea is impossible. Similar to the American Southernism *that dog won't hunt.*

that takes the biscuit BRITISH
Americans would say *that takes the cake*, meaning *isn't that something!*

that takes the rag off the bush AMERICAN (SOUTH)
That beats everything, takes first place, etc.; the expression may have originated with hunters, possibly in the West, who fired at rags that were targets hung on bushes.

that's another pair of shoes BRITISH
That's something entirely different, that's a horse of a different color.

that's how the cow ate the cabbage AMERICAN (OZARK MOUNTAINS)
An expression hillfolk use to indicate that the speaker is laying it on the line, telling it like it is, getting down to brass tacks—with the connotation of telling someone what he or she needs to know but probably doesn't want to hear. The expression has its roots in a story about an elephant that escaped from a zoo and wandered into a woman's cabbage patch. The woman observed the elephant pulling up her cabbages with its trunk and eating them. She called the police to report that there was a cow in her cabbage patch pulling up cabbages with its tail. When the surprised police officer inquired as to what the cow was doing with the cabbages, the woman replied, "You wouldn't believe me if I told you!"

there is a good time coming SCOTTISH
A familiar saying introduced by Sir Walter Scott in his *Rob Roy.*

there's little to come and go on BRITISH
There's little information. In America the shorter form *there's little to go on* is preferred.

thick as Jesse BRITISH
Very thick-skinned or resistant. Another word (like Jumbo) that derives from the name of an elephant—in this case the London Zoo's pachyderm Jesse, a very popular animal in the late nineteenth century.

to thief BAHAMIAN
To steal. "He thief from me." Pronounced *teef.*

thingo   AUSTRALIAN
A thingamabob, thingamajig, gadget, etc. "You put this thingo here in the thingamabob, and put on the thingamajig and it's put together."

thin red line of heroes   BRITISH
"The Russians dashed on toward that thin-red line streak tipped with a line of steel," wrote W. H. Russell, the greatest war correspondent of his day, in reporting the Battle of Balaclava for the *Times* of London. He was describing the 93rd Highland Infantry, which hadn't formed in a defensive square. Rudyard Kipling scoffed at this romantic notion in his poem "Tommy," where his British soldier remarks about a *thin red line of 'eroes* and later adds "We aren't no thin red 'eroes.'" The term has since been used in many countries.

thirl   SCOTTISH
(1) To drill or pierce. (2) To thrill.

thrahin   NORTHERN IRISH
Bad or wicked behavior. "Such thrahin is widely known there."

to thrapple   SCOTTISH
To strangle or throttle. *Thrapple* as a noun means "throat."

360-degree son of a bitch   AMERICAN (WEST)
A complete son of a bitch, someone who is a son of a bitch any way you look at him.

to throw out   HAWAIIAN
Often means to "throw up," as in "The baby throw out his milk."

throw water   NIGERIAN
To bribe or attempt to bribe someone. "Do not let them throw water to you."

to throw words   JAMAICAN
To swear or use off-color language. "He throws words all the time."

to throw words at the moon   JAMAICAN
To insult someone you are with, or who is nearby, by speaking insultingly to the moon. Thus if the person reproaches you, you can say you're not speaking to him, you're just throwing words at the moon.

thuaite   SCOTTISH
A clearing in the wilderness that is used for farming.

thumbtack   AMERICAN
See *push-pin.*

thunderer   AUSTRALIAN
A humorous Aussie name for an outhouse. Also called a *dunnie.*

tickety-boo   BRITISH
Perfectly fine, A-O.K. (q.v.). "Everything's tickety-boo."

tickey-line   SOUTH AFRICAN
A cheap prostitute. "She'll never go home again. She's a tickey-line." A
tickey is an obsolete South African small coin, equal to a threepenny piece.

ticktacktoe   AMERICAN
A popular game for two in which one player marks down X's and the other
marks down O's. The British call the game *noughts and crosses.*

tiddly; tiddlywinks   BRITISH
In British Cockney rhyming slang a *tiddlywink* meant a drink. From the
expression comes *tiddly,* for "a little drink," or "a little drunk," first
recorded in the late nineteenth century. The game *tiddlywinks* is first
recorded in 1870 and may be so named because of the little counters used
in playing it, *tiddly* here perhaps being baby talk for "little."

tight   AMERICAN
(1) Slightly drunk. (2) Close friends, as in "We were tight back then, but
he changed."

tights   BRITISH
What Americans would call women's *pantyhose.*

tiki tour   NEW ZEALAND
A tour of an area with a travel manual as one's only guide.

timeous   SCOTTISH
Timely or early; also spelled *timous.*

Time, please!   BRITISH
A barman's reminder that the pub will soon close, so please finish your drinks.

tinker   BRITISH
In Britain, a child who frequently acts up. "He's a little tinker, isn't he?" In Ireland, a Gypsy.

tinner   AUSTRALIAN
Beer. After the cans in which beer is often sold. "Give us two tinners, mate." See also *tube*.

tip   BRITISH
A garbage dump. "They took a load of rubbish to the tip."

tipper truck   BRITISH
What Americans would call a *dump truck*.

tip the wink   BRITISH
(1) To warn someone, as in "As soon as she comes, I'll tip you the wink."
(2) To give someone inside information. "The jockey tipped the wink to him."

tit   SOUTH AFRICAN
Slang for great, terrific, super. "That's a tit car he has." The origin of the term is unknown, but it probably has no relation to the American vulgar slang *tit* for a breast.

tittle-tattle   BRITISH
Mean gossip. "There's always been a lot of tittle-tattle about the Royals."

titty-biter   JAMAICAN
A small freshwater tadpole that young girls sometimes place on their breasts, believing its bites will make their breasts develop quicker. Also called a *bubby-biter*.

toad strangler   AMERICAN (APPALACHIAN MOUNTAINS)
A very heavy rain. Synonyms are a *goose-drownder* and a *fence lifter*.

tod   SCOTTISH
Heard in Scotland and northern England for a fox or a foxy, crafty person.

toenadering   SOUTH AFRICAN
A political rapprochement, a reestablishing of cordial relations between two countries or groups. From the Afrikaans word *toenader,* to meet halfway.

toff   AUSTRALIAN, BRITISH
Slang for a distinguished person, a swell, a rich person. "Cars like that are just for toffs."

toffee-nosed   BRITISH
Snobbish.

togs   AUSTRALIAN
A bathing suit. See also *cozzie, bathers, swimmers.*

Tokyo trots   AMERICAN
See *Montezuma's revenge.*

in the tom   SOUTH AFRICAN
In the money. "He's been in the tom since he got that nice job." The origin of *tom* for money is unknown.

Tommy   BRITISH
The British Army account or record books in the nineteenth century had a fictitious sample entry in the name of "Private Thomas Atkins" to help soldiers fill in details about themselves. So ubiquitous was Thomas Atkins that he became affectionately known as *Tommy Atkins* and became a nickname for all British soldiers, similar to the American GI Joe. British soldiers were frequently referred to simply as *Tommies* and still are.

too right!   AUSTRALIAN
A synonym for *certainly!,* or, as the British say, *rather!* (q.v.).

toot   AUSTRALIAN
Slang for the toilet or toilet room. "He's in the toot an hour now!"

toque   CANADIAN, BRITISH, AUSTRALIAN
A woolen hat with a small round ball of wool on top, what Americans
would call a *stocking cap.* The British call a *toque* a *bobble hat,* and the
Australians call it a *beanie.*

tor   BRITISH
Tor may be one of the first words spoken in England. Generally held to be
a Celtic term used in place names, it may be a remnant of the prehistoric
language of Bronze Age people on the island. These tribesmen lacked writing to record their language but may have used *tor* as a place name that
the Celts somehow adopted. *Tor* has come to mean "a high rock, a pile of
rocks."

torch   BRITISH
The common term for a flashlight. "Shine your torch in there."

touchous   TRINIDADIAN
To be very touchy, quick to take offense. "He's one touchous mon."

towel rail   BRITISH
What Americans would call a *towel rack.* Similarly, the British *clothes rail*
is the U.S. *clothes rack.*

to tramp   BRITISH
Commonly used for "to hike" in England. "We're going to tramp in those
hills today."

traymobile   AUSTRALIAN
A common synonym for a tea cart that is wheeled from place to place.

trog   BRITISH
To casually walk with someone. "They trogged along with him to the
store."

troppo   AUSTRALIAN
A person who is eccentric, slightly mad, someone affected by *tropical* heat.

truck   NORWEGIAN
Norwegians use the word truck to mean only a *forklift* vehicle.

truckie
AUSTRALIAN

Slang for a truck driver. "All the truckies lost their jobs."

trunk road
BRITISH

A major highway with high speed limits and heavy traffic.

tube
AUSTRALIAN

Another slang term for a can of beer. See also *tinner.*

tucker
AUSTRALIAN, BRITISH

Food, or to eat food. A British term for food is *tuck.*

tumbleweed
AMERICAN

Any of several plants, including the *Amaranthus* genus and Russian this-tle *(Salsola kali)*, whose branching upper parts come loose from the roots and are driven by the wind across the prairie. The plant, like sagebrush, has become a symbol of the American West, as in song lyrics such as "tumbling along with the tumbling tumbleweed." One old belief has it that God put tumbleweed here to show cowboys which way the wind is blowing.

tuna
AMERICAN

See *tunny.*

tunny
BRITISH

Tuna fish. Reportedly, the highest word rate ever paid to a professional author is the fifteen thousand dollars Darryl Zanuck gave American author James Jones for Americanizing a line of dialogue in the film *The Longest Day.* Jones and his wife, Gloria, were sitting on the beach when they changed the line "I can't eat that bloody old box of tunny fish" to "I can't stand this damned old tuna fish." The chore of deleting two words and changing four came to twenty-five hundred dollars a word.

turn the Nelson eye on
BRITISH

To pretend nothing has happened, ignore something, turn a blind eye on. This expression remembers British naval hero Lord Horatio Nelson, who was blinded in one eye during a sea battle. Years later, at the Battle of Copenhagen, he ignored a superior's command to cease fighting by put-ting his telescope to his blind eye and pretending he hadn't received the order. Continuing the action, he defeated the Danes.

turning   BRITISH
The corner of a street. "It's right down there at the turning."

turn-ups   BRITISH
What Americans would call *cuffs* (on men's trousers).

turps   AUSTRALIAN
A humorous term for any alcoholic liquor; from *turpentine.*

tutus   JAMAICAN
Can mean the male sexual organs, or the testicles. Pronounced *tootoos.*
The word's origin is unknown.

twa   SCOTTISH
Two. "She has twa wee children at home."

twicer   AUSTRALIAN
A double-crosser, a cheat. "That twicer would cheat his own mother."

twinkles   AMERICAN (MOUNTAINS)
Heard in the North Carolina mountains and elsewhere for pine needles or
spruce needles.

the twitters   SCOTTISH
Nervousness. "I played a good game despite a bad attack of the twitters."

two-bob   AUSTRALIAN
Very cheap but of little real worth. "That's a two-bob jacket." A *bob* (q.v.)
now means five pence.

twofers   AMERICAN
Twofers has meant two theater tickets for the price of one in America
since about 1948. *Twofer* had previously referred to *two-for-a-nickel* cigars
since as early as 1892.

two-hander   BRITISH
A short play written for two actors. "He and his wife are appearing in a
two-hander."

two lamps burning and no ship at sea   AMERICAN (NEW ENGLAND)
Used to describe a foolishly extravagant person. Someone with ships at
sea in the days of sail was rich and could afford to burn two expensive oil
lamps. Anyone else who burned two lamps was likely a fool. Also *two
lamps burning and no ships out.*

two-up   AUSTRALIAN
A gambling game in which two coins are flipped, the players betting on
two heads or two tails coming up.

U

U   AMERICAN
Mob talk for a thousand dollars. Short for a *thou.* "What would a boat like
that cost?" "A boat like that? Oh, about 300 U's."

ugly   AMERICAN (SOUTH)
(1) Ugliness. "It was ugly, and God don't love ugly." (2) An old term for
sexual intercourse. "He was in jail for throwing bricks at a woman because
she wouldn't do ugly."

Uncle Tom   AMERICAN
A derogatory term for a black person who holds himself or herself sub-
servient to whites. Although the title character of Harriet Beecher Stowe's
Uncle Tom's Cabin (1852) could be easygoing to the point of servility, he
was a noble man who was flogged to death at the end of the book for refusing to reveal the hiding place of two female slaves.

Uncle Tomahawk   AMERICAN
Recent slang for a Native American who is accused of being servile to
whites by other Native Americans; patterned on the older *Uncle Tom*
(q.v.).

under   BAHAMIAN
Younger than. "He have a brother under him."

underdone steak   BRITISH
In America this would be *rare steak.*

undershirt   AMERICAN
See *singlet.*

undertaker   JAMAICAN
A wind that blows from land toward the sea, once thought to be very
unhealthy, a wind that keeps the undertaker busy.

under the doctor   BRITISH
In America this would be *under the doctor's care.*

university man   BRITISH
The usual term for what Americans call a *college graduate.*

until the last dog is hung   AMERICAN (WEST)
Until the end, usually heard in reference to someone staying at a party
until the very last. "We were there until the last dog was hung."

up a gum tree   AUSTRALIAN
To be in trouble, to be very confused, disoriented. *Gum tree* is the popular name for the eucalyptus tree.

up and died   AMERICAN (NEW ENGLAND)
Died suddenly. An old poem goes: "Anna was a lovely bride/But Anna,
damn'er, up and died."

uplift   NEW ZEALAND
To lift up, pick up. "She asked him to uplift the chair."

ups   IRISH
I proceeded to, as in "I ups and clouted him on the chin."

up the pole   BRITISH
To be very drunk, or to be crazed by drink. "You were sure up the pole
last night."

up the spout   BRITISH
Hopeless. Americans would say up the chimney, gone up in smoke.

up with the lark   BRITISH
To be out of bed early in the morning. "I'm up with the lark and to bed
with the dark."

up your street   BRITISH
Said of something someone is very familiar with or knowledgeable about.
"A book on skydiving—that's right up your street." Americans would say
right up your alley.

urge   CANADIAN (NEWFOUNDLAND)
To vomit, throw up. "He urged over the side of the boat."

us   IRISH
Often used instead of the personal pronoun *me*, as in "Give us a smile
now" when one person is addressing another.

used to could   AMERICAN (APPALACHIAN MOUNTAINS)
Used to be able to. "I used to could sing some of 'em old songs."

ute   AUSTRALIAN
Short for a utility truck or a pickup. "He smashed up his new ute."

Vee-dub   AUSTRALIAN
A common nickname for a Volkswagen bug automobile.

verge   BRITISH
The edge, or shoulder, of a road. "The truck was parked on the verge, just
off the road."

the very dinky   AMERICAN (WEST)
Something, usually inanimate, that is the height of perfection. "Boy, that
new saw is the very dinky." Also *the very dinkum*.

very poor man's dinner   AMERICAN (NEW ENGLAND)
A Maine dish made of thinly sliced potatoes and onions fried in the grease
of salt pork. A similar dish made in Massachusetts is called *Necessity
Mess*.

vest   BRITISH
An undershirt. In Britain what Americans call a vest is called a *waistcoat*.

vet   BRITISH, AMERICAN

To check something over. This word has some American usage, as in "His editor vetted the manuscript." The British, however, never use vet to mean a veterinarian, as Americans do.

vexy   JAMAICAN

Annoyed, angry. "Him get very vexy wit me."

vigorish   AMERICAN

A loan shark's margin of profit, 20 percent or more a week, plus late payment penalties and other fees, is called *vigorish,* or *vig,* which also means the percentage or house cut set by a bookmaker in his own favor. *Vigorish* is one of the few words in English with Russian roots, deriving from the Russian *vyigrysh,* "gambling gains or profit," which first passed into Yiddish early in twentieth-century America as *vigorish* and was reinforced by its similarity to *vigor.*

volunteer   AMERICAN (OZARK MOUNTAINS)

A euphemism for an illegitimate child among hillfolk. Possibly based on garden plants called volunteers that spring up in unexpected places. Also called a *wood's colt.*

wabbit   SCOTTISH

Tired, weary, exhausted.

wadge   BRITISH

A thick piece of anything. "He ate a wadge of pie topped with ice cream."

wag   NEW ZEALAND

To skip school or cut classes. "They wagged school yesterday."

waiter   AMERICAN (OZARK MOUNTAINS)

The best man at a wedding, though the term once meant a bridesmaid as well. "John was waiter to his brother at his wedding."

wakey, wakey!   BRITISH

A humorous exclamation meaning "wake up, time to wake up."

to walkabout   AUSTRALIAN
To wander the countryside, take a long walk.

walk good   JAMAICAN
A common farewell. "See you later. Walk good, man."

walking frame   AUSTRALIAN, BRITISH
Americans would call this metal frame with four legs that assists people
who have trouble walking a *walker*. The British call it a *zimmer frame*.

wallah   BRITISH
A now-humorous term for someone with a specific duty. "I'll be the tea
wallah today." ("I'll make the tea today.") The word was brought back by
the British from India and derives from a Hindi word.

Wall Street   AMERICAN
Wall Street, which is an actual street in lower Manhattan and a symbol of
American capitalism in general, takes its name from the defensive wall
that extended along the street in Dutch times. The principal financial institutions of the city have been located there since the early nineteenth century. *Wall Streeter, Wall Street broker, Wall Street plunger,* and *Wall Street
shark* are among American terms to which the street gave birth. *Wall Street
broker* was used as early as 1836, and Wall Street was being called *the
Street* by 1863.

wally   BRITISH
A term of unknown origin for a person who is silly, useless, ineffectual.
"You wally—can't you do anything right!"

to waltz Matilda   AUSTRALIAN
To carry a swag or bedroll, which is also called a *Matilda.*

wanigan   CANADIAN
(1) A clothes storage chest used by lumberjacks. (2) A large, enclosed
supply sled.

wanker   BRITISH, AUSTRALIAN, IRISH
Slang for a stupid, useless man, a fool, a jerk-off. *Wank* is British and Australian slang for to masturbate.

wash-belly JAMAICAN
The last child a woman bears, her youngest. "He my wash-belly child."

washroom CANADIAN
A word favored by Canadians in place of bathroom, lavatory, rest room, etc., as in "I have to go to the washroom."

wasn't IRISH
Frequently used instead of *weren't,* as in "Wasn't the both of you there?"

waur SCOTTISH
Worse. "There nothin' waur than that."

way out BRITISH
Doesn't mean "far out," as it might to Americans. *Way out* signs indicate an exit in Britain.

wedgey, wedgy AMERICAN
A name given in some areas to large sandwiches made of Italian bread and most commonly known as *heroes* in the rest of the United States, although many other names, such as *submarines* and *poor boys,* are used.

wee bit o' skirt SCOTTISH
Slang for a young, attractive girl. "She's a wee bit o' skirt he'd like to meet."

weenie AMERICAN
See *winkie.*

welly BRITISH
Short for a waterproof *Wellington boot.* "Take off those muddy wellies before you come in here."

wendy house BRITISH
A child's playhouse. Named after the Wendy character in *Peter Pan,* who in turn was named after a little girl the playwright J. M. Barrie knew.

went down a treat BRITISH
Was pleasing, very well received. "His victory went down a treat."

the wet   AUSTRALIAN
A common term for the rainy season. "Can't wait for the wet to be over."

whacking good   BRITISH
Excellent. "He had a whacking good part in the play."

whacko   AUSTRALIAN
Good, splendid. "We had a whacko time with our mates." In American
slang a *whacko* is a crazy person, a nut.

whacko-the-diddle-o   AUSTRALIAN
Said of an extremely attractive young woman. "Here she comes—a
whacko-the-diddle-o." The expression is based on the Australian slang
whacko (q.v.).

wharfie   AUSTRALIAN
A longshoreman, someone who works on the wharves or the docks.

what's your game?   BRITISH
"What are you up to?," as Americans would say. "What are your secret
plans?"

wheen   SCOTTISH, BRITISH
(1) A few. (2) A few persons or things. Also heard in northern England.

wheeze   BRITISH
A clever plan designed to make money. "Their latest wheeze is to sell
franchises."

whennie   BRITISH
Recent slang for a boring person who is always talking about his exploits
in the past: "When I was in the army, I . . ."

when the rain is in the nose   ZIMBABWEAN
The time when the rainy season is fast approaching.

where the hoot owl hollers at noon   AMERICAN (OZARK MOUNTAINS)
Used to describe a distant place, so deep in the dark woods that the owls
can't tell day from night.

wherry   SCOTTISH, BRITISH
(1) A one-person skiff. (2) A fishing boat. Also heard in northern England.

whigmaleeree   SCOTTISH
(1) A notion, a whim. (2) A fanciful ornament, a trinket.

whilst   BRITISH
A rather old-fashioned but still frequently heard form of *while*.

to whinge   BRITISH
To whine, complain. The word is also heard in American, mainly in the
expression *stop your whinging and whining* (stop feeling sorry for yourself). A *whinger* is a person who complains a lot.

whisky   BRITISH
The word for Scotch whisky in Britain. Irish *whiskey* is always spelled with
an "e" by the British.

white coffee   BRITISH
The term for what would be *regular coffee* in the United States—that is,
coffee with cream or milk. *Black* means the same as in the United States—
coffee with no cream or milk. "Black or white?" a waitress will ask in
Britain, not "With or without?"

whole meal bread   BRITISH
What Americans would call *whole wheat bread*.

widdershins   SCOTTISH
In a direction opposite to the usual one, counterclockwise. Also *wither-
shins*. "Turn the lock widdershins to open it."

widow maker   AMERICAN (NEW ENGLAND)
(1) A sailing ship's bowsprit or jib boom, so called because sailors who
lost their hold on it while working on the headsails in rough seas often
lost their lives. (2) The sea, because it makes widows of so many women.
(3) A tree in a precarious position that looks as if it will fall and kill a
man.

widow's walk   AMERICAN (NEW ENGLAND)
An elevated observatory atop a dwelling, usually with a railing and affording a good view of the ocean. These watchtowers, often seen on the roofs of old houses in New England, date back to colonial times and were so named because many women walked in vain on them, waiting for incoming ships that never returned. Taking the form of a cupola, railed-in deck, or balcony, they also have been called, less poetically, the *captain's walk, the lookout, the observatory,* and *the walk.*

wifey   BRITISH
An affectionate term for one's wife. "I'm taking the wifey along with me."

wine merchant   BRITISH
See *liquor store.*

wine of ape   BRITISH
Surly or obnoxious drunkenness. One folklorist tells us: "There is a Talmud parable that says that Satan came one day to drink with Noah, and slew a lamb, a lion, a pig, and an ape, to teach Noah that man before wine is in him is a lamb, when he drinks moderately he is a lion, when like a sot he is a swine, but after that any further excess makes him an ape that senselessly chatters and jabbers."

wing   BRITISH
See *fender bender.*

wingey   BAHAMIAN
Small, little. "All I had is one wingey piece."

winkie   BRITISH
Juvenile slang for the penis. The American equivalent term is *weenie,* short for wiener (frankfurter).

Winnipeg couch   CANADIAN
A backless, armless couch that converts into a double bed.

to win the wooden spoon   BRITISH
To come in last, to win the booby prize. Awarding the wooden spoon was an old custom at Cambridge in mathematics competitions.

wiseguy   AMERICAN
Another name for a member of the Mafia; made famous in Nicholas Pileggi and Henry Hill's book *Wiseguys* (1985), which became the movie *Goodfellas* (1990).

within cooee   AUSTRALIAN
To be within hearing distance. *Cooee* is a call Aborigines use in the bush.

wobbly pop   CANADIAN
A colorful name for beer or liquor in Calgary and other places.

wolf juice   CANADIAN
A humorous term for any strong liquor. See also *moose milk*.

wonky   BRITISH
Shaky, groggy, unsteady, feeble, unreliable. "I'm still feeling a bit wonky after last night."

won't be a tic   BRITISH
Won't be a second, a tic on the clock. "Wait for me—I won't be a tic."

wood and water joey   AUSTRALIAN
A handyman hired to do odd jobs.

wooden walls   BRITISH
A historical term for England's warships, which protected the country from invasion like a great wooden wall in the water. *Our watery and wooden walls* was a variation on the phrase.

woolgrower   AUSTRALIAN
Another name for a sheep rancher.

woomera   AUSTRALIAN
(1) A wooden stick used by Aboriginal peoples for hurling a spear. (2) A club.

woop woop   AUSTRALIAN
A term for any small, insignificant town far removed from civilization.

to work back   AUSTRALIAN

To work overtime. "I worked back all week."

worked over with the ugly stick   AMERICAN (WEST)

Beaten up badly; often said of an ugly person. "You look like someone has worked you over with the ugly stick."

worker   JAMAICAN

A servant. "The workers will take care of the dishes."

work like a navvy   BRITISH

To work hard at physical labor. A *navvy* was a man who worked on the many canals that were excavated in England starting in the mid-eighteenth century. These canals were called "navigations," and a laborer working on one was dubbed a "navigator," this soon being shortened to *navvy*, q.v.

wowser   AUSTRALIAN

There has been much speculation over the years about the origin of this term for a puritanical person, a bluenose, or a fanatic. The word appears to have been coined in 1890s Australia to describe fanatic prohibitionists, perhaps even from the initials of a reform organization's slogan: *We Only Want Social Evils Righted*."

WPB   AUSTRALIAN

A common abbreviation for *waste paper bin* (wastebasket). "Toss it in the WPB."

writer   SCOTTISH, AMERICAN

In Scotland, a lawyer or a solicitor, a notary public. In America, *writer* is slang for a graffiti artist.

wrongus   SCOTTISH

A legal term meaning wrongful, unjust.

wuzzy   BRITISH

A good example of how the British have fractured French over the centuries is the London teenage slang *wuzzy*, for "a girl." It was coined in the 1960s from the French word for bird (*bird* being slang for "girl"), which is *oiseau*.

wynd SCOTTISH
A narrow street or a narrow alley off a main thoroughfare.

y

to yabber AUSTRALIAN
To talk or to chat. "He yabbered with his mate for more than an hour." A *paper yabber* is a letter. *Yabber* probably derives from the Australian Aboriginal word *yaba*, to talk. Also *yabber-yabber.*

yabber-yabber AUSTRALIAN PIDGIN
Talk or constant talk. "Him allatime yabber-yabber." For other forms of pidgin see *mary.*

yakka AUSTRALIAN
Work; from an Aboriginal word meaning the same. *Hard yakka* is hard manual labor.

y'all AMERICAN (SOUTH)
You all, the plural of "you." *Y'all* is widely considered the *ne plus ultra* of southern dialect, but this expression, used throughout the South, is much misunderstood. Mainly applied to two or more people, *y'all* can be used when the speaker is addressing one person, but is generally used only when the sentence implies plurality. Most Southerners would not use *y'all* so indiscriminately as to say, "That's a pretty dress y'all are wearing." But a Southerner might well say "How are y'all?"when the question is intended to inquire after the health of you and your entire family or group. Recently the American Southernism *y'all* has been explained, though hardly to the satisfaction of everyone, as a calque (a filling in of an African structure with material) from the West African second person plural *unu*, which is also used in the American black Gullah dialect. This interesting theory is advanced in a study by Jay Edwards in Hancock and Decamp's *Pidgins and Creoles* (1972): "In the white plantation of Louisiana the form *y'all* (semantically *unu*) was probably learned by white children in familiar domestic situations."

yam SCOTTISH
In Scotland, a white potato *(Solanum tuberosum),* not the yam *(Dioscorea* genus) known to most people.

Yank BRITISH, AUSTRALIAN

Commonly used in England today for an American. Also heard in Australia. The word is a shortening of *Yankee*, which has a long, colorful history. The source of *Yankee* has long been disputed and its origin is still uncertain, despite all the research devoted to it. Candidates, among many, have included a slave named Yankee offered for sale in 1725, a Dutch sea captain named Yanky, the Yankos Indians, the Dutch name Janke ("Johnny"), which the Dutch applied to the English, and an Indian mispronunciation *(Yengees)* of the word. The most popular explanation, also unproved, is that Yankee comes from *Jan Kees*, a contemptuous Flemish and German nickname for the Dutch that the English first applied to the Dutch in the New World. *Yankee* seems to have been first applied (contemptuously) to Americans by British soldiers serving under General James Wolfe in the French and Indian War prior to 1758. In any case, *Yankee* described a New Englander by the middle of the eighteenth century and was used by the British to designate any American during the Revolution, the most notable example found in the derisive song "Yankee Doodle" (which was taken up by the Americans as an ironic anthem). Nowadays the British still use the words Yankee (and Yank) for an American, U.S. Southerners use it for Northerners, and Northerners use it for New Englanders, who, despite its early history, remain proud of the designation. The *New York Yankees* are, according to many, the greatest of baseball teams.

Yank tank BRITISH

Usually a disparaging term for any large, gas-guzzling American car.

yap-yap JAMAICAN

Slang for the mouth; probably derives from the British and American slang *yap* meaning the same.

yardie JAMAICAN

The member of a criminal gang or syndicate first based in Jamaica.

the year dot AUSTRALIAN, BRITISH

A very long time ago. "I haven't seen him since the year dot."

yeh IRISH

You (singular). "Get out of here yeh, eejit (idiot)."

yenta   AMERICAN

Yiddish for a gossipy woman who talks too much and can't keep a secret, *yenta* may derive from some unknown blabbermouth named Yenta. The proper name Yenta probably derives from the Italian *gentile.* A talkative character named *Yenta Talabenta* in a play by Sholom Aleichem popularized the term.

yett   SCOTTISH, BRITISH

A gate. Also heard in northern England.

yill   SCOTTISH, BRITISH

A Scottish synonym for "ale." Also heard in northern England.

yin   SCOTTISH

A word used in Scotland for "one."

ying-yang   AMERICAN (MOUNTAINS)

A synonym for penis, heard in the southern mountains.

yins   AMERICAN (APPALACHIAN MOUNTAINS)

A shortening of *you ones,* which means *you.* "Well, we'll see yins."

yirsel   SCOTTISH

You. "Ah, it's yirsel."

yis   IRISH

You (plural). "Is he in there with yis?" See also *youse.*

yo   AMERICAN

Present, or here, often in answer to a roll call. *Yo* is widely used slang in the United States, but actually dates back to fourteenth-century England. *Yo* also is used to call someone's attention, as in "Yo, John!" (Hey, John!). Sometimes *yo* has the meaning of "Here I am!" In this case someone might call, "Hey, John!" and John would answer, "Yo!"

yob   AUSTRALIAN, BRITISH

A rude, offensive, and often violent young person. "There are gangs of yobs with their tattoos and shaved heads all over the country." *Boy,* spelled backward, is the origin of the term.

yonks   AUSTRALIAN, BRITISH
A long time, years ago. "He hasn't been here for yonks."

yonnie   AUSTRALIAN
A small stone or pebble. The term possibly derives from an Aboriginal word.

yopped up   AMERICAN (APPALACHIAN MOUNTAINS)
Messy. "This house is sure all yopped up."

yourself   IRISH
A reflexive pronoun that is often used instead of the personal pronoun, as in "Is it yourself that wants it?" Similarly, *herself* is used the same way ("Was it herself that went?"), as is *himself* ("Himself knows best.")

youse   AMERICAN
Youse—the so-called "generous plural"—is in a class by itself as a New Yorkism, though the expression is definitely heard in several parts of the country, including other eastern cities and the Midwest. *Youse* is usually employed when a speaker is referring to the second person plural, helping the speaker differentiate between one person in the group he or she is speaking to and the group as a whole. It is the New York counterpart of the southern *y'all* (q.v.), the "mountain tawk" *you-uns* and the localized *mongst-ye* heard in Norfolk, Virginia, and on Albemarle Sound. *Youse* also is a feature of Irish speech. See also *yis*.

you-uns   AMERICAN (OZARK MOUNTAINS)
You, singular and plural. "You-uns come down with me." The much-ridiculed *you-uns* of mountain speech can be traced to the *ye ones* of Chaucer's time, and the collective second person *you-together* is sometimes still heard in the British East Anglia dialect.

Z

zack   AUSTRALIAN
Australians use the term to mean five cents, just as Americans use the word *nickel*.

zebra   BRITISH
A pedestrian crossing, marked with black and white stripes. Americans would call it a *crosswalk*. Pronounced *zeh-bra*.

zed BRITISH

The letter *z;* chiefly a British usage.

zimmer frame BRITISH

What Americans would call a *walker* for disabled people.

zing-zang JAMAICAN

A swing; believed to derive from a U.S. Gullah dialect word meaning the same.

zip AUSTRALIAN

Short for *zipper.* "Damn, I caught myself in the zip!"

zip code AMERICAN

The *zip* in *zip code* is an acronym for *z*one *i*mprovement *p*lan. The system and name for it were introduced by the U.S. Post Office in 1963.

zizzer BRITISH

Since at least 1930 *zizz* has meant "to sleep" in the British Navy because the word is suggestive of snoring. From this came the naval slang *zizzer* for "bed," mainly confined to British.

zoon AMERICAN (SOUTH)

To go fast, run fast, often with a hum or a buzz. "He went zooning across the meadow." Also heard as *june.*

zotz AMERICAN

To kill in mob talk. *Zotz* means nothing or zero in slang; thus to *zotz* someone is to make a person nothing, to kill that person.

zut SOUTH AFRICAN

Nothing, zero, zip. "I've got zut money in the bank." The word's origin is unknown.